European Tourism
REGIONS, SPACES AND RESTRUCTURING

Edited by

ARMANDO MONTANARI
University of Rome la Sapienza, Italy and Free University, Brussels, Belgium

and

ALLAN M. WILLIAMS
University of Exeter, UK

JOHN WILEY & SONS
Chichester · New York · Brisbane · Toronto · Singapore

Other Wiley Editorial Offices

John Wiley & Sons, Inc., 605 Third Avenue,
New York, NY 10158–0012, USA

Jacaranda Wiley Ltd, 33 Park Road, Milton,
Queensland 4064, Australia

John Wiley & Sons (Canada) Ltd, 22 Worcester Road,
Rexdale, Ontario M9W 1L1, Canada

John Wiley & Sons (SEA) Pte Ltd, 37 Jalan Pemimpin #05–04,
Block B, Union Industrial Building, Singapore 2057

British Library Cataloguing in Publication Data

A catalogue record for this book is available from the British Library

ISBN 0-471-95286-9

Typeset in 10/12pt Sabon by Dorwyn Ltd, Rowlands Castle, Hants
Printed and bound in Great Britain by Biddles Ltd, Guildford and King's Lynn

This book is printed on acid-free paper responsibly manufactured from sustainable
forestation, for which at least two trees are planted for each one used for paper
production.

Four

Mowforth, M + Munt, M (1998),
Tourism and Sustainability, Routledge
London .

European Tourism

The **European Science Foundation** is an association of its 56 member research councils, academies and institutions devoted to basic scientific research in 20 countries. The ESF assists its Member Organisations in two main ways: by bringing scientists together in its Scientific Programmes, Networks and European Research Conferences, to work on topics of common concern; and through the joint study of issues of strategic importance in European science policy.

The scientific work sponsored by ESF includes basic research in the natural and technical sciences, the medical and biosciences, the humanities and social sciences.

The ESF maintains close relations with other scientific institutions within and outside Europe. By its activities, ESF adds value by cooperation and co-ordination across national frontiers, offers expert scientific advice on strategic issues, and provides the European forum for fundamental science.

This volume arises from the work of the ESF Scientific Programme on Regional and Urban Restructuring in Europe (RURE).

Further information on ESF activities can be obtained from:

European Science Foundation
1, quai Lezay-Marnésia
F-67080 Strasbourg Cedex
France

Tel. (+33) 88 76 71 00
Fax (+33) 88 37 05 32

Contents

List of Contributors

Christoph Becker
Angenwandte Geographie, Universitat Trier, 54286 Trier, Germany

Carles Carreras i Verdaguer
Departamento de Geografia Humana, Facultat de Geografia y Historia, Universitat de Barcelona, Baldiri Reixac s/n, 08028 Barcelona, Spain

Carminda Cavaco
Centro de Estudios Geograficos, Faculdade de Letras, Universidade de Lisboa, 1699 Lisboa, Portugal

Paul Claval
U.E.R. de Geographie, Université de Paris-Sorbonne, 191 rue Saint-Jaques, F-75005 Paris, France

Desmond A. Gillmor
Department of Geography, Trinity College Dublin, Dublin 2, Ireland

Manuel J. Marchena Gómez
Departamento de Geografia, Universidad de Sevilla, c/Maria de Padilla, 41004 Sevilla, Spain

Derek R. Hall
Department of Geography, Faculty of Arts, University of Sunderland, Langham Tower, Ryhope Road, Sunderland SR2 7EE, UK

Russell King
School of European Studies, Arts Building, University of Sussex, Falmer, Brighton BN1 9QN, UK

Armando Montanari
Dipartimento di studi geoeconomici, statistici e storiei per l'analisi regionale, Università di Roma 'La Sapienza', Via del Castro Laurenziano 9, I-00161 Roma, and Eenheid Menselijke Ecologie, Vrije Universiteit Brussel, Laarbeeklaan 103, B-1090 Brussels

Lars Nyberg
Department of Tourism Studies, Mid-Sweden University, S-831 Ostersund, Sweden

Fernando Vera Rebollo
Cavanilles Foundation of Advanced Studies in Tourism, Universidad de Alicante, Rectorado, Apartado Correos, 99, E-03080 Alicante, Spain

Arie Shachar
Institute of Urban and Regional Studies, Hebrew University, Jerusalem, Israel

Allan M. Williams
Department of Geography, University of Exeter, Amory Building, Rennes Drive, Exeter EX4 4RJ, UK

Friedrich M. Zimmermann
Institut fur Geographie, Universitat Klagenfurt, Universitatsstrasse 67, A 9010 Klagenfurt, Austria

Preface

In 1989 the European Science Foundation (ESF) agreed to fund a major re-search programme on Regional and Urban Restructuring in Europe (RURE), directed by A. Shachar and S. Öberg. The programme gave priority to regional and urban restructuring brought about by the transformation in the produc-tion system (Working Group 1), the strategies and operations of multinational companies (Working Group 2), demographic processes (Working Group 3) and the adaptation of the population to economic processes (Working Group 4). During the course of the programme, several new *ad hoc* groups were formed and new projects generated, including the RURETOUR programme concerned with the role of tourism in the wider processes of restructuring which were producing a new map of Europe.

The first two meetings of RURETOUR were held during the RURE congresses at Lisbon (February 1991) and Budapest (February 1992), at the instigation principally of Armando Montanari (chair of RURETOUR), Russell King and Arie Shachar. These meetings generated so much interest that it was decided to change the original *ad hoc* group into a permanent working group with some 20 participants. Further meetings have since been held in Sorrento (October 1992) and in Alicante (February 1994). These meetings were exceptionally helpful in providing an opportunity for detailed discussion of individual papers and of the overall research directions of the group. Their productivity is evident in the fact that these meetings have produced two substantial publications. The first was a collection of papers on European tourism, published as a special theme issue of *Tijdschrift voor Economische en Sociale Geografie* (Vol. 86, Number 1, 1995), under the guest editorship of Armando Montanari and Allan M. Williams. The second publication is this volume.

The main aim of this book is to investigate how changes in the production and consumption of tourism have contributed to a reorganisation of economic and social spaces in Europe, at a number of different geographical scales. Some of these themes are considered by the editors in the introductory chapter. The principal focus of the volume is Western Europe rather than the entire continent, which reflects the fact that the RURE programme was conceived in the era of a divided Europe, as well as the programme's central concern with the restructuring of capitalist relationships. Nevertheless, the chapter by Derek Hall on Central and Eastern Europe provides some counterbalance to this regional concentration.

Given the enormity of the RURETOUR programme, it was decided to ask the contributors to this volume to prepare their individual chapters in the context of one of four principal themes. In the first of these, on regional development and population systems, there are four contributions which examine macro-regions within Europe. These are selective rather than comprehensive in their geographical coverage, but they do illustrate the existence of distinctive subregions within Europe which have experienced some shared structural adjustments in their tourism economies, giving rise thereby to a series of population movements which have contributed to the new demographic map of Europe. In the second section, on the spatial reorganisation of tourism, the focus switches to the systematic consideration of the processes of change in coastal, rural and metropolitan areas. The three chapters in this part of the volume begin to identify some of the distinctive features of production and consumption in particular types of spaces within the larger European mosaic. In the third section, two chapters address the issue of transnationalisation in respect of capital and labour in Europe, which is a strangely neglected theme given the importance of globalisation tendencies, and the way that these mediate the impact of tourism on particular regions and localities. The fourth section is more forward-looking and examines some of the broader social changes and product developments which have shaped and are likely to shape the future restructuring of tourism in Europe. There is no pretence of comprehensiveness in this section given the constraints of space. Instead, three key themes are investigated: mega-events, environmental issues, and tourism changes in Central and Eastern Europe. Finally, a concluding chapter provides an overview of the interlinked processes of economic, cultural and technological change which have remoulded the map of European tourism, thereby contributing to the new map of Europe.

This volume has only been realised through the collective willingness of the individual contributors to adhere to very demanding deadlines and project outlines. In addition, particular thanks are due to the ESF and to those who made possible the Sorrento and the Alicante meetings which facilitated the work of the RURETOUR group: to Armando Montanari who was the local organiser of, and to Scuola Diretta A Fini Speciali Per Operatori Economici Del Turismo, Faculty of Economics, Naval University of Naples who sponsored the first meeting; and to Fernando Vera Rebollo, the local organiser, and the Fundación Cavanilles de Altos Estudios Turísticos, Institut Turistíc Valencià, University of Alicante, the sponsors of the second meeting. The production of this work also received invaluable assistance from Terry Bacon and Helen Jones who drew the maps, and from Jo Small who performed word-processing miracles on the disks and files, with varied specifications, which arrived in Exeter for final editing. However, the responsibility for this work ultimately rests, warts and all, with the authors and editors.

Armando Montanari, *Rome*
Allan M. Williams, *Exeter*   *November 1994*

1 Introduction: Tourism and Economic Restructuring in Europe

ALLAN M. WILLIAMS
University of Exeter, UK
ARMANDO MONTANARI
University of Rome la Sapienza, Italy and Free University, Brussels, Belgium

1.1 INTRODUCTION: TOURISM AND RESTRUCTURING

In the 1950s, through to the early 1970s, there were relatively stable relationships between production and consumption which, arguably, constituted what is known as the Fordist regime of accumulation. By the early 1970s some of the inherent crises in this regime had surfaced in the major recessionary and inflationary difficulties which were triggered by (but not caused by) the oil price crisis of the winter of 1973–74. Thereafter, there was a shift in the regime of accumulation towards more flexible forms of accumulation, which Lash and Urry (1987) term 'disorganised capitalism'. This shift, or in reality these series of shifts—the precise nature of which are contended—have been analysed in terms of the literature on restructuring. That literature has mainly focused on the manufacturing sector, with a belated recognition of the importance of the service sector, but tourism has been conspicuously absent from most of these debates (Montanari and Williams 1994).

One of the central themes of the restructuring literature is the impact of globalisation and Europeanisation on the organisation of production. Global changes—such as new forms of international subcontracting as part of the reorganisation of the labour process—are also linked to market changes and to production/technological changes. The process of restructuring involves deep changes in the geography of production and consumption, influencing regions and localities (see Dicken 1992; Cooke 1989). In turn, the spatial reorganisation of consumption and production is linked to broader processes of economic, social and cultural change. Economic change has generated a series of population dynamics which have influenced economic restructuring. For example, international migration helped sustain the labour processes associated with Fordist mass production, while the latter also contributed to generating the mass international labour migrations of the 1980s.

European Tourism: Regions, Spaces and Restructuring. Edited by A. Montanari and A.M. Williams.
© 1995 European Science Foundation. Published in 1995 by John Wiley & Sons Ltd.

State interventionism has been important as part of the mode of regulation of these different systems of capitalist relations (Dunford 1990). The precise form of interventionism has varied between countries, and over time, in response to the emergence of different economic and political requirements. Examples include the management of international trade, fiscal policies which serve to regulate consumption, and direct state intervention in the spatial organisation of the economy via regional and urban policies. In the period of uncertain economic growth and recurrent crises since the mid 1970s, there has been a change in the role of the state. The role of the central state in economic management has been in decline due to reasons of the economic squeeze on state budgets, competing free market ideologies, and the changing nature of production (especially the shift from mass output to more small-scale and flexible units which have attracted less direct state support) (Albrechts et al. 1989).

These changes are evident at a number of scales and in most of the developed world's macro-regions, but we are particularly concerned here with capitalist Europe. This means that the principal focus is on what traditionally is known as Western Europe, although the post-1989 economic reforms in Eastern and Central Europe, and the impact of these on the West, is also important. Europe is a particularly interesting macro-region for the analysis of restructuring for a number of reasons including: Europe's changing role among the three global superpowers; the increasing level of economic integration in Europe; the immediacy of changes in Eastern Europe; the conjunction of large numbers of developed economies, with late developing and still relatively underdeveloped national and regional economies; and the changing role of state intervention, as neo-liberalism has gained influence at the expense of the previously dominant welfarism of social democracy.

Many of these processes of restructuring have been the focus of the European Science Foundation's Regional and Urban Restructuring in Europe (RURE) project; the main lines of this major research project are described in a special theme issue (1996) of the journal *European Urban and Regional Studies*. Tourism was largely neglected in the early stages of the RURE project, as indeed it has been in the wider literature on restructuring, with a few exceptions such as Britton (1991), Urry (1987) and Montanari and Williams (1995).

This theoretical and empirical neglect is surprising because tourism displays many of the features that have been central to the debates on restructuring. This can be demonstrated by considering the dominant mode of production in tourism, the reorganisation of the labour process in response to rising levels of costs and competition, a shift in the regime of accumulation, and the coexistence of diverse modes of production.

First, it can be argued that, in the 1960s, the dominant mode of production in tourism was mass tourism, which represented a form of mass consumption (Shaw and Williams 1994; Urry 1990). Mass tourism is characterised by a standardised product, and by the domination of markets by producers. Under these conditions, in the 1960s there was the emergence of new monoproduct locations serving the booming market in international mass tourism; these are typified by Spanish resorts such as Torremolinos or Benidorm. This created a new generation of urban structures dedicated to tourism consumption, to set alongside those—such as Blackpool and Scheveningen—which had been created to serve domestic markets at an earlier date. While these centres of mass international tourism were dependent on private sector investments, their creation also required certain forms of state intervention; for example, to regulate production and apply minimum standards to hotels and restaurants, and ensure that minimum sanitary conditions were maintained in the resorts (which was not always the case). The role of the state was also critical in its social investment in facilities such as the transport network (for example airports or motorways) which were essential to guarantee the production of surplus value in the private sector.

The model which emerged was one of state support for, in effect, market dominance by a few companies in the tour and air travel sectors. However, the functioning of these resorts also relied on the existence of very large numbers of small firms, many of which (bus companies, hotels, etc.) were locked into subcontractual relationships with the major tour companies. There is an interresting link here to the debate on the Italian NEC (North East and Centre) model in respect of manufacturing (summarised in Lewis and Williams 1987); were small companies independent and innovative (see Fuá 1983) or were they dependent subcontractors with little capacity for independent growth (Arcangeli et al. 1980)? In our view, mass tourism approximates to the dependency model given the inability of these companies to attract large numbers of tourists independently of the major tour companies.

Secondly, mass tourism was not an invariable form of production and consumption. Instead, there were important changes in mass tourism, partly as a response to changing cultural values (such as a preference for more independent and more active holidays) but also due to the intensification of competition. Given its standardised product (marketing focuses on the generalised attributes of sunshine and sand, or snow and ski-slopes, rather than the particularities of places), competition in mass tourism is essentially at the level of prices. With increasing competition both between tour companies and between countries (for example, from Bulgaria and Turkey) in the 1980s and 1990s, there was pressure for the tour companies to reduce their costs and their prices. This was passed on to their subcontractors and, in the hotel sector, one reaction to this was a shift to greater self-provisioning (Urry 1987), whether in the forms of self-catering, or the introduction of self-service in hotel restaurants. Another strategy was for some subcontractors to operate in the unregistered or informal sector, thereby reducing their labour and other costs; this was particularly important in the growth of tourism in Greece in the 1980s (Leontidou 1991). In many countries, especially Spain and Italy, the availability of Third World immigrant labour—a part of which was illegal—also served to reduce labour costs (see Montanari and Cortese 1993a; and King, Chapter 10).

Thirdly, while firms in the mass tourism sector sought to adjust to changes in both consumer preferences and in production requirements, there were more fundamental shifts in tourism. In particular, there was a change in the mode of production, with at least a relative shift from Fordism to post-Fordism (Urry 1990). This shift was predominantly driven by changes in consumption, that is a greater emphasis on more individualistic or on specialised forms of holidays; this demanded smaller-scale and more flexible provision which created niche markets that provided opportunities for small companies. The shift to post-Fordist forms was also facilitated by production-side changes; for example, many smaller establishments had the advantages of relying on lower cost (a form of self-exploitation) and more flexible family labour (see Williams et al. 1989). Improvements in computer technology and in information technology also allowed many small companies to compete in sophisticated and internationalised niche markets. Changes in the form of state intervention, with the decline in the role of state intervention and increased levels of regional and local interventions, also contributed to this shift in the mode of production of tourism. As local economic development strategies became virtually universalised in Western Europe in the 1980s, many of these incorporated tourism as a central instrument of economic policy, as for example, in Glasgow, Manchester and Barcelona (Law 1994).

Fourthly, care must be taken not to oversimplify the changes which occurred in the mode of production of tourism services. There was no simple linear and universal shift from Fordism to post-Fordism. Instead, as Hudson (1989) has argued in the case of manufacturing, there was typically the coexistence of different modes or forms of production at any one time. Some sectors—for example, rural tourism—never experienced mass production and consumption. Not even coastal tourism was universally constructed as a mass tourism product and experience; instead, many small villages on the coast of Italy, France and Greece relied almost entirely on individual travellers. Similarly, while urban tourism was essentially a specialised and/or individualistic market, some segments—such as international holiday tourism to major cities such as Rome, London and Paris—were dominated by mass consumption and production. And when the shift from mass tourism to post-modernism did occur in the 1980s and 1990s (Urry 1990), its impact was uneven and relative. Indeed, many traditional centres of mass tourism—such as Benidorm—appeared to experience a revival in the 1990s at the same time as there was also growth in more specialised holiday markets elsewhere in Spain.

For all of these reasons, it is clear that analyses of tourism cannot, and should not, be isolated from attempts to analyse the broader processes of restructuring in the European economy. In the next section we consider some of the implications for regional and local development.

1.2 TOURISM AND REGIONAL AND LOCAL DEVELOPMENT

Tourism has important implications for development at all scales. It is of course an important industry in the European Union (EU), accounting for 5.5% of GDP in 1985 and for 8.1% of final private consumption (Lowyck and Wanhill 1992, p. 232). While there has been a tendency to the universalisation of tourism in the 1980s and 1990s, assisted by its widespread adoption as a key element of local development strategies, its distribution is inherently uneven (Williams and Shaw 1991b). It is place-specific for two main reasons. Firstly, because of the inherent nature of the tourist gaze (Urry 1990, 1992); the places that tourists wish to gaze upon are culturally determined, and although they change over time they are inherently selective. Secondly, the economics of mass tourism dictate concentration; this applies both to the requirement for social investment by the state in infrastructure and to the promotional and other operating costs of the large airline and tour companies in the private sector (see Shaw and Williams 1994, Chapter 9). In both cases, economies of scale encourage spatial polarisation. Temporal polarisation in mass tourism (whether the object is winter snow, summer sunshine or attendance at mega-events (see Carreras, Chapter 11) only serves to reinforce the effects of spatial polarisation (see Shaw and Williams 1994, Chapter 1).

While it is recognised that tourism has an uneven distribution, there is no simple or inevitable outcome in terms of the resultant regional patterns. These are subject to specificities of place and time. For example, Claval (Chapter 14) has shown that there have been a number of long-term changes since the seventeenth century in the macro-regional distribution of different types of tourism within Europe. These have been dictated by changes in the geography of production and disposable income within the continent, as well as in transport modes and networks, and in fashions and values. As a result, there have been changes in the social construction of tourism and in the perceived tourism value of particular regions (see Montanari on the Mediterranean (Chapter 3) and Zimmermann on the Alps (Chapter 2).

There have also been changes in the regional distribution of tourism over the shorter term, in consequence of the shift from mass tourism to post-modernist tourism. Post-modernist tourism is much more evenly spread spatially, and touches almost all urban and rural areas. The post-modernist tourism product by its very nature—emphasising individualistic or specialised holidays—is small scale and geographically dispersed. Hence, there is less polarisation, less need for social investment (in large-scale infrastructure) to support the ability of private companies to realise surplus values, and less need to assemble large pools of immigrant labour given that there is greater reliance on local labour (see Montanari and Williams 1995). Empirical analyses in the UK and Ireland (see Williams and Gillmor, Chapter 4) confirm that these shifts in the form of tourism have important implications for the regional distribution of the industry.

Even if there were not these shifts in mode of production, there would be changes within particular modes related to the evolution of particular tourism product cycles, or what Butler terms 'the resort cycle model'. While the Butler (1980) model is a useful descriptive device, which draws attention to the maturing and potential decline of particular tourist destinations, this has been extensively criticised. For example, Wolfe (1983) argues that Butler ignores the environmental dimensions of the growth, maturity and decline of the tourist product, and uses Torremolinos to exemplify this. Cooper (1990a) argues that Butler fails to identify clearly the criteria which delineate different stages and turning points in the product cycle. And Agarwal (1994) stresses that the model fails to appreciate the 'impossibility' of passive decline of resorts in the modern economy. This can also be explained in terms of legitimation, which demands that the local state should intervene to try and modernise the local tourism product given the lack of alternative economic futures for most resorts.

The identification of changes in the degree of polarisation of tourism activity does not in itself indicate whether tourism contributes to the intensification or amelioration of wider patterns of regional inequality (see Williams and Shaw 1994; Williams and Gillmor, Chapter 4). The social construction of tourism—with an emphasis especially in mass tourism on the 'flight' from the pressures of working and urban life—have meant that 'peripheral' areas (in contrast to the dominant and prosperous 'core') have been important tourist destinations. This operates at both the national and international scales. However, there is no inevitability in this pattern; while international mass tourism to Portugal largely favours what had been poorer regions (the Algarve and Madeira), international tourism to the UK favours the most prosperous regions, especially London (Williams 1994). Therefore, in the question of the contribution of tourism to regional inequalities, it remains difficult to generalise; instead, attention must be paid to the specificities of each case.

However, there is a further layer of complexity in these arguments concerning polarisation and regional distributions. Much of the debate is couched in overly simplistic terms because it relies on narrow definitions of tourism, that is it concentrates on the direct and on the localised indirect and induced multiplier effects. This means that the full multiplier effects of tourism, which involve the purchase of material and service inputs from a wide geographical area, are ignored. Yet multiplier studies (Henderson 1975) have shown that there are distinctive spatial patterns of indirect linkages. There is leakage from the local economy to the rest of the region (for example, via labour commuting from the surrounding hinterland), the rest of the national economy (for example, purchases of advertising and accountancy services, or of material inputs such as food and furniture), and internationally (to tour companies, the owners of airlines and hotel chains, etc.). In other words, there are spatial divisions of labour associated with tourism which have as yet been little explored.

As a result of these multiplier effects, there is greater spatial dispersion of tourism impacts in reality than is suggested by the initial assessment of a high degree of polarisation. Secondly, there is greater spatial continuity in the indirect impacts of tourism than in the direct ones. The Butler model suggests that there will be a decline in particular resorts, especially because of competition from new destinations. However, the net effects on the large tour and airline companies may be neutral if they are simply redistributing their market share among destinations. If the headquarters of these companies are in metropolitan areas such as London and Frankfurt, there will be little change in their economic impact in these areas, even if particular destinations experience dramatic declines. Similarly, taking into account these indirect effects reduces the extreme temporal polarisation that is initially observed. Even if individual resorts close down seasonally, there may be year-round jobs in the headquarters of the tour companies, in travel agencies selling holidays, or in factories making non-perishable tourist souvenirs.

Another complexity comes from the need to consider the idea that economies are cumulative outcome of rounds of investments (Massey 1984). There are successive rounds of investment over time, each one of which influences the next round. Massey sees this as the relationship between structure and process. Such an approach also reminds us that tourism is just one of the economic activities in a locality (except for a few cases of extreme monoindustrial structures). Hence, the economic impact of tourism depends on its relationship to other economic sectors, such as its linkages to these in terms of inputs, or the competition/complementarity of its seasonal demand for labour, especially in relation to agriculture in rural areas. But the relationship of tourism to these other sectors goes further than this. Because tourism is the object of the tourist gaze (Urry 1990), its configuration in relation to other sectors of the economy is critical. Thus 'dirty' industry in a neighbouring area can blight the tourism product (see Gilg 1991 on the particular effects on tourism of decentralised planning in Switzerland in this respect). However, this relationship also works in the other direction: tourism can be used to create or reshape place images, thus repositioning localities on the European economic map (see Law 1994 on urban tourism, or Carreras, Chapter 11, on the Barcelona Olympics).

In summary, tourism is now one of the most widespread and most powerful influences shaping the economic futures of regions and localities in Europe. Moreover, the nature of tourism—essentially it is a series of host–guest and environment–guest relationships—means that the impact of tourism on these areas extends far beyond the narrowly economic. These were some of the issues which were addressed by the Lancaster locality study (Bagguley et al. 1989), but there remain considerable gaps in our theoretical and empirical understanding of the role of tourism in local and regional development.

1.3   TOURISM, CAPITAL AND LABOUR

In order to understand more fully the role of tourism in restructuring, we need to examine the relationships between capital and labour in the tourism industry.

This subject is surprisingly under-researched (Shaw and Williams 1994; Chapters 9 and 10 this volume), even though the processes of restructuring of investment and of labour markets in the wider economy are closely linked with changes in the tourism sector. For example, tourism companies have been the subject of takeover bids by non-tourism companies (such as ITT and Midland Bank) as parts of their diversification strategies. Changes in tourism labour markets—such as increased part-time working—are also linked to the restructuring of the labour process in other sectors.

This theoretical neglect of labour market issues in respect of tourism is surprising given that one of the particular attractions of tourism as an object of local and regional development strategies is its capacity for generating employment (Williams and Shaw 1988). For example, it is estimated that there were 7.5 million tourism jobs in the EU in the 1980s, accounting for 6.5% of total employment (Lowyck and Wanhill 1992). Given that there has also been sustained employment growth in tourism, the importance of this sector cannot be overestimated in context of the overall economic restructuring and structural unemployment which have characterised the European economy since the mid 1970s.

The global picture of an expanding tourism sector is, however, misleading in that there is also restructuring within the industry. The key to understanding this is the intense competition which exists in tourist markets; for example, between and among mass resorts, rural and urban destinations and, indeed, among all destinations. There are some specialist niche markets, such as pilgrimages, in which competition is limited. But most destinations are in competition with all others for limited amounts of leisure time and disposable income in their potential markets. The globalisation of information and the widening of accessibility also means that this competition increasingly is over larger and larger areas. Furthermore, Urry (1990) argues that post-modernist shifts in leisure and in culture mean that tourism is also subject to pressures from new forms of locally based entertainment (new leisure centres with new forms of mixed media entertainment, for example).

One of the ways in which tourism firms respond to these pressures is the reorganisation of the labour process; this, in turn, may have a significant effect on the impact of tourism on local economies and its contribution to local employment.

There are several ways in which individual firms are able to reorganise the labour process. One of these is reliance on the informal sector, as a means of reducing costs directly and, also, of pressurising downwards prices in the formal labour market. There has always been a high degree of informality in the organisation of tourism and, for example, many areas of mass tourism had their origins in the letting of rooms by individual households (see Dawes and D'Elia, 1995, on Naples and Sorrento). More generally, Bishop and Hoggett (1989) argue that there are three types of informal labour organisation, and each of these exists in the tourism sector. Firstly, there is outworking, which can be identified in catering, for example, in the form of cooks working at home to supply restaurants with pre-prepared dishes. Secondly, there is communal self-help involving the exchange of goods between households; an example of this in tourism is the exchange of tasks such as the cleaning of holiday cottages, or the passing on of visitors from a guest-house which is full to one which still has vacancies. A third form of informal organisation is the production and consumption of goods within the home itself, a notion that is also common to Gershuny and Miles's (1983) concept of the self-service economy. Examples in the tourism sector include doing maintenance work on a caravan or camping wagon, and rehabilitation of dilapidated cottages—which may have been inherited by first-generation urban immigrants from their rural families—as second homes (see Cavaco, Chapter 7). The balance between the formal and informal sectors may change over time, especially in response to macro-economic changes; for example, the economic crisis in Romania in the early 1990s has seen a shift from hotel-based holidays to camping.

To some degree informalisation is a characteristic shared with many other economic sectors, especially in southern Europe where late development, political and agricultural structures have been conducive to this form of organisation (Mingione 1991). But in tourism informalisation is not only long established but continues to be widespread throughout Europe, both north and south.

There are a number of reasons for the pervasiveness of informalisation in the tourism sector. Perhaps the most important is the nature of tourism; tourism services have to be provided at specific places and times. This means that the demand for tourism services is very uneven or 'lumpy' and varies during the day, the week and the year. Demand is also variable among tourism subsectors at different times; for example, demand peaks for beach services between mid-morning and mid-afternoon, for restaurants in the early evening, and for discos at night. Considerable labour market flexibility is required in response to this uneven demand. This can be theorised in terms of numerical and functional flexibility (Atkinson 1984) and, to a lesser extent, the degree of openness in labour markets (Simms et al. 1988). As a result, part-time, seasonal and casual forms of employment are widespread in the tourism sector (see Shaw and Williams 1994, Chapter 7). These are present in virtually all tourism regions and destinations but the precise employment mix depends on the structure of the local economy (for example, whether it is combined with farm work) and on demand (the proportion of day visitors versus weekend or long holidays, etc.).

Informalisation is also one response to intense competition in mass tourism. In this sector, the nature of mass tourism—essentially a homogeneous product—means that competition is almost entirely on the basis of prices and therefore of costs. Informalisation is one response to cost cutting. One notable example is Greece where unregistered hotels and apartments even appear in the brochures of northern European tour companies (Leontidou 1991).

While informalisation is important in the tourism industry, it is only one of the competitive strategies available to individual firms. Also of importance are the gendering and other forms of social construction of occupations, reliance on subcontracting, the substitution of capital for labour (and occasionally vice versa) depending on factor prices, and self-provisioning.

The gender construction of occupations is particularly strong in tourism. Many jobs are socially constructed as being 'female jobs', such as cleaning, making beds and, in some countries, cooking. There is, of course, nothing inherently female in these jobs. Instead, women carry over into the paid labour market their domestic roles which, in turn, were also socially constructed. There has also been a tendency for women to work part-time, which is also related to social assumptions about their dual roles in the home and the workplace; this is yet another social construction. The net effect of these social constructions has been to allow employers to reduce wages. The social construction of jobs as being suitable for 'women', 'young people' or for 'immigrants' provides similar means for reducing total labour costs.

Large tourism companies, especially tour companies, can also reduce their operating costs through subcontracting to large numbers of small firms (hotels, etc.). This is particularly evident in the strategies of the tour companies, which have adopted and refined a system of package holidays first introduced by the pioneer of organised tours, Thomas Cook. There are some similarities here with the strategies of Benetton and other companies in the manufacturing sector, which have used networks of large numbers of competing small-scale suppliers to reduce their costs (Williams 1987). Such strategies are not exclusive to mass tourism; they may also be observed even in areas of more élitist rural tourism: for example, in the UK, the Country Cottages company rents more than 6000 cottages on behalf of their owners, using sophisticated IT systems to manage this large stock. The owners of these cottages are responsible for their cleaning and stocking, which usually involves family labour or employing 'local women' (another social construction).

Another strategy to reduce costs is the substitution of capital for labour, usually linked to technology changes. In the UK catering industry there have been two main technology-led waves of substitution of capital for labour (Bagguley 1990). The first of these was the introduction of automatic dishwashers in the 1950s and 1960s which reduced the demand for unskilled kitchen assistants, and the second was the introduction of cook–chill technology in the 1980s which reduced the need for skilled chefs.

Self-provisioning has been another strategy for reducing costs. This is evident in the rapid growth of self-catering forms of accommodation in the 1980s and 1990s in both domestic and international European markets; this may involve either renting accommodation or the purchase of second homes (perhaps linked to long-term retirement plans). Self-provisioning is also a strategy for reducing costs in the serviced sector; for example, via introducing self-service meals or direct dialling facilities in hotels.

Most of these trends are common to many other sectors of the economy. But two things are distinctive, even if not unique, in the case of tourism. Firstly, there is a close interdependence between a few large companies and large numbers of small companies. In effect there are oligopsonistic relationships which allow dominant companies to squeeze the prices and profit margins of a multitude of small-scale suppliers. Secondly, there is the fact that there has always been a large degree of flexible production in tourism because of the nature of demand and of the product. The shift to post-modernist tourism may intensify this and have important regional implications, but flexibility is not new.

It should also not be assumed that the growth in post-modernist tourism means that there is a decline—absolute or relative—in the position of the large companies. Instead, there continue to be substantial economies of scale for airlines and tour companies. In addition, the demand for more exotic holiday destinations tends to make tourists more dependent on organised travel, even if this is compensated for by increased independent travel to places such as Spain which were once considered to be exotic destinations but which are now more familiar and have large numbers of internationally owned second homes. The global scan of increasingly mobile capital also reinforces the position of large-scale capital in the tourism sector. Examples include the takeover of the Netherlands-based Center Parcs by British brewing capital, the investment in Disneyland Paris, and (the now bankrupt) Brent Walker group investments in marinas in Spain and Portugal.

1.4 TOURISM AND STATE INTERVENTION

The state is a social force in its own right and state policies do not simply reflect the dynamics of either the economy or of civil society. Hence, the state may introduce and enforce policies—such as minimum standards of safety and of consumers' rights—even if these are in opposition to the interests of tourist firms. This is not to say that the state is an entirely independent force in either the economy or in civil society. Instead, different groups have differential power and resources for pursuing their interests through the state. In much of Europe—especially northern Europe—the tourism industry has been far less effective than, say, agriculture or manufacturing in terms of influencing the state. There are a number of reasons for this, including the fragmented and competitive nature of the industry (especially firms serving domestic versus foreign markets), the general neglect of the service sector until recently, relatively strong growth in most tourism subsectors (taken to signify the absence of any compelling logic for interventionism), and the apparent 'candy floss' or superficial nature (Williams and Shaw 1988) of its economic contribution.

In recent years, tourism has attracted greater attention from the state (Williams and Shaw 1988). One of the main reasons for this is the fact that capitalist societies are inherently crisis prone even if they are non-problematically reproduced for much of the time (see Dunford 1990). In the 1980, as most other sectors seemed to offer zero prospects for growth in much of Europe, tourism came to be seen as a 'solution' to some endemic crises such as unemployment, even if it was also conceived of as the cause of others, for example, road congestion and environmental pollution.

This does not mean that tourism had been totally neglected by the state prior to the unstable and recessionary conditions that have prevailed since the mid 1970s (Williams and Shaw 1991b). There is strong territoriality in the mode of operation of the state. This has meant that it has been active in most European countries in supporting national tourism industries against foreign competitors. According to the OECD (1974) there have been three distinctive phases of tourism policies in the post-Second World War period: in the 1940s and 1950s the emphasis was on removing or lowering international barriers to tourism; after the 1950s there was greater emphasis on the promotion of national tourism industries as a contribution to current account balances; and by the 1970s the state was becoming more involved with the resolution of some of the social and environmental contradictions of tourism.

The state plays a key role in social reproduction in most capitalist societies, and this encompasses tourism in some respects. Its role is limited by its position in the international economic and political order. However, this is not to adopt a reductionist view, for there are important national specificities in state intervention in tourism. This is evident in a comparison of the UK's minimalist approach to tourism policies and the more positive and encompassing approach of the state in, say, Austria. State intervention in tourism is therefore best viewed as the outcome of wider international contingencies, and of the interaction of national interests in and around the state (see Greenwood 1992 for a discussion of the role of pressure groups in this respect).

In the regulationist view there are regimes of accumulation (stable relations between production and consumption) and modes of regulation (beliefs, norms, etc. which support the regime of accumulation). The state has a role to play in respect of both of these, and in particular to ensure that consumption and production are maintained in a consistent relationship. This is achieved by a variety of means, such as social and income redistributive policies (including minimum statutory holiday entitlements), and macro-economic fiscal policies and exchange rate management. Other forms of state intervention include spatial economic planning, minimum health and safety standards, and social investments in airports and other forms of social infrastructure. All such policies potentially can influence tourism. The state also assumes responsibility for ensuring that the mode of regulation is itself successfully reproduced (via health and educational policies) which may also influence tourism via (in some countries) social tourism schemes and, more widely, the reinforcement of particular beliefs about the role of tourism and leisure in European societies. It is above all concerned with successful reproduction of the mode of regulation and the avoidance of crises in both this and in the regime of accumulation.

State intervention does not mean the end of crises in capitalist societies, only that they are internalised. The state itself is subject to rationality crises such as which criteria should govern state action, most significantly whether equity or efficiency should be the primary objective. An example in tourism would be the criteria used to determine the locations of state investment in transport, or in establishing national parks. There are also legitimation crises if, for example, the outcomes of state policies are very different from their intended aims. There are also fiscal crises within the state, and these have been particularly intense during the early 1990s. These can lead to the redrawing of public versus private boundaries in health and social services. They may also lead to cuts in direct state support to production, as for example happened in the UK where Section 4 grants to tourism businesses were eliminated at the same time as there was a major reduction in expenditure on all forms of regional policy in the late 1980s.

One of the most important instruments for state intervention in tourism has been regional policy. Tourism occupies a different position in this in different countries; for example, it has been relatively strong in Italy and relatively weak in the UK (see Yuill et al. 1991). In the late 1980s and early 1990s the scope and content of regional policy have, however, been reduced in most European countries, because of fiscal crises in the state, and ideological shifts in the debate over the role of the state. To some extent, central government initiatives have been replaced by local and regional development initiatives. In many instances this has actually increased the prominence given to tourism in local economic and cultural strategies (see Law 1994 on urban tourism).

There has also been a redrawing of the boundaries of state intervention as a result of the expanding role of the EU. Tourism has largely had a 'Cinderella' status in respect of the EU, as previously had been the case in national policies. EU tourism policy was either very weak or non-existent until the mid 1980s. Even them, tourism was mainly a matter for discussion and relatively few resources were devoted to specific tourism initiatives (Williams and Shaw 1994). Instead, EU policy for tourism has been most effective where it has been incorporated into other fields of policy concern. One example is transport where EU attempts to liberalise air passenger movements and to build a European super rail and road network could eventually change the face of tourism in Europe. Tourism has achieved considerable attention in the Fifth Action Plan for the Environment (Blacksell 1994) and, as a result, significant flows of funds are being directed to the sector. Finally, since the 1970s tourism has attracted funds within the European Regional and Development Fund programme, and latterly in the Community Support Frameworks. In 1989–93 this accounted for 5.5% of the total aid for Objective 1 (peripheral) regions, 7.5% of that for Objective 2 regions (urban decline) and 6.8% of that for Objective 5b regions (rural under-development) (see Lowyck and Wanhill 1992).

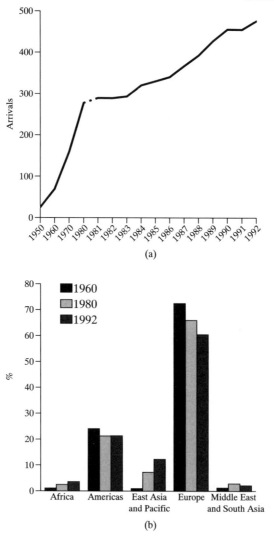

Figure 1.1. International tourism 1950–92. Source: WTO (1993)

1.5 FUTURE PERSPECTIVES

Tourism has been subject to a number of processes of restructuring in recent years, and one of the principal forces of change has been globalisation. It is likely that international competition will further intensify in future. Urry (1990, p. 40) writes that '. . . while the producers are to a significant extent spatially fixed, in that they have to provide particular services in particular places, consumers are increasingly mobile, able to consume tourist services on a global basis'. The tourist industry has been subject to large increases in international movements since the 1960s (Figure 1.1(a)), which confirms that there is a tendency to greater globalisation. However, it is still largely dominated by regionalisation (Figure 1.1(b)), with Europe dominating both international arrivals and departures.

The question is how future changes in tourism will impact upon the European economic and social space. According to the World Tourism Organisation (WTO) (1991), while there will continue to be strong absolute growth in Europe, its share of the world market will decline, particularly because of stronger growth rates in the Pacific Rim. Northern Europe already has relatively strong participation in tourism. Therefore, unless there is a major redistribution of income (by either the market or the state—neither of which seems likely) growth will in future be relatively modest, while access to tourism continues to be highly socially polarised. There are, however, prospects for growth in Southern and Eastern Europe, where until recently participation in tourism—especially international tourism—has been limited. There are already signs of incipient growth in the former Eastern bloc countries which are reviving some traditional forms of mass tourism in the Alps (see Zimmermann, Chapter 2) but further expansion is contingent on economic political developments.

With respect to restructuring, the major question centres on whether (or perhaps when) and where crises of overproduction will be evident in the tourism sector. There are already signs that this is happening in particular localities such as the North Sea resorts and some Spanish resorts (see Marchena Gómez and Vera Rebollo, Chapter 6). But there is also the possibility of a more globalised crisis given the enormous amount of investment in almost all forms of tourism during the 1980s and 1990s. It may well be that in the next decade tourist destinations will figure less as centres of accumulation and more as localities in crisis, requiring new forms of economic activity to allow diversification away from over-reliance on a crisis-affected tourism sector. At present, however, such a scenario seems over-pessimistic given the prominent role of tourism in so many local and regional strategies, even if the main reason for this remains the lack of viable alternatives.

The key to interpreting some of the future restructuring issues for tourism is to identify how it interacts with other interests and sectors. It is, for example, unique in the way it impacts upon local cultural and environmental systems, and in the way it interacts with other economic sectors (for example, the seasonal, weekly and daily interchange of labour with agriculture in the case of farm tourism). It is also used as an instrument for changing the images of places so as to reposition them on the economic map of Europe. This means that the resolution of the many crises attendant on tourism development will require broad strategies which encompass all of these particular roles and interests.

Part I

REGIONAL DEVELOPMENT AND POPULATION SYSTEMS

2 The Alpine Region: Regional Restructuring Opportunities and Constraints in a Fragile Environment

FRIEDRICH M. ZIMMERMANN
University of Klagenfurt, Austria

2.1 INTRODUCTON: THE ALPS IN THE 1990S

The Alpine Arc is a mountain system with an area of 240 000 sq. km. It is approximately 1000 km in length and 130–250 km in width, and encompasses parts of France, Italy, Switzerland, Austria, Germany, Liechtenstein and Slovenia. This is one of the most important tourist regions not only in Europe but, indeed, in the world. Nevertheless, it is a region which is subject to immense restructuring pressures.

The present-day socio-economic situation of the Alps can be characterised by the following features:

- A macro-region which was formerly the preserve of mountain agriculture has become the 'roof garden of Europe', providing a major recreation and sports area for the continent's urban population.
- The importance of traditional sustainable agriculture has been and is decreasing, and is becoming concentrated on the valley floors where production conditions are more favourable.
- The exponential growth of tourism and the spatial diffusion of facilities since the 1960s has led to the physical and economic predominance of tourism in many Alpine areas. About 25% of global tourism turnover is generated in the Alps.
- Favourable conditions for the production of tourism services, and the unique market position of the Alps, have resulted in a one-sided winter dependence with associated risks of economic failure and disintegration tendencies for the local socio-economic and ecological systems. The presence of 50 million tourists, who spend more than 300 million overnight

European Tourism: Regions, Spaces and Restructuring. Edited by A. Montanari and A.M. Williams.
© 1995 European Science Foundation. Published in 1995 by John Wiley & Sons Ltd.

stays in the Alps, and of more than 150 million short-term (one-day to weekend) visitors per year is indicative of the types of pressures experienced in this macro-region.

- There is intense land-use competition between agriculture and the supra- and infrastructural needs of tourism. The latter are illustrated by some basic tourism statistics: there is a supply of 3 million beds in the tourism industry, and there are approximately 12 000 ski-lifts which are able to transfer 1.2 million persons to the mountain tops to use more than 40 000 ski-slopes with an extent of 1000 sq. km and a length of 120 000 km.
- The intensive use of the Alpine region for tourism causes ecological prob- lems, such as scarring of the ground, noise and pollution. There is a real danger that existing mass tourism activities will destroy the basis for future tourism developments.
- The Alps are criss-crossed by 405 000 km of transportation lines, connect- ing some of the major economic areas of Europe. Tourist traffic is superim- posed on a heavy base of transit traffic (e.g. 13 million cars and trucks use the Brenner freeway every year), leading to sharp conflicts with the local population and the environment.
- Local populations in Alpine areas face the threat of becoming more and more economically dependent on tourism, and of losing their cultural identity and their traditional economic base (with its associated social relationships).

Although there are a number of shared features of Alpine tourism, developments in individual countries over the last two decades have been typified by contrasting tourism ideologies, as is illustrated by the cases of the Swiss, Austrian and Bavarian Alps. In Switzerland, Alpine tourism has had a long and successful tradition, and today the Swiss tourism industry is well known for its high-level resorts with grand hotels, self-catering apartments and second homes. When traditional tourism structures encountered difficulties in the 1980s, this initiated an intensive discus- sion of economic and ecological issues, partly based upon research projects con- ducted on behalf of the UNESCO Man and Biosphere (MAB) programme. Austrian tourism development has followed a different course. In consequence of the effects of two world wars, many areas in Austria had to restart their tourist industries in the 1950s and made substantial profits out of mass tourism develop- ment in the 1970s and 1980s. The development of cableways and ski-lifts was particularly dynamic until the end of the 1980s, when ecological concerns led to a politically initiated end of quantitative growth. In Germany a restrictive tourism development strategy for the Bavarian Alps was introduced at a much earlier date: at the beginning of the 1970s the *Alpenplan* was created so as to protect certain Alpine areas (see Bayerisches Staats-Ministerium für Landesentwicklung und Um- weltfragen 1980). In France the pattern of Alpine development was also different, essentially being an *ex-nihilo* creation in high-altitude zones with very weak links to local economies and societies.

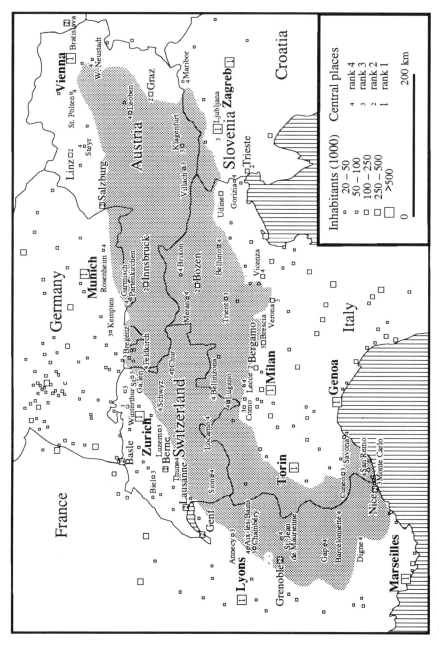

Figure 2.1. The Alps. Source: Bätzing (1993)

Having briefly outlined some of the major issues and the recent development of Alpine tourism, the remainder of this chapter focuses in more detail on some of the wider processes impacting on the industry, and considers the options for restructuring tourism in ways which are compatible with long-term sustainable development. First, however, it is necessary to note some of the difficulties involved in analysing such a large, diverse and politically fragmented region.

Given that the Alpine Arc encompasses several countries with different political, legal and organisational frameworks, it is not surprising that it is virtually impossible to assemble a single harmonised database which serves to describe the entire region on a comparable basis. The defined borders of the Alps (see Figure 2.1) are based on physio-geographic parameters, which do not accord with political borders on a state or federal level. Using Eurostat annual tourism statistics would mean working with the following regions/nations: France (Rhône–Alpes, Provence–Alps–Côte d'Azure); Italy (Piedmont, Lombardy, Trentino–Alto Adige); Germany (Bavaria); Switzerland; Liechtenstein; Austria; and Slovenia. These offer, at best, very crude approximations of the Alpine region. Coming down to the level of local communities, tourism-based data are partly if not consistently available but anyway are not directly comparable because of differences in the ways that they are collected. Therefore, certain aspects of this study will have to rely on a case-study approach.

2.2 THE ALPINE TOURISM PRODUCT

2.2.1 New challenges for the production and delivery of services

Important changes in the social and demographic profile of Western European visitors have generated new challenges for the Alpine tourism industry at all levels. A number of significant themes have been identified in the literature on social change, such as the move to shorter and more flexible working hours, dynamic development of the right to holidays, high and increasing levels of individual vehicle ownership, creation of a 'new middle class' with particular interests in leisure and recreation, saturation in the consumer sector, recurrent and perhaps structural unemployment problems, and extremely rapid developments in the communication media (see Krippendorf 1980; Bernt and Pauer 1988; Smeral 1985, 1986; Opaschowski 1987, 1988, 1992; Steinecke 1989). These developments, in the context of post-industrial society, have had a lasting effect on tourism structures in the Alps, revealing the following specific characteristics:

● Changes in the demographic life-cycle in Western Europe have affected the main pattern of holiday travel into the Alpine regions in a negative way. This is due to a decline in the number of young people (and therefore a decline in the supply of potential skiers), an increase of active senior citizens (greater travel experience is encouraging long-distance trips). There has also been an increase in the number of single households, which are independent financially, institutionally and timewise; they increasingly tend to favour long-distance or overseas travel activities.

- There have been changes in the style of holidays due to social shifts such as increased experience of travelling, reductions in linguistic barriers, the multiplication of competitive tourism products, new preferences and tastes, a search for freedom and adventure and for what may be termed a 'sense of life', escape from and compensation for everyday routine, and increased personal body consciousness, and environmental awareness. This leads to fragmentation of the main holiday structure into a number of shorter holidays, the motives for this being as varied as the places visited. However, these shifts have been counterbalanced to some extent by a parallel development, in that the opening-up of Central and Eastern Europe has created a new potential demand group. The opening-up of this new market has had an unexpected consequence in the lengthening, or rather the revival, of the product cycle of the traditional 'long main holiday taken once a year'.

- As an obvious expression of the rising expectations with respect to values and standards, increasing attention will have to be paid in tourism to the environment. It can be expected that, in future, the quality of the environment will be an (or even the) essential criterion for tourists when they make decisions as to where to spend their holidays. So far, there are only minimal signs that the necessary process of reorientation is under way in respect of the tourism supply. However, a short-sighted concern with profit maximisation should be supplemented by greater ecological consciousness in planning and development.

In addition to the social process outlined within the field of demand, there were also important changes in the supply of tourism services and products in the 1980s. Social change has left an indelible imprint on the Alpine living area, where modern society—with all its recreational activities—has overlapped with the traditional Alpine farming society. The post-war generation has been superseded by a younger generation which has been influenced by their guests' way and style of life, and which is no longer willing to work in tourism without free time and leisure, and opportunities for family life. An increasing number of low-quality family-run enterprises face the problem of generational succession. In seeking a successor inside or outside the family, quality and profitability are the decisive factors. However, even where these are positive, the necessity for considerable investments and high risk levels and indebtedness may serve to deter potential investors.

One of the critical impacts of these tourism developments is to be seen in the local housing market. There are significant connections between the importance and quality of tourism (at least in terms of image) in a place and real estate prices. Not least, the enormous pressure of leisure homes on the local real estate market may lead to extremely high housing price levels which pose

many problems for young people in the local community. In practice, they
have little opportunity to buy real estate and to remain in their native communities. The consequence is that areas tend to become overwhelmed by external
and, sometimes, foreign influences (via the owners of second homes, seasonal
employees, etc.) which do not identify with the region and the local culture;
there is a real danger that the strains of mass tourism and reduced quality of
life can lead to the loss of a 'sense of place' among the local population.

2.2.2   Developments in Alpine tourism products

Until recently the winter tourism season seemed to have its own dynamic, with
a continuous growth in demand and average increase of more than 10% per
annum from the late 1960s. This reflected the suitability of the Alpine regions
for touristic activities in winter, for which there was virtually no effective
competition in Europe, the growing number of second and third holidays as
well as short trips, and the development of a 'new' middle class with potent
market power. Subsequently the rate of growth has slowed down, leading to
suggestions that the development of the winter season has reached its limits,
and that the mature phase of the traditional 'winter sports product' has been
entered. Additionally discussions about 'global climatic change and the need
for machine-made snow', 'ski-slopes and forest decline', 'avalanches and
floods', etc. have led to an increasing ecological consciousness, especially
among the young generation which is the main potential source of demand for
Alpine skiing (70% of all skiers are younger than 40 years old).

In contrast, the summer season—with all its long traditions—has been characterised by very strong fluctuations since the beginning of the 1970s and, up
to the middle of the 1980s, by dramatic recessions. Up to 1972 the annual rates
of increase were almost 10%, but then the first losses were recorded followed
by a short but vigorous phase of recovery with a peak of overnight stays at the
beginning of the 1980s. The following years were characterised by heavy falls
in demand, with a resulting decrease of income, and ensuing serious problems
for those involved with the production of summer tourism services in the Alps.
By the middle of the 1980s, overnight stays had dropped to the level they had
attained in 1970. The success of new marketing strategies, improvements in
the supply of summer tourism services (rafting, parachuting, hang-gliding,
etc.), and the effects of the opening to Central and Eastern Europe led to a
stabilisation of summer tourism in the Alps. By the beginning of the 1990s the
following tendencies were observable:

- The touristic product that can be termed 'summer holidays in the Alps' in its
  traditional form seems to have lost much of its dynamism. For example, in 1980
  Austria was still the preferred destination for the long-stay holidays of Germans,
  but by 1990 it had fallen to third place behind Italy and Spain. One important
  exception to this is the attraction of guests from Central and Eastern European

countries, who tend to take their first tourism experience in Western Europe in the form of a long summer holiday trip; this serves to revitalise the traditional form of mass tourism behaviour in Western Europe just when this had seemed to be entering a phase of significant if not terminal decline.

- The leisure behaviour of Western European tourists has been changing because of the aforementioned socio-economic, demographic and social trends. This has led to holiday time being subdivided into three or more shorter holidays with more specialised motivations and different locations (e.g. a winter holiday in the Alps, a summer vacation, and a specific profile of activities being spent elsewhere in culture-oriented city tours, non-European destinations, etc.).

- The Alps are subject to extensive international competition. Losses in the summer season are increasingly important for the so-called 'mountain summer' tourism product in regions with an excellent winter image. This may herald, in some areas, possible development towards a single winter season with virtually no summer tourism, and with considerable attendant negative economic effects.

- Beside the factors already mentioned, there are other reasons for the negative summer development: to mention but one there is a loss of attractive countryside for summer activities due to the building of large hotels, cableways and ski-lifts, ski-slopes, leisure homes, roads, etc.

- In the 1970s and the early 1980s many kinds of resources (investments, subsidies, publicity, etc.) have been reallocated to the winter season, while the summer season has been increasingly neglected. However, new ways of thinking within tourism policy and the economy since the middle of the 1980s have been responsible for an improvement in the situation.

In addition to the seasonal rhythm of demand peaks in long-term tourism, there are also short-term tourism rhythms caused by a dynamic development of day trips and short-term visits. While this offers advantages for the winter season, it requires greater flexibility in the accommodation sector, and many regions are increasingly faced with the problem of utilisation conflicts. It is expected that the future development of short-term tourism in the Alps will involve a quantitative increase in day trips and short holidays, with demand from Germany being particularly strong. The tourism industry will have to pay special attention to this fact, above all given that there is the danger of utilisation conflicts with long-term tourism.

2.3   THE REGIONAL DISTRIBUTION OF TOURISM IN THE ALPS

2.3.1   Uneven regional tourism development

The development of tourism in the Alps had already begun in the eighteenth century, when artists, writers, poets and members of the aristocracy travelled

for educational, religious or health reasons. Tourism as a form of mass phenomenon started in the second half of the nineteenth century with the first
railroads crossing the Alps (Brenner 1867; Gotthard 1881; Tauern 1909).
Besides the previously mentioned motivations for travelling, summer recreation and mountain climbing started to become important. In 1863 Thomas
Cook led the first package tour to Switzerland and, at the same time, climbers
began to explore the peaks of the Alps. Reacting to the increasing number of
tourists, cableways were established (Rigi 1873, Berner Oberland-Bahn 1890,
Schafberg 1893). By the early twentieth century Switzerland was the most
important destination within the Alps and the Swiss tourist industry consisted
of three main types of tourism: (1) high-level tourism in the grand hotels along
the shores of the pre-Alpine lakes like Geneva and Thun (e.g. Montreux); (2)
mountaineering in Alpine valley resorts like Grindelwald or Zermatt; and (3)
tourism devoted to health cures (notably tuberculosis) in resorts placed on
sunny Alpine terraces above the fog level (like Davos).

In Austria the product cycles are comparable with: upper-class tourism,
associated with the Austrian–Hungarian aristocracy, especially in the Salz-
kammergut; mountain-climbing and summer recreation in the mountains, enforced by the Alpenverein, an association dedicated to leisure activities in the
Alps, e.g. around the Großglockner or the Semmering; and health resorts based
on thermal water like Badgastein and Bad Ischl.

Towards the end of the nineteenth century, tourism was influenced by innovations in sport and recreation. Skiing and ice-skating were invented as new
types of recreation among Swiss youth. While at first this was the preserve of
the wealthy, the increasing popularity of winter sports changed the nature of
Alpine tourism after the First World War. The opportunity to build up a
second season, and to diversify the supply of tourism away from existing
nuclei, increased the economic impact of tourism and contributed to stemming
population losses in the harsh environment of the Alps. New openings and
challenges were created for Alpine farming society.

While the Swiss, German and Austrian development of winter sports resorts
was associated with the enlargement of existing rural settlements, development
within the French Alps is mostly an *ex-nihilo* creation in high-altitude areas.
Three stages are clearly identifiable, associated with particular resorts:

1. First generation (Alpe d'Huez)
2. Second generation (Courchevel)
3. Third generation (La Plagne, Tignes) (see Haimayer 1984, Barbier 1978).

This kind of tourism is a development of recent decades, characterised by the
building of new resorts and the extension of existing centres, the increasing
importance of large multinational companies, and limited environmental
awareness with the major transformation of many Alpine areas. Changes are
apparent in the landscape, in modern and purpose-built chalets, in apartments,

hotels and restaurants, in ski-lifts and ski-slopes in high-altitude areas. Agriculture has largely disappeared because of the exodus of population and the shift of the remaining residents to tertiary-sector jobs. Tourism has been the underlying reason for a fundamental change in society in these areas (see Tuppen 1991).

2.3.2   The Alps and the spatial matrix of tourism flows

Turning first to the origins of Alpine tourists, it is clear that foreign demand is the dynamic factor in Alpine tourism. The Alps have secured a very distinctive market profile, among international destinations, in terms of the origin of its tourists. Austria's special position in the international market stems from two particular features. One is the extremely high share (77%) of foreigners in the total of about 124 million overnight stays per year. By comparison, the proportion in Switzerland is 46%, and in Italy only 29%. Secondly, there is a very high level of dependency on guests from a single country of origin, that is, Germany, which accounts for 60% of all foreign overnight stays in Austria; in Switzerland or Italy the comparable values are about 40%. The foreign market segment generally has a positive effect on both the tourist trade as well as the national budget. This dependency can be problematic in the event of global, European or sectoral recession and unemployment. However, the converse is also true for, as long as the values and standards of this very significant market segment are stable, then the Alpine tourism industry does not face major difficulties. The question is, of course, whether they are largely invariable or in the process of transformation.

The destinations of the tourists in the Alps are somewhat more complex. This is illustrated by the case of Austria, where the development of tourism since the Second World War has been extremely dynamic (see Figures 2.2 and 2.3). Dynamism in Austria has meant an exceptionally high level of development of winter tourism in Alpine areas, which has caused an extremely polarised distribution of tourism in favour of the western Alpine areas. The demand for winter tourism services has strongly impacted, with differing degrees of intensity, on virtually all those regions with some capacity for winter recreational activities. The majority of tourists are polarised in just three provinces—Vorarlberg, Tyrol and Salzburg—which together account for more than two-thirds of all guests visiting Austria; furthermore, the degree of spatial concentration is continuing to intensify. This reshaping of the spatial matrix of tourism flows has had a differential impact on the three main types of destinations within Austria, and more generally the Alpine system. Firstly, there are the mountain communities which are characterised by a combination of summer and winter tourism, by a preponderance of foreign tourists, and significant levels of demand for short-term tourism. Included among these are some monofunctional winter regions in the areas of Arlberg, the Paznaun and the Radstätter Tauern. The second main area within the Alps are lake

28

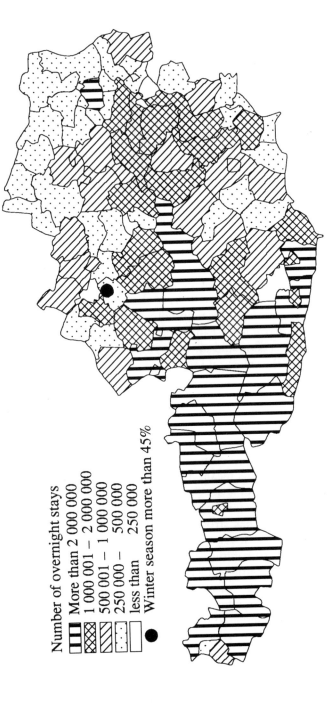

Figure 2.2. Tourism in Austria in 1970. Source: Prepared by author on the basis of data provided by Osterreichisches Statistisches Zentralamt (1970)

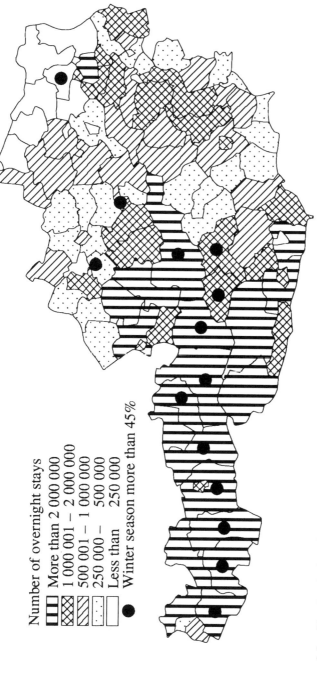

Figure 2.3. Tourism in Austria in 1992. Source: Prepared by the author on the basis of data provided by Osterreichisches Statistisches Zentralamt (1992)

30

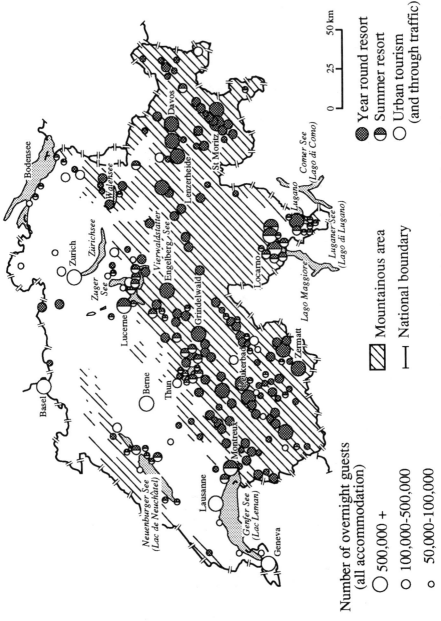

Figure 2.4. Tourism in Switzerland in 1991. Source: Bundesamt für Statistik Länderbericht Schweiz (1991)

communities with long-established tourism traditions. Their existing economic, social and built structures make it difficult to respond to the new structures of demand, not least because of the effect of inertia. The third main area of demand are the spas, which have survived the different phases of tourism development by adapting their specialist facilities to modern market circumstances, in some cases even including the development of winter sports activities.

To complete this picture of tourism in the region, it is necessary to mention that within or at the edge of the Alps, there are cities which offer either important cultural activities and sights, like Salzburg or Vienna, or have been able to enhance their image by hosting international sporting events, like Innsbruck, the venue of the Olympic Games in 1964 and 1976. Significantly, an attempt to mount an application for the Olympics in 2002 failed because of a negative popular referendum. This was very much a consequence of ecological consciousness which had been boosted by the negative effects of the 1992 Olympic Games in Albertville (France). Last but not least, there are also many smaller recreation communities, which mostly lie either close to the major tourist centres and take advantage of their infrastructure, or offer alternative, small-scale supplies of tourism services and products.

The importance of the Alpine Arc for tourism in the adjacent states cannot be overemphasised, as is illustrated by the example of Switzerland (Figure 2.4): more than 80% of all overnight stays in Switzerland are spent in resorts located within the Alps. Most of the Alpine resorts are visited in summer and winter but, in spite of their image as winter recreational spaces, there is a predominance of summer tourism which accounts for approximately 55% of all tourism overnight stays. The leading tourism regions of Switzerland are Graubünden with 6.5 million, Wallis with 4.3 million, and the Berner Oberland with 3.7 million overnight stays out of a Swiss total of 35 million. In summary, therefore, although the importance of the Alps to the tourism economy of a much larger macro-region is unquestionable, its precise impact— notably in terms of spatial and temporal polarisation—is uneven and highly intricate.

2.4 THE ECONOMIC IMPACT OF ALPINE TOURISM

Whatever difficulties exist in securing comparable statistics on tourism flows within the Alps, these are magnified when it comes to analysing the economic impact of tourism. For this reason, this section adopts a case-study approach, concentrating on Austria and Switzerland.

2.4.1 The case of Austria

Austria's international tourism receipts are valued at more than $13 billion (1992). Domestic tourism is also economically significant. There are more than

6 million domestic tourists, who account for 29 million tourist nights per year, and they make an important contribution to total tourism receipts. More significant, however, is Austria's position within the international market for tourism. When looked at in terms of average tourist receipts per inhabitant, Austria has the leading world position with $1700 per person, followed by Switzerland ($1100), Spain ($550), Italy and Greece.

The economic impact of tourism is mediated by the structure of the industry. The organisation of the tourism industry in Austria—and there are similar structures in the Alpine areas of Bavaria, Italy and in some cases in Slovenia too—can be characterised as small to medium scale, while the sources of capital are mostly private and family enterprises are dominant. There has been only limited direct multinational investment, and venture capital is of restricted importance within Austrian tourism. In the case of the accommodation sector, for example, development is due to strong demand pressure dating back to the early 1960s. From an initial number of approximately 200 000 guest beds in 1950, the supply had increased to more than 1.2 million by 1992. This development is not evenly distributed in respect of either the seasons or individual groups of establishments. While high-quality five- and four-star

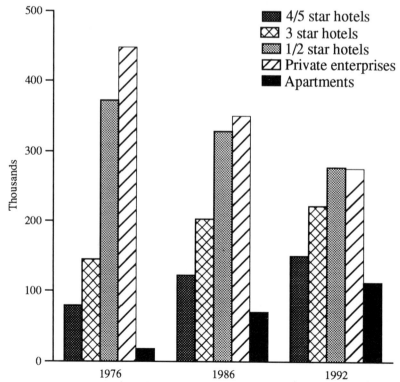

Figure 2.5. Tourism beds, by category, in Austria. Source: Prepared by the author on the basis of data provided by Osterreichisches Statistisches Zentralamt (1970–)

establishments with about 150 000 beds increased by 90% between 1976 and 1992, medium-quality three-star establishments (160 000 beds) also increased by around 60%. In contrast, two- and one-star establishments, which are still predominant in Austria's commercial supply, with 275 000 beds, have declined by 40% (see Figure 2.5).

In contrast to Switzerland, where the letting of private rooms is of little importance in the supply of tourism services, this sector is of critical significance in Austria. It has contributed significantly to the diffusion of tourism to peripheral regions and the sector functions as an important reserve of accommodation for peak periods, hence increasing the flexibility of the supply side. However, it is precisely the letting of private rooms which has been most severely affected by losses (of the order of 40% between 1976 and 1992). The strong expansion of this sector up to the mid 1970s peaked in the summer of 1976 with an absolute total of 470 000 beds and a share of 40% of the total bed potential. The market share of less than 25% in the mid 1990s is due to a greater demand for quality and to dynamic development in the case of apartments (Zimmermann 1991b).

This brief sketch of development in the accommodation sector shows how the present economic structure has evolved. The profitability of establishments has held up if their quality level is adequate and if there is a possibility of operating in two seasons. However, profit margins have decreased elsewhere, and the constant need to innovate to maintain standards requires continuous reinvestment. The situation is worse in those establishments which do not provide a high level of amenities and in the tourist regions which operate in one season only; here incomes are too low to maintain or achieve the necessary quality standards. There is in effect a negative downward spiral, for only better quality guarantees an adequate market share in modern Alpine tourism. These shifts in the accommodation sector also have distinctive distributional impacts for particular regions and segments are differentially affected by the uneven pattern of change.

2.4.2 The case of Switzerland

At the beginning of the 1950s Swiss tourism accounted for about 15 million tourist nights, while 40 years later the numbers are around 75 million (including hotels, apartments, camping, etc.). In 1992 the receipts from international tourism were around $9 billion (Schweizer Tourismus-Verband 1993). However, in contrast to Austria, the modern tourism scene in Switzerland was clearly established by the 1970s. Since then demand has remained fairly static.

The static demand of the last 20 years caused a number of problems within the Swiss tourism industry, such as regional imbalances caused by an increasing emphasis on the winter season within a static overall market share. Other issues relate to an increase in self-catering and, in consequence, a lower level of

Table 2.1. Economic dependency on tourism—the case of four Man and Biosphere test regions

	Pays-d'Enhaut	Aletsch	Grindelwald	Davos
Tourism-dependent jobs (%)	35	80	90	80–90
Tourist nights	600 000	700 000	1 200 000	2 500 000
Local population	4 200	1 000	3 500	10 500
Accommodation capacity (beds)	6 700	13 600	9 400	20 500
Economic sectors[a] 1950 (%)	P 42	P 69	P 38	P 8
	S 22	S 12	S 20	S 22
	T 37	T 19	T 42	T 70
Economic sectors 1980 (%)	P 22	P 14	P 11	P 4
	S 21	S 22	S 21	S 19
	T 57	T 64	T 68	T 77
General characteristics	Rural recreation area	Growing tourism and service region	Traditional and international resort	International tourism and congress city

[a] P = primary; S = secondary; T = tertiary.
Source: Messerli (1989).

economic revenue, as well as the increased influence of foreign capital, foreign ownership and foreign workers. The Swiss tourism industry is characterised by a decreasing importance of the hotel sector (capacity 266 000 beds), which had previously played such a positive role in creating the strong 'image-factor' of Swiss tourism. This change is partly a result of the growing tendency towards self-provisioning in the Swiss domestic holiday sector, which contributes to an increasing number of self-catering apartments and second homes (about 400 000 beds). Another reason for the restructuring of the production and delivery of tourism services lies in foreign exchange movements which leads to the partly accurate perception of foreign visitors that Switzerland is an expensive country to visit. The various forms of restructuring have also contributed to a regional redistribution. The position of the Alpine resorts has been strengthened because of the increasing demand for winter sports activities (Gilg 1991). However, this raises a different issue: in the regions of rapid tourism expansion, fears are increasing about the danger of a monostructural economy. This is illustrated by Messerli (1989) who has identified economic dependency in four Man and Biosphere test regions (Table 2.1).

Economic development in all four areas is highly tourism oriented. There has been a decrease of more than 40% in the number of agricultural enterprises since 1950, and there is an extreme job dependency on tourism, with the exception of Pays-d'Enhaut. The dependency can also be expressed in terms of the ratio of capacity (beds) to local people, which is 13 : 1 in Aletsch, 3 : 1 in Grindelwald, 2 : 1 in Davos and 1.5 : 1 in Pays-d'Enhaut.

2.5 FUTURE TRENDS IN ALPINE TOURISM

2.5.1 Influences on future development

Ecological challenges

One of the most important negative aspects of Alpine tourism, and one which is cited equally by both guests and residents, is the ecological situation. The increase in environmental consciousness is underlined by the fact that, in 1985, only 30% of tourists recognised ecological problems as being of consequence, while in 1990 the share was almost 90%. The following eight problems are the most important to be overcome if future tourism development is not to be endangered (Zimmermann 1992a):

1. The exploitation of nature by tourist infra- and suprastructures, especially as winter sports resorts reach their load-bearing capacity. This has already led to a change in politicians' views. For example, the province of Vorarlberg halted the development of cableways in their Alpine zones in 1978, while the most important winter province, Tyrol, ordered a 'meditation phase' of 3 years to allow reassessment of ecological and social problems and costs.
2. The spoilation of the countryside, and in consequence of cultivation, together with land speculation have led to the expansion of settlement into ecologically sensitive zones and to the necessity to regulate the drainage network.
3. Because of these developments, the consequences of elemental forces have intensified, with a significant increase in the risk of floods, landslides, avalanches, etc. Also important in this is the careless exploitation of natural resources, e.g. clearing of woodland, devastation of protective forests, damage to soil, opening-up of glaciers for winter sports activities, road-building, etc.
4. The decline of agriculture and, in consequence, the lack of attention to preserving and shaping the landscape, have impaired the natural scenery which is such an important element in the social construction of the summer season. Furthermore, with the decline of agriculture, there is a loss of one of the stabilising factors in rural social structure. This opens the possibility that relatively harmonious traditional social structures will be displaced by non-local structures and architectural styles. In short, traditional culture and ways of life may give way to a 'Lederhosen mentality'.
5. The Alpine woodlands are threatened by utilisation conflicts and the increasing space requirements of tourism. The decline in the forest area makes essential the better protection of the remaining reserves. Otherwise the leisure function of the woodlands will be lost for the future.
6. Waste separation, avoidance and utilisation will be a central problem in the future because there is increasingly fierce local resistance to the development of new refuse pits.

7. The transit traffic is one of the most evident problems within the Alpine area. In several regions local populations' endurance levels have already been reached or exceeded.
8. The electric power-supply companies will have to rethink their strategies. There is a clear conflict between ecology-orientated tourism and the construction of power stations, the transfer of water from several Alpine valleys to one huge central power station, and the disfigurement of the landscape by high-tension power lines, for example.

It is essential that the ecological problems outlined should be resolved by appropriate means, whether these are legal, financial, involve training measures, the creation of environmental models and cooperation concepts, or investments in 'human capital' in the form of consultation where individual solutions to problems are required. By the year 2000 nature and the environment will almost certainly be the main factors in reconstructed high-quality tourism.

Economic challenges

In the 'New Europe' the future development of tourism will be influenced by two major external effects. First, the EU membership of Austria will affect the structure of supply in this country. A number of processes are likely to be triggered, the most important of which are spatial polarisation, commodification and external control:

- Spatial concentration in the west, commercialisation of supply and greater professional management will increase the pressure on small-scale family enterprises.
- Increasing foreign investments, together with a rising demand for leisure homes (especially from southern Germany), will result in greater external control over the development of tourism. *In extremis*, there could be a shift towards a spatial separation of the local and the tourism societies, as has already happened in the French Alps.

At the same time, there are few signs of a dynamic self-sustaining growth in Austria's capacity to attract tourists. Considerable refinement of the supply of tourism products and services, combined with sophisticated marketing strategies, are required in order to attract guests from Western European countries (see Zimmermann 1989, 1991a).

The second major factor affecting future tourism trends is the new dimension added to tourism flows by the opening of Central and Eastern Europe. Up to the year 1990, tourism policy in the Alps was almost universally oriented towards enhancing the quality of the supply side of tourism. The tourism industry is now faced by the dynamic development of demand. This is illustrated by the fact that 73% of the former GDR population, compared to 68% of the West Germans, and more than 50% of the Czech and Slovak citizens, did participate in at least one tourism activity of 5 days or longer in 1990. As a result, the demand for cheap and low-quality bed and breakfast services has increased, especially in areas surrounding well-known tourist places with attractive leisure infrastructures. The outcome has been intense competition between guests from Western industrial nations and Eastern European guests, with an underlying tendency in some areas for mass tourism to exclude high-quality tourism.

2.5.2 Growth perspectives

The future perspectives of Alpine tourism can be assessed from two surveys of expert opinions (Krippendorf 1980; Müller et al. 1991; Zimmermann 1992b). These reveal that there are several advantages of the Alpine tourism industry such as a central location in Europe (close to major tourism markets) with a varied nature and countryside, a healthy climate and positive prerequisites for winter activities. There is rich cultural and educational provision, there are organically grown structures with long experience and tradition of the tourist trade, and a wide understanding of the role of tourism in raising the standard and quality of life. Last but not least, there is a varied, high-quality supply with a positive settlement structure.

The point on which experts disagreed most was the question about the further development of tourism in the Alps. Approximately one-half think that the peak of growth has not yet been attained, while the other 50% considered the peak of the boom has already been reached or even passed. The arguments for continuing growth may be listed as follows:

- the potential of increased leisure time and of growing numbers of people participating in tourism (especially more active elderly people)
- growth possibilities in the winter season, due to an increase in short holidays
- Eastern European visitors providing a new market
- improvements in marketing (internationalisation and a policy of filling market gaps)
- support of target group-oriented activities (new forms of service provision)
- greater consciousness of the environment will bring advantages, as against the disadvantages of competition
- innovations are making the tourism products more sophisticated
- guests with more flexible holiday patterns will make an extension of the season possible, if they are appropriately catered for

But there are also counter-arguments which suggest that the end of quantitative growth may be likely:

- strong and innovative international competition (especially recreation in 'sunshine destinations' in winter)

- climatic change
- supply outstripping demand
- the opening-up of new—and competing—tourism regions in Eastern Europe
- an absolute decline in the number of tourists in Europe due to decreasing population levels
- changing holiday habits because of social, demographic and economic changes
- decreasing demand for traditional summer tourism products in the Alps
- a failure to attract the youth
- readjustment of structures will result in losses of visitors (a consequence of operating a high-price policy within a low-price competition)
- the end of expansion in some regions as the limits of environmental exploitation have been reached, and the supply of winter tourism services cannot be expanded further
- welfare state reforms in Western Europe may lead to reduced old-age pension provision which, in turn, may restrict tourism by the elderly
- shorter working hours will make the tourist products more expensive
- the trend for Western European tourists to spend their holidays in more distant destinations may result in a decrease in the number of those spending their leisure time in the Alps

2.5.3   Tourism and regional development: concentration versus diversification?

The previous discussion leads to the question of the future distribution of tourism in the Alps, and in particular whether tourism has the capacity to restructure Alpine economies and thereby reduce regional disparities. A review of historical trends, exemplified by the case of the Austrian provinces, provides a first answer: the data in Table 2.2 show that tourism income has contributed to a reduction in regional disparities, especially during the take-off period when combined with the introduction of new tourism products. The winter tourism-dominated areas of Tyrol, Salzburg and Vorarlberg increased their GDP between 1970 and 1992 substantially more than the other provinces, especially compared to the province of Carinthia which experienced its peak period in the summer-dominated tourism in the 1960s and the early 1970s, and which has subsequently faced stagnation. Additionally, some areas in the east of Austria, especially in Lower Austria and the Burgenland, faced an increase in the importance of tourism activities due to the diffusion effects of growth in the recreational activities of the Viennese population and the importance of Vienna as an international tourism centre.

In a future perspective, the trends identified point to an increasing process of concentration of touristic activities. International competition necessitates an intensification of capital, and this will tend to make investment more selective. Therefore, it is likely that not all existing tourism regions will be able to survive

Table 2.2. The influence of tourism on regional economies in Austria, 1970–93

Province	GDP 1992 ($billion)	% of 1970 GDP	No. of beds 1973 ('000s)	% of 1973 beds	Overnight stays 1993 ('000s)	% of 1973 overnights
Burgenland	3.4	535	12.8	160	1 030.9	175
Carinthia	8.7	465	104.4	90	9 106.3	105
Lower Austria	25.1	490	44.2	110	4 243.1	130
Upper Austria	25.7	530	45.3	90	4 262.4	98
Salzburg	11.3	610	105.9	110	14 213.0	130
Styria	19.0	480	55.3	100	5 495.3	115
Tyrol	13.2	600	211.3	130	28 779.7	160
Vorarlberg	7.2	585	33.1	110	4 734.3	135
Vienna	47.0	550	38.6	190	6 084.8	170

Source: Prepared by the author on the basis of data provided by Österreichisches Statistisches Zentralamt (1970ff.).

the international competitive struggle. However, although concentration is considered appropriate for reasons of managerial, economic and market strategies, almost 60% of all Austrian experts disapprove of the concentration of subsidies in favour of 'central tourist regions'. Austria as a whole must survive as a tourism-oriented economy and a ghettoisation of the industry must be prevented. Some conditions do favour the provision of assistance for small-scale tourism regions and these are mostly arguments for supporting new and alternative forms of tourism services (Zimmermann 1992b):

- 'Tourism is not a universal therapy' but can only successfully be applied when certain basic conditions as well as a concept of development exist. The objective needs to be target group-oriented marketing linked to the construction of unique tourism images.
- Tourism strategies must involve cooperation concepts, professional management and positive foreseeable effects for the regional economy, especially for the local population.
- Subsidies should be available only 'to help self-help' in those cases where there is adequate local initiative, endogeneous development pressure and the availability of positive local resources.
- Each development should be based on a positive cost–profit calculation including ecological and social parameters.

If there is a role for the state to play in diversification, this begs the question of what form it should take. Expert opinion emphasises the importance of investment in 'human capital': for example, consultation where individual solutions are required, drawing up of appropriate multifunctional concepts so as to maintain the quality of the environment and of everyday life, development of new models of organisation, regional management strategies and a policy of filling market gaps and pilot-project guidance. In addition, there are arguments for investments in basic and recreational infrastructure at the communal level. Improvements to the quality of life for tourists and local people should also be sought via revitalising service outlets, restructuring villages, preservation of agriculture, and advanced training programmes.

2.5.4   Future Alpine tourism products

There are three main products which have good prospects for success in the future development of tourism in Alpine areas:

1. *Health.* With an increase in the number of older people, health tourism is likely to see growth, especially in view of the fact that the elderly are turning increasingly to prophylactic measures and activities for their health. At the same time, health tourism will also benefit from the growing environmental awareness and body consciousness by younger people. The integrity of nature and the environment will be of special importance for this kind of social construction of tourism.
2. *Sports.* In the course of the new health wave, sports activities will attain new levels of participation. The potential market among young seniors suggests growth tendencies heading towards 'soft and gentle' activities (such as cross-country skiing, hiking, bicycle-riding, horse-riding, etc.) with a major dimension being the enjoyment of nature.
3. *Adventure and commercial attractions.* On the one hand a policy of filling market gaps, aiming at sporting adventure (mountain-climbing, para-gliding, rafting, etc.) promises a dynamic development as, on the other hand, do attractions with a good quality base and professional know-how (recreation centres, theme parks, themed packages, etc.).

Consistent orientation towards new product developments requires large-scale specialisation of provision, as well as adaptation to the holiday styles of seg-mented target groups. Packages have to allow for holidays which are as varied as possible, and must be innovative (new leisure technologies) and sociable (indi-vidualised provision, personal contacts, opportunities to enjoy culture, to study according to individual interests). The central message at the end of the twentieth century is that Alpine tourism must present a touristic 'life style' if it is to prosper in the face of wider social and economic processes of restructuring.

3 The Mediterranean Region: Europe's Summer Leisure Space

ARMANDO MONTANARI

University of Rome la Sapienza, Italy and Free University, Brussels, Belgium

3.1 INTRODUCTION

It is well known that the Mediterranean is the most important tourist destination in the world, accounting for a third of all international tourist movements. Even so there is no specific Mediterranean product on the holiday market (instead there are a series of national products) and international organisations do not publish statistics relating to the area as a whole. The reason for this apparent paradox is that the major destinations within this macro-tourist region (Portugal, Spain, France, Italy and Greece) have hitherto competed against each other and against the countries on the southern and eastern rims of the Mediterranean. Consequently, these holiday markets have developed in competition with one another instead of there being a strategy to develop a policy based on assimilation, equality and collaboration. There is also an institutional problem in that the five major tourist destinations—listed above—are members of the European Union (EU). This has meant that most studies, research and policies have had a European rather than a Mediterranean perspective. The overall result is that there is no clear-cut definition of, or commercialisation of, the Mediterranean tourist product as such in any of the five countries. However, even if the Mediterranean tourism concept does not exist at present, there is no reason why it could not be created. One of the tasks for researchers, in this respect, is to identify the principal characteristics and specificities of this macro-tourist region; this chapter seeks to contribute to this project.

The Mediterranean region has long been familiar to tourists because of its good climate and as the site of extensive ancient historical remains. However, past growth and attractiveness are not necessarily a guide to the future, and the Mediterranean tourist industry cannot assume an untroubled and guaranteed outlook. Instead, it is under threat because of political instability, terrorist attacks, civil conflict and religious fundamentalism in much of the area.

European Tourism: Regions, Spaces and Restructuring. Edited by A. Montanari and A.M. Williams.
© 1995 European Science Foundation. Published in 1995 by John Wiley & Sons Ltd.

3.2   GENERAL CHARACTERISTICS OF TOURIST SUPPLY AND DEMAND IN THE MEDITERRANEAN

A sunny place by the seaside is the core of the stereotypical image of the Mediterranean holiday. This invokes images of the journeys (sometimes only imaginary) of writers, philosophers and artists to 'the south', a cultural phenomenon which has constituted one of the 'myths' of industrial society. In fact, the prevailing 'classical myth' has its origins in literary and artistic works inspired by the places and regions of the Mediterranean. Over time the cultural interest in the region has been supplemented by an interest in its other resources: the sun, the sea and entertainment services (Thurot 1982).

The Mediterranean Sea is almost enclosed and covers an area of 3 million sq. km. Eighteen countries share its coastline:

Spain	France	Monaco
Italy	Malta	the former Yugoslavia
Albania	Greece	Turkey
Cyprus	Syria	Lebanon
Israel	Egypt	Libya
Tunisia	Algeria	Morocco

This definition of the Mediterranean countries was formulated by the Mediterranean Action Plan (MAP) which was established in order to protect the Mediterranean environment. It was adopted in 1976 by the rim countries under the auspices of the United Nations Environment Programme (UNEP). Part of the MAP consisted of the now famous Blue Plan. This aimed to analyse the socio-economic situation of the coastal countries in order to identify potential development projects in various economic sectors including tourism. The first finding of the MAP was that approximately 60 million foreign visitors arrived in Mediterranean countries in 1973; this figure was the equivalent of one-third of all international tourism. Furthermore, between 1960 and 1971 tourist arrivals had increased by two and a half times. The highest rates of increase were registered in Greece, Israel and Turkey (fourfold growth), Cyprus and the former Yugoslavia (fivefold), Malta (eightfold) and Tunisia (tenfold). As a result, MAP requested that the Mediterranean countries should identify new tourism models which have less damaging implications for the environment (Tangi 1977). Subsequently, aggregate numbers of tourist arrivals in the 18 Mediterranean countries rose from 86 million in 1975, to 125 million in 1985, and to over 200 million in 1990. Numbers declined in 1991 to 187 million as a result of the Gulf War and international economic recession. Thus defined, the Mediterranean is the world's main tourist destination, accounting for 45% of all international tourist arrivals and 28% of all tourism revenue.

Obtaining a precise definition of the Mediterranean region is more difficult than is suggested by these national-level data. An Economist Intelligence Unit report (Jenner and Smith 1993) distinguished between the 18 countries bordering the Mediterranean and the tourist regions within those countries. Consequently, they excluded the Atlantic coasts and hinterlands of Spain and France, the Alpine and Piedmont regions in France and Italy, the Atlantic coast of Morocco, and the hinterlands of Morocco, Algeria, Tunisia, Syria, Turkey and Yugoslavia, as well as cities such as Paris, Madrid and Milan. The report was uncertain as to whether to classify Florence as a Mediterranean city. On this basis it was calculated that just over 60% of tourism in Mediterranean countries involved coastal areas. There is no explanation as to how this figure was calculated, its statistical basis or as to precisely which year it refers to. The figure is then used in the analysis of chronological data and to modify qualitative data. Within these limitations, Jenner and Smith have produced a useful report. They have attempted to use, and, arguably, perhaps even to 'force' official statistical data into their framework, in order to provide a more precise picture of tourism in the Mediterranean. On the basis of these statistics, international tourist arrivals in the coastal regions of the Mediterranean rose from 111 million in 1987 to 126 million in 1990. Numbers declined to 113 million in 1991. By adding the internal flows—approximately 65 million in 1990, or 52% of international arrivals—and undocumented tourist flows (the latter are estimated to be equivalent to 5–10% of the market), Jenner and Smith calculate that over 200 million tourists visit the Mediterranean every year. Given that these flows are in fact concentrated on a relatively small part (the coastal fringe) of the Mediterranean region, their economic, social and environmental impacts are immense.

3.3 THE MEDITERRANEAN TOURIST REGION: ITS DIMENSIONS AND CHARACTERISTICS

In order to identify the elements of urban and regional restructuring attendant on tourism in the Mediterranean area, it is essential to quantify the region's tourist flows as accurately as possible. To date, the data gathered and analysed by the World Tourism Organisation (WTO) are the only conventional source which is widely accepted. The data are inaccurate, above all because of the scale of undocumented tourism. A comparison of official statistical data with the results of fieldwork carried out in major Italian tourist resorts led Becheri (1993) to the conclusion that it is necessary to take three types of data into account. First, official statistics; in Italy these are calculated by ISTAT (Italian National Statistical Institute) for the WTO. Second, so-called 'market' statistics, or the combination of data, estimates and surveys compiled by public bodies responsible for tourism. Third, 'undocumented' sources; these are acquired mainly through figures relating to rented properties and holiday homes. In Italy, for example, the insertion of the above figures into an econometric model generates the following estimates: over and above the official figure of 252 million Italian and foreign tourist nights in 1991, should be added a further 120 million from 'market' sources, and a further 400 million from undocumented sources, making a total of 772 million tourists in hotels and other accommodation (Becheri 1993). This is equivalent to about 138 million arrivals.

A study carried out by the Spanish General Secretariat for Tourism (Secretaria General de Turismo 1990) analyses the amount of accommodation being used or potentially used for tourist purposes. This amounted in 1989 to 1.9 million in use and to 4.2 million for that potentially in use. This makes a total of 6 million lodgings, which is equivalent to approximately 23 million beds. The same study identified 19 million undocumented tourists. In particular, it was discovered that less than 2% of tourists rented accommodation legally in the regions of Asturia, Galicia, Murcia and the Basque Country, 4% rented legally on the Balearic Islands and in Valencia, 7% in Andalusia and 88% on the Canary Islands. Despite the significant use of rented tourist accommodation, the figures relating to this are largely underestimated. In Spain, in 1990, of just under 10 million tourist beds, only 22% were located in hotels, while 78% were in tourist lodgings which were classified by the Spanish authorities (MICYT 1992) as non-regulated supply (*Oferta non reglada*). The situation was similar in Italy where out of 17 million beds, 83% were in tourist lodgings, and in France where out of 19 million beds, 76% were in lodgings (Simonazzi 1993).

The geographical dimension of the Mediterranean tourist region constitutes another element which requires definition. To limit the research exclusively to the countries located around the rim seems too restrictive for an analysis of tourism in the Mediterranean. Studies which include Portugal and Jordan, making a total of 20 countries (Joannon and Tirone 1990) also seem inadequate to our purpose. In this last study, the option of including countries facing on to the Black Sea was also considered. However, it was rejected because of the difficulty of obtaining data and the incompatibility of the available statistical information.

Even if, at first sight, Mediterranean tourism offers sun, sea and beaches, and therefore satisfies a demand for bathing holidays, it is not correct to assume that only the Mediterranean coastal areas are suitable for development. In fact the success of the first Mediterranean tourist resorts led to the development of other bordering tourist areas sharing similar characteristics. This was the case for the south-west coast of the Iberian peninsula, the north-west Moroccan coast facing the Atlantic Ocean, the north coast of Turkey, Bulgaria and south-west Romania, and the Black Sea coast of the Crimea.

The Mediterranean is known, above all, for the remains of ancient and diverse civilisations which overlapped throughout the millenia and bequeathed a heterogeneous cultural legacy to the region. While the traditional beach holiday is experiencing a crisis (Montanari 1993a), the principal tourist regions in the Mediterranean are attempting to 'rediscover' the cultural and natural riches which lie further inland: agritourism, tourism in protected areas, at archaeological sites and historic cities. The initiative has been captured in a

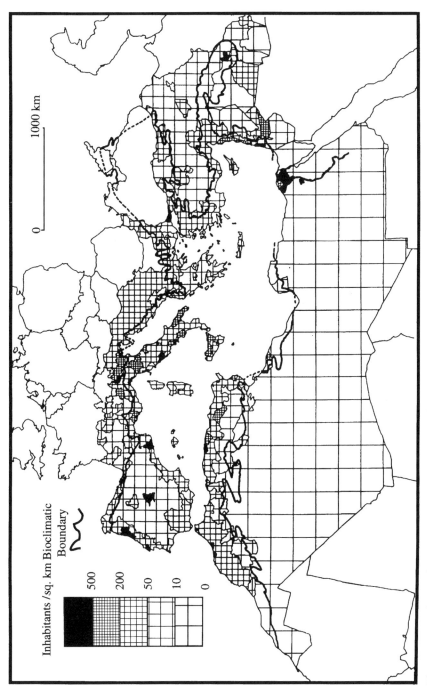

Figure 3.1. The Mediterranean tourist region: population density in relation to the bioclimatic boundary

46

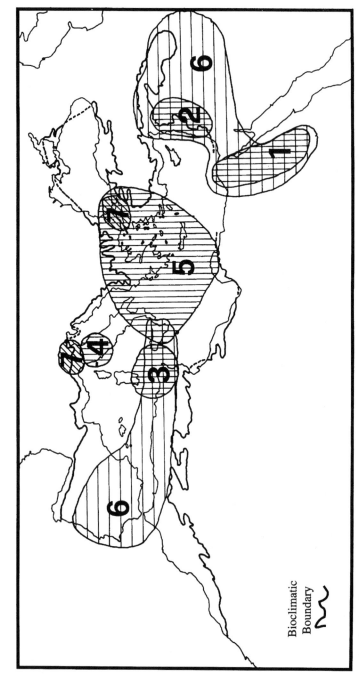

Figure 3.2. The Mediterranean region: the principal concentrations of the remains of ancient Mediterranean civilisations: 1 = Egyptian; 2 = Phoenician; 3 = Carthaginian; 4 = Etruscan; 5 = Greek; 6 = Arab; 7 = Byzantine

slogan which appeared in the press in 1994: 'as the beaches empty, the museums fill up'.

A natural boundary which may be used to identify Mediterranean tourism is formed by the Mediterranean climatic region. This is characterised by warm, rainy winters due to the proximity of relatively warm seas. Typical January temperatures vary between 7 and 12 °C. The northwards shift of the anti-cyclone from the Azores ensures hot, dry summers with average temperatures varying between 22 and 28 °C in July. The diffusion of the olive tree also helps to define the areas of typical Mediterranean vegetation. The olive tree, the quince and the oak are the most common features of the Mediterranean coun-tryside. There are also some distinctive geological features of the Medi-terranean which are caused by friction between the African and Eurasian continental plates: rolling hills, seismic faults, volcanoes, earthquakes and springs (another important tourist attraction), but this is less helpful for defini-tional purposes. The relationship between the natural definition of the Medi-terranean and the pattern of human settlement is illustrated by Figure 3.1 which shows the bioclimatic limits superimposed on population density (in-habitants per square kilometre) by region and province.

Despite the attractions of a relatively simple bioclimatic approach, Mediter-ranean tourism cannot be based uniquely on such criteria. Equally important are the areas and regions which conserve the vestiges of previously important Mediterranean civilisations. A Mediterranean tourist area therefore must in-clude areas of previous Egyptian, Phoenician, Persian, Greek, Etruscan, Car-thaginian, Roman, Arab and Byzantine culture. Figure 3.2 shows the areas with the highest density of ancient remains compared with the limits of the Mediterranean bioclimatic area. Roman remains have not been included on the map as they are so widely distributed throughout the area.

The Mediterranean region also houses the centres of the three major mono-theist religions: Judaism, Christianity and Islam. This is important not only because of the resulting landscape, characterised by domes, minarets and bell towers, but also because of the resulting religious tourism. This focuses on two kinds of pilgrimage according to Cohen (1992): formal and popular. The most famous formal pilgrimage sites are the Wailing Wall of Jerusalem, the Nativity Church in Bethlehem and Saint Peter's in Rome. However, a multitude of sanctuaries and religious sites may be included among popular pilgrimage sites. In 1991 the 20 most visited sanctuaries in Italy (including Assisi, Padua, Pompeii, Loreto and Montecassino) were visited by almost 35 million Italians and foreigners. Some visitors may be defined as pilgrims whose prime motives were religious, while others were perhaps motivated by a more general cultural interest. Religious tourism involves the movement of about 100 million people per year (1991). Italy leads in this sector, ahead of France, Germany, Poland and Spain.

Defined in a broader way which takes into account these cultural and bio-climatic criteria, the Mediterranean tourist region includes 24 countries: the

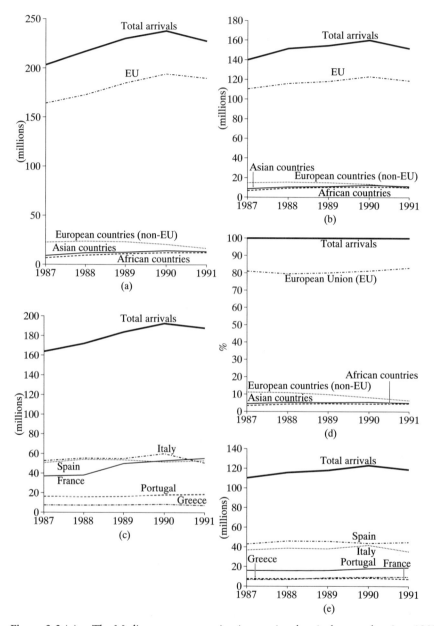

Figure 3.3.(a). The Mediterranean countries: international arrivals per subregion, 1987–91; (b) the Mediterranean macro tourist region: international arrivals per subregion, 1987–91; (c) the Mediterranean macro tourist region: international arrivals in the EU subregion, 1987–91; (d) the Mediterranean region: percentage variation in international arrivals per subregion, 1987–91; (e) the Mediterranean macro tourist region: international arrivals in EU countries, 1987–91. Source: Prepared by the author on the basis of data in WTO (1992b)

18 countries around the Mediterranean rim, together with Portugal, Bulgaria, Romania, Ukraine (Crimean Republic), Jordan and Iraq. In these countries tourist arrivals increased from just over 200 million in 1987 (Figure 3.3(a)) to almost 240 million in 1990. This figure fell in 1991 to just under 230 million (WTO 1993). Such a broad definition of the Mediterranean tourist region may seem exaggerated in the present climate of tourist supply and demand. However, in this respect it is useful to consider the example of the Crimea and, in particular, its south-eastern coast which shares a similar climate to that of the Côte d'Azur in France (Durbiano and Radvanyi 1987). It was the destination for 10 million visitors in 1990. The tourists were accommodated in huge anonymous blocks similar to those found in the worst suburbs of the former Soviet Union. There was no transport infrastructure and no facilities for private boat owners. In the present restructuring of Europe, significant international investments in the tourist sector imply that the Crimea may receive as many as 16–20 million annual visitors over the next 10 years (Cabanne 1993).

If consideration is to be limited exclusively to areas typified by more narrowly defined Mediterranean features, the following points need to be observed. Portugal, Albania, Greece, Lebanon, Israel, Malta and Cyprus should be considered in their entirety. Most of Spain should be considered (excluding the provinces of Pontevedra, La Coruña, Lugo, Asturias, Cantabria, Vizcaya, Guipuzcoa, and some of the provinces in the Pyrenees). The same applies to Italy (excluding the regions of Piedmont, Valle d'Aosta, Lombardy, Trentino–Alto Adige and Belluno province) and Turkey (excluding the provinces of Afyon, Agri, Ankara, Artvin, Bilecik, Bingol, Bitlis, Çankiri, Çorum, Elazig, Erzincan, Erzurum, Eskisehir, Gümüshane, Hakkari, Isparta, Kars, Kastamonu, Kayseri, Konhia, Malatya, Mus, Nevsehir, Nigde, Rize, Sivas, Tunceli, Van, Yozgat). Most inhabited and habitable areas in Syria, Libya, Tunisia, Algeria and Morocco are located near the coast and therefore these countries should be considered in their entirety. The whole of Egypt has also been considered both for cultural reasons and because its settlements are distributed along the banks of the Nile, which for our purposes represents a sort of cultural and climatic fjord. Parts of Iraq and Jordan, and the Mediterranean coast of France (Languedoc–Roussillon, Provence–Alpes–Côte d'Azure, Corsica), Slovenia (Istria), Croatia (Istria and Dalmatia) and Montenegro have been considered. A large part of the coastal areas of the Black Sea have also been considered, in particular Turkey, Bulgaria, Romania (as far as the Danube Delta). In the Ukraine, only the part relating to the Crimea has been considered. As it is not possible to calculate the numbers of tourists visiting each Mediterranean region, the number of tourist beds in hotels in 1990 was measured.

These data were integrated with statistics relating to tourist arrivals and the numbers of people in hotels. It was assumed that any underestimation of numbers would be evenly distributed over the territory. In this way the approximate tourist flow to the tourist regions of the Mediterranean was calculated. Included in the Mediterranean tourist area were 18% of tourist flows in France, 50% in Romania and Iraq, 60% in the former Yugoslavia, 70% in Italy, 80% in Bulgaria, 85% in Spain, 94% in Turkey and 100% in the remaining countries. Using this formula it was calculated that there were 160 million tourist arrivals in the Mediterranean in 1990 (Figure 13.3(b)). Just under 80% of these were in the EU. In 1991 Spain was the main tourist destination in the Mediterranean with over 40 million arrivals. Italy followed with just under 40 million. Next was Portugal with about 20 million, and then France and Greece with about 10 million each (Figure 3.3(c)). Bulgaria followed with about 6 million and then Turkey with 5 million. All the other countries registered fewer than 5 million arrivals. Turkey experienced the fastest growth between 1987 and 1991. In this period the numbers of arrivals doubled. If one adds to 160 million international tourist arrivals, almost 85 million national arrivals plus a conservative 80% for figures for 'black market' and 'undocumented' tourism, one can arrive at an aggregate total of about 450 million tourist arrivals in the Mediterranean area in 1990.

3.4   REGIONAL DISTRIBUTION OF TOURISM

The Mediterranean tourist area may be subdivided into four subregions: EU members, non-EU European countries, Asian countries on the eastern rim of the Mediterranean and African countries on the southern rim. EU countries absorb over 80% of the arrivals, while the remainder is divided equally between the other three subregions (Figure 3.3(d)). Italy was the first Mediterranean country to experience mass tourism before the First World War. Approximately 900 000 tourists visited Italy in 1911. In 1910 revenue from tourism amounted to 450 million lire, equivalent to 24% of total exports (Stringher 1912), a remarkable figure for such an early date. Italy's dominance peaked in the 1950s when it attracted almost 80% of foreign tourists visiting the Mediterranean. Italy's share, however, was drastically cut in successive decades as other countries such as Spain, Yugoslavia and Greece entered the tourism market (Anastasopoulos 1989).

3.4.1   Mediterranean countries in the EU

The Mediterranean EU countries (Portugal, Spain, France, Italy and Greece) dominate the Mediterranean tourist market. With over 120 million tourist arrivals they account for about 80% of the market (Figure 3.3(e)). During the 1980s, these countries passed through two phases of development: 1984–87 and 1988–90. During the first period, annual average figures were positive for all countries with a maximum of 8% registered in France and a minimum of 2% in Greece. In the second period the annual average variance was negative in Spain (–5.0%). In Italy it was 0.3% while in Portugal the variance was almost 5% (Eurostat 1991). The success registered in the first phase may be attributed, above all, to foreign tourist arrivals. Annual numbers rose by over 10% in Portugal, over 9% in France, but just over 2% in Spain. The collapse in the industry during the second phase is similarly attributable to a fall in foreign visitors: −14% per year in Spain, and −4% in Italy. This fall was partly compensated by a rise in domestic tourist figures both in Spain (8.4%) and in Italy (3.2%).

In Spain the crisis of 1988–90 mainly affected the numbers of people staying in hotels. This fall was compensated for, however, by the numbers of people staying in non-hotel accommodation. This tendency was exactly the opposite of the trends registered in the other countries, where an increase in numbers using hotel accommodation (7.7% in France and 5.8% in Portugal) was balanced by a decline in numbers staying in other kinds of accommodation (−5% in Greece and −3.5% in France). In 1990 Italy had the most hotel beds (about 1.7 million) followed by France with 1.1 million, then Spain with 930 000, Greece with 440 000 and finally Portugal with 180 000. Other forms of accommodation (camping and tourist villages) were most frequent in France with 2.6 million beds, Italy with 1.2 million, Spain with 570 000, Portugal with 260 000 and Greece with 82 000.

If one takes the entire EU Mediterranean coastline from Portugal to Greece it becomes clear that the tourist infrastructures (hotels, camping sites and tourist villages) are concentrated in a limited number of areas. These are Lisbon and the Algarve in Portugal; Costa del Sol, Costa Blanca, Costa del Azahar, Costa Dorada, Balearic Islands and Canary Islands in Spain; Languedoc–Roussillon and Côte d'Azur in France; the Ligurian Riviera, Versilia, the Sorrentine peninsula and the islands in the Gulf of Naples, the Costa Smeralda, Adriatic coast of Romagna and Veneto in Italy; and the Aegean and Ionian Islands in Greece.

In order to highlight the relative significance that the tourist sector has for each economic locality, the number of inhabitants has been compared to the number of beds available in hotel and non-hotel accommodation. In Portugal in 1987 (Figure 3.4) the number of free rooms in hotels per 1000 inhabitants was calculated in each tourist area; the NUTS territorial division in Portugal (Nomenclatura das Unidades Territoriais para Fins Estatísticas) was used as the basis for analysing data produced at a national level (INE 1988). To these official data were added estimates of the large unregistered sector comprising rented houses and private apartments, equivalent to two and a half times the official figures. The areas of most intense tourism in relation to residential population were found in the Algarve, Alentejo Litoral and Greater Lisbon–North. The importance of the Fatima Sanctuary as a tourist destination has also been noted by researchers (Lewis and Williams 1988).

In Greece in 1988 the tourist supply (number of rooms in hotels per 1000 inhabitants) (Figure 3.5) was processed per commune using statistics supplied by the EOT (Ellenikós Organismós Turismoû). The communes with an index of over 50 per 1000 are located on the island of Corfu, in a few communes on

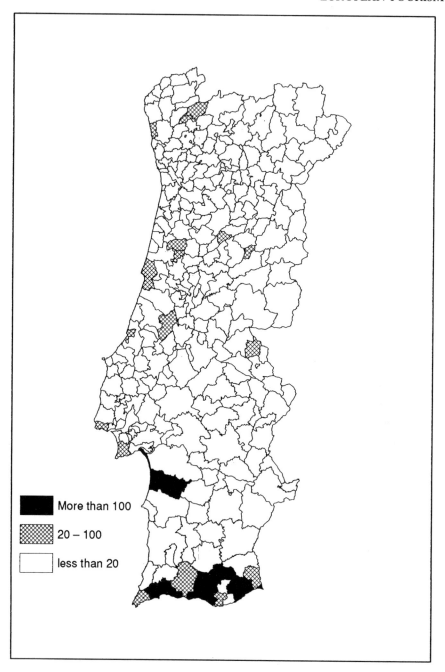

Figure 3.4. Portugal: tourism supply (number of hotel rooms per 1000 inhabitants) per NUTS region, 1987 (NUTS = Nomenclature das Unidades Territoriais para Fins Estatísticos). Source: Prepared by the author on the basis of data in INE (1988)

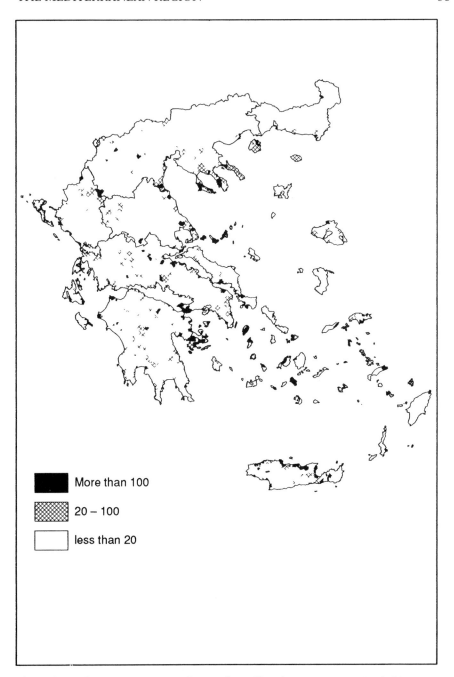

Figure 3.5. Greece: tourism supply (number of hotel rooms per 1000 inhabitants) per commune, 1988. Source: Prepared by the author on the basis of unpublished data provided by Ellenikós Organismós Turismoû

the northern coast of Crete, in the peninsular region of Macedonia, Thessaly and Argolis, near Corinth and on numerous Aegean islands. A comparison with data for 1981 reveals an increase in the tourist supply especially on the Aegean and Ionian Islands and on Crete. In absolute terms the tourist supply increased from 22 000 in 1981 to 48 000 rooms in 1988 in the Aegean Islands region, from 12 000 to 19 000 rooms in the Ionian Islands region, and from 15 000 to 30 000 rooms in the Crete region. Within Crete, the number of rooms in the Nomoi of Iraklion, where the biggest town on the island is located and where the ruins of Knossos are to be found, rose from 1500 in 1971, to 9000 in 1981 and 17 000 in 1988.

In Spain the number of hotel (and hostel) beds in 1992 was calculated on the basis of data supplied by the General Secretariat for Tourism of the Ministry of Industry, Commerce and Tourism in Madrid (Figure 3.6). Various areas of concentration of the tourist supply in relation to numbers of inhabitants were identified on the Andalusian coast between Malaga and Marbella, on the coast in the region of Valencia between Benidorm and Cabo de la Nao, and between Peñiscola and Vinaroz, on the coast of Catalonia between Lloret del Mar and the French border, and in the Pyrenees between Puigcerdá, Andorra, Viella and Panticosa.

In Italy it has also been possible to calculate the number of hotel beds per commune on the basis of official data for 1989 (ISTAT 1991). There is considerable variation between the North and South of the country (Figure 3.7). In the South the most concentrated supply of tourist services is located on the north-east coast of Sardinia, between Palinuro and Praia a Mare on the Tyrrhenian coast, and around the Gargan peninsula on the Adriatic coast. In the North there were also identifiable areas. The largest is located in the Alpine communes with a high concentration of hotels in the Trentino–Alto Adige region stretching as far as Lake Garda. This line continues along the Apennine ridge in Umbria, Tuscany and Emilia-Romagna. A third is located on the Adriatic coast in all communes from Marche as far as Friuli-Venezia Giulia.

In many EU countries there were considerable changes in consumption levels and patterns of holiday-taking in the 1980s. Together with the increase in tourist arrivals, there was an even greater increase in tourists leaving the country as more and more people became accustomed to spending their holidays abroad. In 1990 tourism revenue in France, Italy and Spain was about 15 000 million ECUs, a figure corresponding to approximately 7, 10 and 22% of total revenue respectively in these countries. In Portugal and Greece revenue was about 2500 million ECUs, representing between 16 and 23% of total revenue respectively. A surprising result was that Greek tourism revenue was almost 20% lower than Portugal's, even though Greece has twice as much hotel accommodation as Portugal. This may derive from the type of tourists who visit Greece—in general tourists in Greece are considered to be poorer and less spendthrift than those visiting other parts of the EU—or from the way in which the revenue was calculated (Williams 1993b).

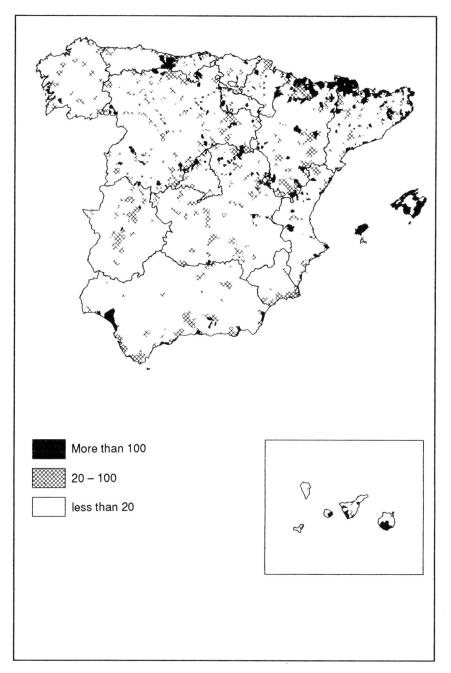

Figure 3.6. Spain: tourism supply (number of hotel rooms per 1000 inhabitants) per commune, 1992. Source: Prepared by the author on the basis of unpublished data provided by the Secretaría General de Turismo

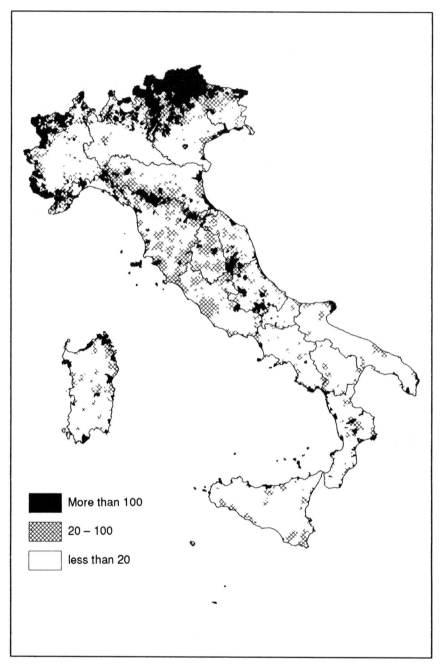

Figure 3.7. Italy: tourism supply (number of hotel rooms per 1000 inhabitants) per commune, 1989. Source: Prepared by the author on the basis of unpublished data provided by the ISTAT (1991)

The tourism growth rates for the period 1984–90 are different. Greece registered a growth rate of 40%, Italy and Spain less than 50%, France, 65% and Portugal 130%. The largest tourist expenditure was in 1990 in Italy, almost 11 000 million ECUs. French tourist expenditure was a little less than 10 million, while in Spain it was 3.3 million and less than 1 million in Greece and Portugal. The most surprising variation was registered in Italy where between 1984 and 1990 tourist expenditure rose by almost five times. In Spain expenditure tripled while in Portugal, Greece and France it doubled. The tourist balance of payments was still significant in Spain, France, Portugal and Greece (respectively standing at 11 billion, 6.1 billion, 2.1 billion and 1.3 billion ECUs) where it had increased since 1984. In Italy, however, the balance had fallen by 44% and stood at 4700 million ECUs.

There are no data relating to how many people work either directly or indirectly in the tourist sector. On the basis of Eurostat and OECD figures, tourism is thought to account for 4% of employment in Portugal, Italy and France and between 5 and 6% in Spain, where the figure becomes 11% if related service industry is taken into account. In the five countries considered, tourism accounts for over 2.5 million jobs and perhaps as many again in indirectly related sectors. Employment is very spatially concentrated.

Most tourists come from elsewhere in the EU. In Portugal EU tourists account for 94% of all the foreign market, in Spain 82%, and in France and Greece 72%. In Italy only 50% or tourists come from inside the EU. Significant numbers come from Switzerland, from ex-Yugoslavia, the United States, Australia and Japan.

3.4.2 Non-EU European countries

The non-EU countries included are Albania, Bulgaria, the Ukraine (Crimea), Romania and the countries of the former Yugoslavia (Figure 3.8(a)). Until recently all these countries had planned economies. They will be discussed further in Chapter 13. Malta has been included in this group. In 1991 almost 900 000 foreign tourists visited this small island with 137 km of developed coastline. Tourism developed rapidly in the 1970s but fell into decline between 1980 and 1985. During this period overnight tourists decreased by 34% and the revenue generated from tourism fell by over one-half (Central Bureau of Statistics, various years). This was mainly because the island was considered to have little to offer tourists and was too highly priced. Water and electricity supplies were also insufficient. Tourism on the island began to pick up again after 1985. Today it generates a revenue equivalent to $560 million representing 22% of GDP. Initially most tourists visiting Malta were British but between 1980 and 1990 their share dropped from 72 to 52%. German tourism is on the increase. During the same period their share of the market rose from 4 to 15%. Italian and French tourism is also on the increase.

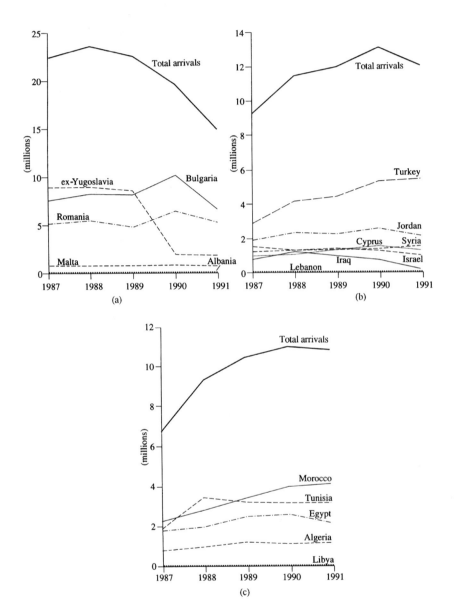

Figure 3.8.(a). The Mediterranean: international arrivals in non-EU European countries, 1987–91; (b) the Mediterranean: international arrivals in Asian countries, 1987–91; (c) the Mediterranean: international arrivals in African countries, 1987–91. Source: Prepared by the author on the basis of data in WTO (1992b)

3.4.3 Mediterranean Asia

Included in this group are: Turkey, with over 5 million international arrivals in 1991; Jordan, Syria, Cyprus and Israel, with an influx of between 1 and 2 million each. Iraq and the Lebanon are also included but tourist movements cannot be quantified (Figure 3.8(b)). This is because Iraq has been and is at the time of writing still at war, and the Lebanon is still suffering from a long civil war. Other crises which have affected the development of tourism in this area have been recurrent political and economic turmoil in Turkey at the beginning of the 1970s and the beginning of the 1980s, the partition of Cyprus the Middle East conflict and subsequent war and guerrilla warfare, and more recently the Gulf War.

In Turkey the number of tourist arrivals remained stable at about 1 million until the beginning of the 1980s. Between 1980 and 1984 the number of arrivals doubled. They doubled again between 1984 and 1988 and then grew by 30% until 1991. The numbers of arrivals in Cyprus rose by 46% between 1987 and 1991. In Israel the numbers of arrivals rose from just under 500 000 in 1970 to 1.165 million in 1980. Numbers exceeded 1.5 million in 1987, only to drop to just over 1.1 million in 1991 (Central Bureau of Statistics, various years). In Syria arrivals exceeded 1 million throughout the 1970s, but decreased to below the million mark during the 1980s, peaking, however at approximately 1.5 million arrivals in 1987 (SAR, various years). Arrivals in Jordan rose by 40% between 1985 and 1990, but decreased by 15% between 1990 and 1991. In Iraq, development of the tourist sector was promoted during the 1970s leading to a rise in tourist arrivals from 360 000 in 1970, to 482 000 in 1975, and to over 2 million in 1982. Lebanon registered approximately 1.7 million international tourist arrivals in 1970 rising to 2.3 million in 1972. It was the fifth most popular destination in the Mediterranean at the beginning of the 1970s.

Between 1980 and 1991 revenue from tourism in Turkey increased tenfold to US$3400 million. This figure is much greater than similar revenue in either Greece or Portugal and is equivalent to 25% of exports. Cyprus' tourism revenue exceeded US$1000 million and represented almost 40% of exports. Tourism revenue in Israel represented about 8% of exports. Of tourists visiting Turkey in 1991, 49% were from the EU, especially from Germany, Greece and the UK. EU tourists, especially the British, make up the majority in Cyprus where they account for almost 70% of all tourists. In Israel EU tourists account for 40% of tourism while 27% are American. Americans constituted 38% of the arrivals in 1970, 27% in 1975 and 24% in 1980.

3.4.4. Mediterranean Africa

Morocco and Tunisia are the two main tourist destinations with over 3 million tourist arrivals in 1991 (Figure 3.8(c)). While Morocco concentrated on the development of cultural tourism both on the coast and inland, Tunisia focused attention on the development of tourist resorts on the coast. Between 1972 and 1981 tourist arrivals to Morocco doubled to over 2 million. Tunisia achieved over a million tourist arrivals by 1975 and reached the 2 million mark in 1981. In Egypt, the wars of 1967 and 1973 with Israel hindered the development of tourism. However by 1977 Egypt had achieved 1 million arrivals which had doubled by 1988 and continued to increase in 1989 and 1990 to 2.6 million. Arrivals fell by 15% in 1991 as a result of the Gulf War. Algeria and Libya made no attempt to develop international tourism. Morocco's tourism revenue rose from US$933 million in 1987 to almost US$1400 million in 1991, a figure equivalent to 20% of exports. In Egypt, on the other hand, a smaller statistical presence yielded US$600 million in 1987 and almost $2000 million in 1990, representing about 22% of exports. During the year of the Gulf War it lost almost US$500 million. Of international arrivals in Egypt in 1991, 30% originated in the EU, as did 24% of arrivals in Morocco and 31% in Tunisia.

3.4.5   Regional distribution of tourism growth: a summary

Since the 1960s, the increase in foreign tourist arrivals has been intense but not constant. All countries in the region were adversely affected by the oil crisis in 1973/74, which caused a 6% drop in arrivals in 1974. These picked up again almost immediately in 1975, however, increasing by 9%. The following decade was characterised by a succession of years of even greater positive growth such as 1988 (9%). These alternated with years such as 1983 which was beset by economic crisis and with a succession of tourist seasons compromised by various geopolitical crises: terrorist attacks in 1986, the Gulf War (1990/91) and the Yugoslavian conflict (since 1992/93). These events had a negative effect on tourism all over the Mediterranean area, but particularly in the countries on the southern and eastern rim of the Mediterranean.

3.5   TOURISM, LABOUR MARKETS AND POPULATION MOBILITY IN THE MEDITERRANEAN

It is important to remember that in the literature on tourism (see Kemper 1978) the word 'tourism', in its modern usage, was first used in the English langauge; it in fact has a classical origin. The Latin term *tornus* derives from the Greek *tópvos* which originally referred to a rotating machine but came to mean 'travel around, turn around, go back to the starting place'. Another term which has already been referred to above is 'pilgrim', from the Latin *peregrinus*. This means 'foreigner, stranger or exotic'. Without going into details about the numerous definitions of this series of words which are included in the contemporary meaning of tourist or pilgrim (Smith 1992), it is possible to generalise that tourism in the Mediterranean is at the base of, or is perhaps the consequence of, a whole series of processes which directly or indirectly affect population mobility in the area.

At the beginning of the 1990s, the population of the Mediterranean tourist area was 390 million, equivalent to about 14% of the world population. Until 1985 half of the Mediterranean population was in European countries, and the other half was roughly divided between African and Asian countries. From the end of the Second World War until 1985, the European population rose by only 30% while the population in the rest of the area rose by 150%. The clear division between the rates of growth between the rich northern countries and the less well-off countries in the rest of the region has become clearer in recent years. The 'youthening' of the populations in African and Asian countries is matched by ageing populations in European countries. For a long time, and particularly at the end of the Second World War, all Mediterranean countries, with the exception of France, were emigration countries (King 1993).

It was only at the end of the 1970s and beginning of the 1980s that southern Europe, which had exported labour for many decades, became the object of migratory flows, mainly from other Mediterranean countries (Montanari and Cortese 1993b). Migration and tourism have developed contemporaneously in the Mediterranean region. It was between the 1970s and 1980s that non-European Mediterranean countries (Morocco, Tunisia, Egypt, Israel, Jordan, Cyprus and Turkey) established their presence on the world tourist market. Wars, political conflict, and terrorism which have reduced the tourist potential of the area have had the opposite effect on migratory flows. There are almost 10 million immigrants in the EU, a figure equivalent to the population of Belgium. The majority of these come from the Mediterranean area and might be compared to the equivalent of an additional EU member state in terms of journeys, family reunion and visits to family members in Mediterranean countries of origin. Equally relevant and innovative is the migratory phenomenon involving pensioners from north-western Europe who move for extended periods to the Mediterranean. There are no exact statistics for this kind of movement, because the move is not usually definitive and on the whole is undocumented. According to surveys carried out in the Spanish Mediterranean, an estimated 1.5 million pensioners are present (Jurdao and Sanchez 1990). There is a marked increase in the tendency for European pensioners to travel (Wheatcroft and Seekings 1993) even if this sector of the market is dominated by a few countries (Germany, the UK, France, Belgium, the Netherlands, Italy and Sweden) which account for 80% of the market.

The potential for employment creation in the tourism sector could make it a decisive instrument in reducing the so-called economic migration which is expected to increase over the next few decades (Montanari and Cortese 1993b). Tourism is particularly significant because of its labour-intensive nature and its potential to attract foreign capital. According to statistics published by the OECD, the creation of a job in manufacturing industry requires seven times more investment than to create a job in the tourist industry. In a simple interpretation, this means that with the same investment it is possible to create seven times more jobs in tourism than in manufacturing. There are no exact data on the number of employees working directly or indirectly in tourism because the methods of measurement vary greatly. Sessa (1983), for example, takes into consideration 10 categories of activities in which jobs derive directly from tourism: the creation and the maintenance of infrastructure and services, the production and processing of agricultural products, transport, commercial services, the building of receptive infrastructure and relevant public administration. At best, it is only possible to obtain statistical information about the last three of this wide range of activities.

Employment in the hotel industry is characterised by a significant presence of part-time workers (Shaw and Williams 1994) and even if it is only possible to obtain statistical data in a few countries, it is clear from the OECD study that the hotel industry and other tourist services employ a large quota of female and young employees (OECD, annual reports on tourism). In Portugal the female workforce accounts for just under 50% of the total employed and in Greece, for almost 40%. These are particularly high values for Mediterranean countries where the rate of female occupation is particularly low.

It is even more difficult to quantify and qualify tourist sector employees in non-EU Mediterranean countries. On the basis of figures supplied by the relevant national authorities, it is possible to estimate that there are about 1 million employees in the tourist sector, with the same number again working in related sectors. Small-scale studies carried out in individual tourist resorts are more reliable. They enable us to relate the number of rooms to the numbers of jobs in the hotel industry. A ratio of 1 in Europe and other industrialised countries rises to between 1 and 2 in developing countries because labour is cheaper. Sessa (1983) maintains that a middle-ranking hotel with 1000 beds in an industrialised country will employ about 135 specialised personnel and 60 auxiliary staff; one job for every five beds. The ratio rises in smaller hotels offering a better quality service. In developing countries, however, one may calculate on the basis of one job one bed.

In the 24 Mediterranean countries under consideration in 1990, there were about 6 million beds in approximately 3 million hotel rooms or similar receiving infrastructures (hotels and similar establishments; WTO, annual statistics). One may estimate that hotels alone account for 3 million employees, of which 70% are in the EU countries. This obviously does not take into account the numbers employed in the other nine categories providing jobs for tourist personnel. On the basis of data gathered in southern Europe, Renucci (1990) states that a hotel supply of between 3 and 5 beds corresponds to 1 job in the hotel industry and to between 2 and 8 jobs in the rest of the tourist sector. On the basis of these parameters it may be estimated that 6 million hotel beds represent a tourism labour market of 9 million in the region.

A research project carried out at Agadir, the main tourist location in Morocco, provides an example of labour market parameters. In 1980 the ratio of beds to number of jobs in five-star hotels was 0.59%, in four-star hotels 0.41%, in three-star hotels 0.26%, for two-star hotels 0.27% and for one-star hotels 0.12%. Furthermore over 50% of the staff were younger than 30 and over 20% were women. Only 23% of the employees were born in Agadir; the rest (26%) were immigrants from rural areas in the province, or neighbouring provinces, or from the rest of Morocco. This was the case, above all, for the most specialised and experienced staff. Confirmation was found, in that in luxury hotels and tourist villages, the percentage of native Agadians was less than 20% (Berriane 1983). The development of tourism in Agadir triggered commuter movements from the rural hinterland of Agadir and migration of more qualified workers from the rest of the country, similar to the process noted in the Algarve region (Cavaco 1980).

Since the 1950s, in the Balearic Islands, the development of tourism has triggered various forms of migration from the Spanish continent, especially from the southern provinces. In 1986 almost a quarter of the resident population was born in the rest of Spain, especially in Andalusia (42%), Albacete and Murcia (Salvá i Tomás 1991). A project carried out in the summer of 1982, in Corsica, discovered that out of 15 000 workers in the tourist sector just under 70% were resident in Corsica, but only 40% had actually been born there. The shortage of local personnel was compensated for by the importation of personnel from the rest of France, especially medium and highly specialised personnel (Renucci 1985). In asking the questions whether and how tourism could become a signifi-cant part of the development of the Mezzogiorno, Barucci and Becheri (1990) discover that only non-qualified personnel are recruited in southern Italy, while the rest came from central and northern Italy, or at least they are trained and gain experience in these regions. This functional deficit had been noted in other sectors of the advanced services in Italy (Formez 1982).

In a study of Italian migration flows from 1980 to 1991, highly educated Italians came predominantly from the tourist municipalities like the tourist resorts: Bordighera, Ospedaletti, Ventimiglia, Diano Marina, San Remo, Al-assio, Albissola, Chiavari, Rapall e Lerici in Liguria and Taormina and Giar-dini Nazos, in Sicily (Montanari 1993c). If intermediate-level tourism gives rise to migration of the workforce on a national level, then, at the managerial level, the flux is predominantly international.

3.6   MEDITERRANEAN TOURISM: RESOURCES, RISKS AND PREDICTIONS

The previously mentioned Blue Plan has outlined the main possibilities for the development of tourism to the years 2000 and 2025 and its consequences for the Mediterranean environment. By the year 2000 it is estimated that arrivals in the 18 countries could vary from between 268 million and 409 million, representing an increase of between 40 and 120% according to varying hypo-theses for economic development. By 2025 arrivals could reach between 379 million and 758 million (Grenon and Batisse 1989). The Economist Intelligence Unit (EIU) Research report (Jenner and Smith 1993) estimates a total of 330 million arrivals in the same 18 countries by the year 2000. This represents an increase of 76% over 9 years. The EIU prediction for numbers of arrivals in the year 2000 in the coastal regions of the Mediterranean is 205 million, representing an increase of 81% compared to 1991.

If the Mediterranean tourist region is taken to include 24 countries, 290 million arrivals are predicted for the year 2000. This figure does not take into account undocumented tourism. The United Nations predict that the population in the 24 countries concerned will be 460 million in the year 2000.

The Mediterranean environment is extremely fragile and sensitive both to the quantitative and qualitative presence of human activity. Such a rapid increase in the population of the region, changes in life style and an increase in tourist flows cannot fail to take their toll on the environment. The availability and consumption of drinking water are likely to be a source of international political friction, especially in the Mediterranean where countries are able to identify water shortages and implement national strategies for its capture and exploitation. Conflicts of interest may also occur between different consumers within countries, given that annual water consumption per person does not exceed 1.8–3.6 cu. m of water for the nomadic populations in Africa, reaches 18–36 cu. m per person in developing countries and 90–180 cu. m in more developed and urbanised regions of Mediterranean Europe. In contrast, according to UNEP the daily consumption of water per tourist in a five-star hotel on the Mediterranean coast is between 0.6 and 1 cu. m per day. The countries in the northern Mediterranean have the most water, while those in the south have only 1000 cu. m of water per person per year. With the increase in the population and in the tourist flows, the quantity of water available will not be enough to satisfy the needs of the resident population let alone the consumption required for agriculture and other productive activities (Montanari 1993b).

The only solution to the water problem, as with many other environmental problems in the Mediterranean, seems to be collaboration between countries in the region to achieve a common management of natural resources. Tourism may benefit both from sustainable management of natural resources and from forms of cooperation in the region which will reduce the risk of conflict and war. Even if forms of competition within the tourist region can and must be perpetuated, it will still be necessary to find ways of appreciating the Mediterranean as a single entity.

The estimated number of tourists for the year 2000 varies according to a set of different scenarios as does the effect that these may have at a territorial level. A scenario predicting a world economic recession, high levels of pollution and deterioration in environmental standards, and further outbreaks of conflict in the Middle East and the Balkans, would divert Europeans to new destinations or even accelerate the tendency towards new forms of 'virtual' tourism (Cohen

1993). This situation would have a negative impact on all Mediterranean countries and could lead to as much as a 25% reduction in arrivals.

On the other hand, the year 2000 might be characterised by global political and economic stability, dominated by a solid and expanded EU including the countries of Central Europe and able to control and reduce conflict via cooperation with Mediterranean countries. The scenario presupposes a greater control of environmental conditions and pollution, and an equal division of the increased cost of transport which are considered to be too low at present. An EU comprising 430 million inhabitants living in comfortable economic conditions would stimulate tourist demand, and an increase in transport costs would direct it towards the more accessible Mediterranean countries. Such a scenario could credibly lead to anything from a 40 to 120% increase in arrivals as indicated in the Blue Plan. The Blue Plan, which was conceived so as to evaluate the maximum impact that tourist activities could have on the environment, was excessively optimistic in this respect.

Certain commentators, such as Lozato-Giotart (1993), point to possible intermediate solutions for the next decade. The scenario is dominated by an increase in, and the diversification of, demand in a region which is still beset by sporadic crises. The increase in tourist flows would therefore be concentrated in the countries of the north-western Mediterranean, because of their ability to resolve already serious environmental problems, and in the north-east providing they are able to ensure peace and security. In terms of utilisation of territory we are heading towards a polarisation of the supply which, in the areas where tourism is already developed, requires substantial restructuring. It is therefore probable that the Mediterranean cities will bear the burden of the new tourist influx (Mespelier-Pinet 1993).

While the characteristics and means of tourism development remain the subject of debate over the next few decades, the United Nations prediction that the population of the 24 Mediterranean countries will be 460 million by the year 2000 would seem to be a virtual certainty.

ACKNOWLEDGEMENTS

Figures 3.4–3.7 were prepared by A. Montanari with the Geographical Information System assistance of C. Magnarapa. The equipment was provided by CNUCE/CNR.

4 The British Isles: Tourism and Regional Development

ALLAN M. WILLIAMS
University of Exeter, UK
DESMOND A. GILLMOR
Trinity College, Dublin, Ireland

4.1 INTRODUCTION: TOURISM IN THE UK AND THE REPUBLIC OF IRELAND

Tourism is of increasing importance to economic development and cultural formation throughout Europe. It is also an industry which binds countries together in increasingly complex ways. This is illustrated by the British Isles— the United Kingdom and the Republic of Ireland—where tourism has been both shaped by economic growth and the emergence of new forms of mass consumption, and has contributed to these. This is particularly evident in the positions of these countries in international tourism, and especially in the shifting balance between their roles as countries of origins and destinations. In addition, the relationship between the UK and Ireland is itself of interest; over time there has been a decrease in the dependency of Ireland on the UK market, which also reflects the more general reorientation of the Irish economy.

In the UK there has been a gradual extension of mass tourism throughout most of the twentieth century. This has had two distinctive peaks. The first, in the 1950s, was the emergence of a genuinely mass domestic tourism market, linked to the growth of mass consumption (Urry 1990) in a period of rapid growth during the early years of the post-war social democratic consensus. This was characterised as the 'golden years' of the British seaside resorts, when the majority—but not all—of the working class aspired to and were able to realise one- or two-week seaside holidays as part of emergent consumerist life styles. By the 1960s mass tourism was becoming increasingly internationalised and this constituted the second peak in the UK's experience. While international tourism had existed in various forms over several centuries, it was in this decade that it began to change from being an élitist experience to being a form of mass consumption. The reasons for this are well known, especially the key role of international tour companies which revolutionised the economics

European Tourism: Regions, Spaces and Restructuring. Edited by A. Montanari and A.M. Williams.
© 1995 European Science Foundation. Published in 1995 by John Wiley & Sons Ltd.

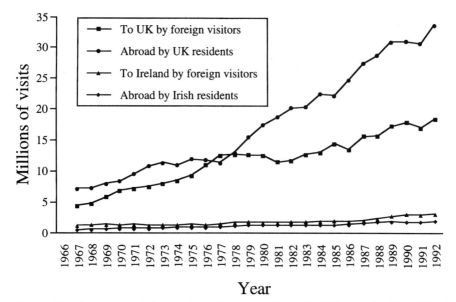

Figure 4.1. International flows of tourists to and from the UK and the Republic of Ireland. Sources: Prepared by the authors on the basis of data from the British Tourist Authority and Bord Fáilte (Irish Tourist Board)

of international holiday travel (see Shaw and Williams 1994). The high elasticity of demand for international tourism meant that over the medium term its growth was relatively independent of economic growth, hence the strong and sustained expansion evident in the 1980s (Figure 4.1), despite the highly uneven economic growth rates in this decade.

The 1970s was a key point in UK international tourism. After recovery from the 1973–74 oil crisis and economic recession, international departures from the UK rose sharply and overtook international arrivals. However, there has also been strong growth of international tourism to the UK in most years, with the exception of the early 1980s recession. This has been facilitated by a series of devaluations of the UK currency. The attractions of the UK as a tourist destination are twofold. Firstly, they are cultural, hence the pre-eminence of London as a destination, but also the importance of Edinburgh, Oxford, Stratford-upon-Avon and other cities. There is a high degree of mass consumption in the way that this sector is organised, evident in the importance of organised tours. Secondly, there is the attraction of relatively unspoilt countryside in the more peripheral regions of the UK, such as western Scotland, Wales, the Lake District and the West Country; this type of tourism has been characterised by more individual forms of travel. Both types have been among the growth sectors of international and domestic mass tourism in the 1980s.

The origins of the UK's international market are shown in Table 4.1. While there have been some fluctuations, there have been no significant shifts in

Table 4.1.   Origins of overseas visitors to the UK, 1980–92

(a) Overall (% of total)

	North America	Europe	Other	Total
1980	16.8	63.7	19.6	100.0
1985	26.3	54.5	19.3	100.0
1990	20.5	59.6	19.9	100.0
1992	18.2	63.4	18.4	100.0

Source: BTA/ETB (1993).

(b) Main countries of origin, 1992

	Visits ('000s)	Spending (£m.)
USA	2748	1490
France	2483	420
Germany	2268	636
Irish Republic	1416	424
Netherlands	996	239

Source: Data provided by the British Tourist Authority.

market share during the period 1980–92. By far the most important market is Europe, followed by North America. Three countries alone account for more than 7 million tourist visits, making the UK relatively vulnerable to changes in any one market segment, such as terrorist-inspired cancellations in the USA, or recession in mainland Europe. In practice, however, the overall growth of foreign arrivals in the UK has been remarkably resilient (Figure 4.1).

There are some parallels in the growth of tourism in the Irish Republic, although there are also many differences and the industry is on a smaller scale in absolute if not relative terms. Throughout the twentieth century, Ireland has been host to more international tourists than it has sent abroad. This reflects relatively low levels of economic development until the internationalisation of the economy in the 1960s led to increased real incomes, which was reinforced by the benefits which followed EC membership in 1973. Rising standards of living meant that there was a steady increase in the numbers of Irish people able and choosing to take holidays abroad (Figure 4.1). As in the UK, this was facilitated by the growth of charter tours, which accounted for more than one-half of the holidays to mainland Europe (Gillmor 1993b). Ireland, itself, did not emerge as a significant tourist destination until quite recently, mainly because it lacked the (climatic) conditions for mass tourism. In addition, even the modest growth of international tourist arrivals was disrupted by the international media attention given to the 'troubles' in Northern Ireland; as a result the rates of growth for foreign arrivals were among the lowest in Europe during much of the 1970s. The effect on tourism in Northern Ireland was even more disastrous, with tourist arrivals falling by more than one-half between 1969 and 1972.

In the 1980s, however, there was strong recovery in the Republic of Ireland international tourist industry (although numbers in Northern Ireland did not

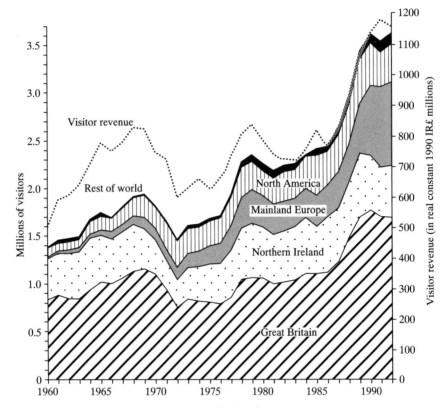

Figure 4.2. Visitors to the Republic of Ireland, 1960–92. Source: See Figure 4.1

regain their 1969 level until the 1990s). The recovery in Ireland has been facilitated by improvements to international transport links, and by reduced access fares and price inflation (Gillmor 1993a). Ireland also has those tourist products which have been increasingly attractive in recent decades: unspoilt rural areas and coastline, especially in the west, and cultural tourism in Dublin, Kilkenny, the Rock of Cashel and many other sites. This is confirmed by opinion surveys which show that sightseeing and the scenery are the leading holiday activities, being cited by 57% of respondents in a 1988 survey of the reasons why people chose to visit Ireland (Central Marketing Department 1988): This was followed in rank order by the reasons of 'new experiences', visiting friends and relatives, restfulness, meeting Irish people, and cultural/ historic reasons (19% gave this last reason). Also important is language study, which accounts for about 9% of the visitors from mainland Europe.

The recovery in international tourism was also associated with a change in market composition. In particular, there has been a decline in the share of the UK, and a major increase in the share of the rest of Europe (Figure 4.2). This

Table 4.2.   Some characteristics of overseas visitors in the Republic of Ireland, 1992

Characteristics	Britain	Mainland Europe	North America	Other areas	All overseas
Expenditure per visitor (IR£)	199	373	374	392	279
Main purpose of visit (%):					
Holiday only	18	50	46	41	32
Holiday plus other reasons	14	7	17	15	12
Visiting friends/relatives	34	10	17	21	24
Business/conference	20	18	12	12	18
Study/personal/other reasons	14	15	8	11	14
Proportions of bed-nights (%):					
Staying with friends/relatives	57	15	36	29	36
Hotels and other serviced accommodation	23	28	43	23	28
Rented/caravan/camping/ youth hostel and other accommodation	29	57	21	48	36

Source: Prepared by the authors on the basis of data provided by Bord Fáilte.

shift has reduced the dependency of Ireland on a single market. It also reflects the increasing competitiveness of Ireland in the international market, precisely because it offers the kind of individually organised rural and or cultural tourism which is still a strong segment of market expansion. The decline in the British market share also reflects the diminishing relative importance of the emigrant market. One-third of the British market is made up of people visiting friends and relatives, and one-half are staying with friends and relatives (Table 4.2). This is a useful market in that it is a relatively assured niche, it is not open to competition, and it is less seasonal than other holidaying. It is, however, dependent on continuing high levels of emigration from the Republic, and generates relatively low levels of expenditure per visitor.

The importance of tourism in the economies of both the Republic of Ireland and the UK has increased sharply in recent years. This is reflected in the statistics on GDP, exports and employment (Table 4.3). While there are difficulties in the estimation of all of these totals—linked to the problems of defining tourism and of data inadequacies—they mark out tourism as one of the largest individual sectors in both countries. In many respects it is true that recent growth in

Table 4.3.   Tourism and the national economies of Ireland and the UK, 1992

	Ireland	UK
% of GDP	7.1	3.4
% of all exports	4.7	4.7
% of all employment	7.1[a]	6.0[b]

[a] 1991. [b] 1991; for employees in tourism-related industries.

Source: See Table 4.2.

tourism has helped to offset the decline and stagnation evident in other parts of the economy; this is particularly true of tourism given the labour-intensive nature of the industry. However, the impact of tourism has been highly uneven geographically, and in both countries this has had a strong regional dimension.

4.2 TOURISM AND REGIONAL DEVELOPMENT: SOME ISSUES

Tourism has characteristics which distinguish it from other service industries. These relate to the nature of the services on offer and the conditions under which they are consumed. In addition, there has been a shift in tourism in recent years, from mass consumption to more customised and flexible products (Urry 1987). Each of these features is considered here but see Shaw and Williams (1994) for further detail. These features of tourism have implications for regional development. These are, of course, contingent upon local, regional and national conditions which are themselves subject to processes of short- and long-term change. However, on the basis of the preceding discussion, it is possible to draw out some general implications for regional development.

Firstly, tourism is not a product which can be stored or transported, but instead has to be consumed at the point of production. It is true that a series of ancillary industries have grown up around tourism, such as shops selling travel books and tourist 'loot' (souvenirs, etc.; see Williams and Shaw 1992). However, the principal object of tourism—the visual gaze (Urry 1992)—can be experienced only at particular locations. As the supply points—leastways for mass tourism—are spatially fixed, this means that tourism is subject to a high degree of spatial polarisation. In part this is related to the climatic and geomorphological distribution of the objects of mass tourism, in particular beaches/sunshine and snow/mountains. However, this is also conditioned by the social construction of the tourism gaze. Urry (1990, p. 47) argued that 'The contemporary tourist gaze is increasingly signposted. There are markers which distinguish the things and places worthy of our gaze. Such signposting identifies a relatively small number of tourist nodes.' Signposting is influenced by the media and the advertising industries as well as by wider cultural values, and the socio-pychological determinants of tourism behaviour (Iso-Ahola 1980). Such signposting has pointed in the direction of beach holidays, skiing vacations or rural 'retreats' during much of the twentieth century, as was verified in a recent EC-wide survey of holiday behaviour (CEC 1987). In addition, economies of scale in developing tourism infrastructure (airports, etc.) as well as in investment in tourism attractions (e.g. theme parks) and accommodation, are also conducive to spatial polarisation.

However, the growth of mass tourism at any one point in space potentially contains the seed of its own decline. This was formalised by Butler (1980) in his descriptive model of the tourist resort cycle, based on changing powers of attraction as well as the negative implications of the congestion which accompanies polarisation. He suggested that there were six stages in the evolution of tourist destination areas. In the fifth stage, which he labelled 'stagnation', numbers peak and there is a high turnover of business properties. This is followed by the sixth stage in which attractiveness continues to decline; this may become long term and terminal unless action is taken to rejuvenate the area. While flawed, the resort life-cycle model does provide a perspective on the rise and decline of resorts and potentially, therefore, shifts in the regional distribution of tourism. It does not, however, provide any pointers as to either the initial rich region versus poor region distribution, or to the direction of any subsequent changes.

The second key feature of tourism is that it is subject to restructuring tendencies (see Urry 1987). There have been two important shifts in recent decades. The first was the competition offered by Mediterranean resorts to traditional seaside resorts in the British Isles, such as Torquay, Southend and the south-east resorts in Ireland. The social reconstruction of what constituted desirable mass tourism products, together with a change in social access to these, had profound implications for these traditional domestic resorts. Their growth was depressed and in some cases they entered the decline phase of the resort cycle. The second major process of restructuring has centred on the relative shift from mass tourism to post-modernist tourism (Urry 1990). In particular, there has been increasing emphasis on individualised products, and on mixed media/cultural experiences. As a result, there has been a challenge in northern Europe to the dominance of the traditional object of mass tourism, the seaside holiday. This has been reinforced by an increasing capacity to market a wider range of objects for tourist consumption, whether this be industrial archaeology (e.g. Wigan Pier), cultural distinctiveness (e.g. the Asian community in Bradford, or the early Christian communities in Ireland), modern industrial production (e.g. Waterford crystal), garden festivals (e.g. Ebbw Vale), or the possibilities for contact with an open and friendly host community (as in most of Ireland).

The implication is that tourist resorts—as with any locality—are subject to restructuring. This may involve labour market reorganisation, increased capital intensity, product innovation or—in the case of failure to adapt and compete—terminal decline. Taken together, these changes in the fortunes of individual resorts, can lead to major regional shifts. In particular, tourism can contribute to the changing overall pattern of development between rich and poor regions. This can be partly understood in terms of the changing balance between mass consumption and post-modernism. Mass tourism, as a form of mass consumption, primarily (but not exclusively) serves the needs of the populations in the rich regions which have critical mass in terms of population and income. Given the way in which mass tourism is socially constructed as a flight from the pressures of everyday life and the attraction of relaxing beaches and countryside, it has traditionally been viewed (e.g. Peters 1969, p. 11) as an activity located in peripheral regions.

This traditional pattern of rich region/poor region relationships is, however, challenged by the post-modernist developments in tourism referred to earlier. There are many different forms of tourism in the developed world in the 1990s, and these encompass culture, industrial heritage exhibitions and many other objects of the tourist gaze. All of these types of tourism have distinctive spatial forms, and have quite different regional implications. Some forms of tourism focus on capital cities (almost invariably located in richer regions), while the growth of short-break tourism (which is constrained by geographical accessibility to the major markets) also favours destinations in or adjacent to the rich region. However, the growing interest in industrial heritage tends to favour older industrial cities and regions, which are often located in the poor regions. In effect, therefore, the simple dichotomy between 'cores of origins' and 'peripheries of destinations', which was never an adequate conceptualisation of the polarisation tendencies in tourism, has further declined in relevance given the growth of new forms of tourism activities.

Another set of considerations hinges on the impact of the internationalisation of tourism. Within Europe the growth of international mass tourism, especially to the Mediterranean region, has been well documented (see Williams 1993a) and this is only one part of much wider globalisation of tourism (Shaw and Williams 1994, Chapter 2). This has important regional implications for any one country, depending on three conditions. Firstly, there is a displacement effect; has the growth of international departures displaced tourism growth which would otherwise have been directed at domestic destinations, and if so, which regions are most affected? Secondly, there is a substitution effect; are there significant numbers of foreign tourist arrivals, and if so, what are their regional destinations? Thirdly, there is a balancing effect; what is the net regional outcome of the processes of international arrivals and departures? The answers to these questions are highly contingent, as has been argued in a comparative study of the regional impact of international tourist arrivals in Portugal and the UK (Williams 1994). The assessment of the regional impact of internationalisation is therefore a matter for empirical investigation rather than theoretical prediction. However, it is clear that it does have strong implications for tourism in the UK and Ireland, and within these countries.

4.3   THE REGIONAL DISTRIBUTION OF TOURISM IN THE BRITISH ISLES

In this section the impact of tourism on regional development in the UK and Ireland is examined. The discussion is focused on the conceptual issues that have been identified earlier. The emphasis here is on the broad regional distributions but this is not to deny that there are complex spatial patterns at the local level. These subregional trends have been analysed elsewhere (Townsend 1992; Pollard 1989; O'Cinneide and Walsh 1990–91) and, in the space available here, concentration is on the larger regional scale within the British Isles.

Tourism in the UK is a highly polarised activity, and this is evident even at the aggregate scale of the 12 English Tourist Boards, and those for Wales, Scotland and Northern Ireland (Table 4.4). There are, however, important

Table 4.4.   Regional distribution of domestic and foreign tourists

(a) UK 1992

Region	% of total visits	
	Domestic	Foreign
Cumbria	2.7	1.7
Northumbria	3.3	1.9
North-west	7.7	5.6
Yorkshire and Humberside	7.8	4.9
Heart of England	7.7	6.8
East Midlands	6.1	3.4
East Anglia	9.5	6.9
London	7.3	53.8
West Country	13.7	7.9
Southern	9.9	9.8
South-east	7.2	10.5
Scotland	9.3	9.7
Wales	8.7	3.6
Northern Ireland	1.1	0.5
All regions	100.0	100.0[a]

[a] Also includes Channel Islands and Isle of Man.

(b) Ireland 1992

Region	% of total visits	
	Domestic	Foreign
Dublin	14.7	24.6
Midlands/East	12.7	9.1
South-east	16.5	10.4
South-west	18.8	17.9
Mid-west	13.2	12.9
West	16.6	15.0
North-west	7.5	10.1
All regions	100.0	100.0

Source: See Figure 4.1.

differences between domestic and foreign tourism. In terms of the domestic market, the leading UK tourist region is the West Country with a 14% share. It is followed, at some distance, by Southern, East Anglia, Scotland and Wales with 9–10% each. Geographical concentration in a few regions, then, is matched by a relatively even spread of tourists among the other regions. Clearly, if the scale of analysis were reduced to individual counties, or cities and towns, an even higher degree of polarisation could be identified.

This apparently simple pattern is made more complex if the international context is considered. UK regions compete for visitors—both international and domestic—with foreign regions. In particular, since the 1960s there has been the growth of international air charter tourism in Europe, and this market has been dominated by flows from the UK and Germany to the Mediterranean countries (see Pearce 1987c). There is no doubt that this has displaced some of the growth which might otherwise have accrued to the UK domestic tourist industry. However, the aggregate impact of the growth of overseas tourism from the UK has often been exaggerated, not least because it ignores the substitution effect, that is the incoming tourist flows (see Shaw et al. 1991). As can be seen from Figure 4.1, it was only in the mid 1970s that there was a decisive divergence in the growth of foreign tourism to and from the UK. By the late 1980s the ratio between the two was almost two to one in terms of visitor numbers, although this overestimates the economic impact as the per capita expenditure of visitors to the UK is considerably higher than that of the British abroad.

There is, however, a distinctive regional dimension to these relative shifts in outward and inward tourism. If it is assumed that outward tourists would have had the same regional distribution of holidays within the UK as domestic tourists, then internationalisation of tourism has had a major regional impact (see Table 4.4). London is the principal destination of foreign tourists, accounting for 54% of the total. In second place is the South-east with 10% of the total. In contrast, East Anglia, the West Country and Wales which are important destinations in the domestic tourism market, attract relatively few foreign tourists. The net effect of these two-way international flows of tourists has been to reduce polarisation in traditional tourism regions.

Turning to the Republic of Ireland, there are similar differences to note between domestic and foreign tourism (Table 4.4). Domestic tourism is remarkably evenly spread throughout the regions of Ireland; only the North-west has a share which is not within the 10–20% range. The most popular regions are the South-west and the West with their outstanding coastlines and rural landscapes. They are closely followed by the South-east, which has the advantage of proximity to the main market, Dublin. Dublin itself attracts only 14.7% of domestic holiday tourists.

There are marked differences in the distribution of foreign tourists, although some of these are exaggerated in that the data relate to all tourism trips, including business ones (Table 4.4). Dublin is a strong pole of attraction within the Republic of Ireland, but less so than London is within the UK. Even so, one-quarter of all foreign tourists visit the capital. The second most important region is the South-west, for the same reason as for domestic tourism. The South-east is relatively unimportant to this market segment, as also is the Midlands. The North-west is relatively more attractive to foreign tourists than to domestic ones. These figures, however, have to be disaggregated so as to take into account the strong element of emigrants returning from the UK for holidays. For the American sub-market the main attraction is Dublin, followed by the western region; the reverse applies to visitors from mainland Europe.

Table 4.5. Regional role of tourism employment in the British Isles

(a) Distribution of tourism and related leisure employment in standard L_

	% of all tourism employment 1989	% of all employment in 1989	Tourism over (+) or under (−) represented
South-east	38	34	+
East Anglia	3	3	
South-west	9	7	+
West Midlands	7	10	−
East Midlands	6	7	−
Yorkshire and Humberside	7	9	−
North-west	11	11	
North	5	5	
Wales	4	4	
Scotland	10	9	+
Total	100	100	

a Northern Ireland excluded.

Source: Prepared by the authors on the basis of data provided by Central Statistical Office (1991) and English Tourist Board.

(b) Estimated tourism-related employment by region in Republic of Ireland 1990

Region	Number	As % of national tourism-related employment	As % of region's total employment
Dublin/East	29 193	36.5	6.1
South-east	6 868	8.6	5.8
South-west	16 023	20.0	9.7
Mid-west	7 534	9.4	7.8
West	8 947	11.2	9.5
North-west	6 144	7.7	10.8
Midlands	5 291	6.6	4.7
Total	80 000	100.0	7.1

Note: These employment data relate to the pre-1989 tourism regions.
Source: Prepared by the authors on the basis of data provided by Bord Fáilte and Tansey, Webster and Associates (1991).

4.4 TOURISM AND REGIONAL DEVELOPMENT

The contribution of tourism to the regional economies is difficult to assess because of the lack of reliable regional economic data and multiplier estimates. However, some idea of the relative economic contribution of tourism in the UK can be obtained from employment data. While tourism employment data *per se* are not available for UK regions, it is possible to estimate tourism and related leisure employment for standard economic planning regions which are different to tourism regions (Table 4.5). These data show that there is a high degree of polarisation with 38% of all such jobs being in the South-east. This is followed by the North-west, Scotland and the South-west with 11, 10 and 9% respectively, while no other region has more than 7%. The wider definition employed here, which includes local leisure activities, is bound to reflect the distribution of regional populations, as well as central place hierarchies, and therefore may exaggerate the importance of the South-east. However, if these data are compared to the percentage of total employment in each region, then the polarising effects of tourism are evident. Tourism and leisure-related employment is over-represented only in the South-east (a special case for the reasons outlined above), Scotland and the South-west (Table 4.5). While the latter is usually considered to be one of the rich regions of the UK, in this case—as with the West Country (tourism region)—it can be considered as poor given that the more westerly Devon and Cornwall dominate its tourism industry. In contrast, the Midlands, and (non-core) Yorkshire and Humberside all have under-representations of tourism and related jobs.

In the case of the Republic of Ireland, Dublin/East and the South-west together account for more than one-half of total tourism employment and other regions—except the West—account for less than one-tenth (Table 4.5). There is therefore a relative polarisation of tourism employment within the regional system, although the use of 'tourism-related' employment estimates means that the share of Dublin tends to be exaggerated. The contribution of tourism measured as a proportionate share of these regional economies does, however, reveal a different pattern. Tourism is of greatest relative importance in the North-west, where in absolute terms it is of far less importance (Table 4.5). It also has a considerable impact on the other western regions, and is of relatively limited importance in the Dublin/East and South-east regions; this is, of course, the inverse of the index of industrial and overall economic development. This simple pattern is, however, spoilt by the case of the Midlands, Ireland's poorest region, where tourism has generated relatively few jobs.

This discussion of employment leads on to the related question of the contribution of tourism to the redistribution of income between rich and poor regions. Rich and poor are, of course, static and rather simplistic terms and, as such, are of limited value. However, this framework does provide a descriptive device for identifying whether tourism contributes significantly more to the economies of the richer or the poorer regions. In the UK the three most prosperous regions in terms of household incomes, wealth and low unemployment are East Anglia, the South-east and the South-west (Hudson and Williams 1989). The South-west is problematic because the aggregate data are inflated by the relatively dynamic Bristol subregion. The foreign tourism distribution is complex, and is difficult to interpret given the enormous domination of London. But this concentration does mean that tourism contributes most to the economies of the richest regions. It does also make a disproportionate contribution to the economies of the West Country (South-west) and Scotland, but this is insignificant compared to the concentration of more than one-half of all visits in London. In contrast, the poorer regions do rather better in terms of the domestic

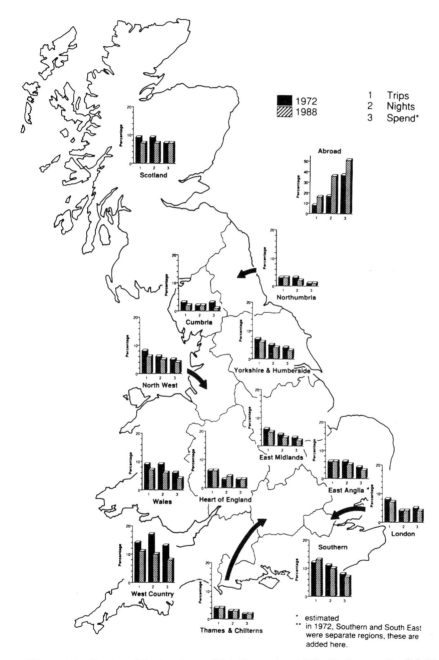

Figure 4.3. Regional destinations of British tourist, 1972–88. Source: English Tourist Board

market, although the effects are still mixed: two of the regions which are most attractive to domestic tourists—the West Country (seen as dominated by Devon and Cornwall) and Wales—are among the poorest regions in the UK. Therefore, while the overall pattern is complex it can be summarised as follows: domestic tourism tends to redistribute income from rich to poor regions, but this is counteracted by the concentration of foreign tourism in London.

Although there is some evidence that the distribution of domestic tourism has favoured the poor regions, it can be argued that the shift from mass tourism to post-modernist forms of consumption may have resulted in a relative shift of growth to the rich regions. It is not possible to operationalise and quantify precisely the concept of post-modernist tourism (Urry 1990), but it is possible to identify some growth trends in non-traditional forms of tourism: heritage based, business and short break. Heritage sites, museums, gardens and country parks have all become more important as tourism venues, and most of the top 10 most popular attractions in each of these categories are in the South-east and London. Business tourism has become relatively more important in recent years, and accounted for 22% of all trips within the UK in 1991. By its very nature business tourism is likely to be concentrated in the core regions (see Shaw and Williams 1994, Chapter 5). There has also been a sharp increase in the relative importance of short holiday tourist visits (three or less nights). By 1991 there were 53.8 million nights spent on short holidays and 242.1 million on longer holidays. Market research indicates that there is consumer resistance to travelling more than 2 hours on short holiday breaks, and that these second and third holidays are—to a far greater extent than main holidays—concentrated among the middle classes. These changes in sub-markets strongly suggest that the destinations for this growing market segment are disproportionately concentrated in the south of the UK, that is in or near the rich regions.

These changes in the nature of UK domestic tourism have led to a major regional redistribution of the industry from poor to rich regions. Between 1972 and 1988 the shares of all domestic trips and nights spent in poor regions such as Scotland and Wales have decreased sharply (Figure 4.3). The sharpest fall has been in the West Country. In contrast, the smallest declines were in southern England while the market share of the West Midlands (Heart of England) actually increased. There would therefore appear to have been a relative shift from poorer to richer regions. The increase in the number of foreign tourists from 4 million in 1967 to 16.6 million in 1992 will also have reinforced the poor region to rich region shift, given their strong geographical concentration in London and the South-east. In this sense, the internationalisation of tourism after the 1960s, with the increase in foreign tourists arriving in the UK and the displacement of millions of traditional long summer holidays from the UK to abroad, has contributed to rich region–poor region divergence.

The regional shift in tourism has, of course, had an impact on the distribution of tourism employment. Between 1981 and 1989 there were increases of 60% or more in tourism and leisure employment in the Midlands, the

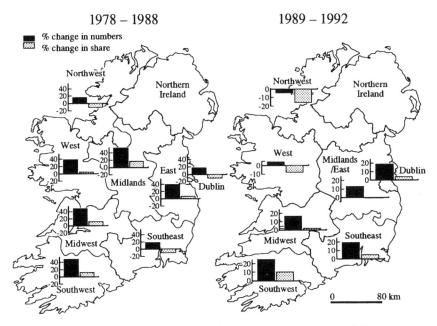

Figure 4.4.   Percentage change in share of external visitors to Ireland, by region, 1978–88 and 1989–92. Source: See Table 4.2

South-east and East Anglia, while the increases were less than 45% in most of the northern regions. While this partly reflects differential rates of population growth and local demand for leisure, it is also the product of differential tourism growth. Working with county-level data, Townsend (1992) provided clear evidence that the pattern of change is intraregional as well as inter-regional. In particular, he identified a 'coast-to-cities' shift in hotel jobs, as well as high growth rates for all leisure and tourism jobs in rural areas. Moreover, the problem should not be thought of as being limited to the large seaside resorts. A report by the English Tourist Board (1991a) suggested that the smaller seaside resorts have lost at least one-half of their overnight visitor market since the 1970s. Therefore, the changing structure of tourism consumption has had intraregional effects as well as interregional ones.

The analysis of regional shifts in Ireland is as problematic as in the UK, because of a lack of regional data in the past and a number of changes in geographical definitions. However, Figure 4.4 gives some idea of changes in the distribution of tourists, 1978–88 (regional data are not available prior to these dates). In this period, and probably for the previous decade also, tourism would seem to have contributed to regional convergence; this is substantiated by the large gains in the share of foreign visitors accounted for by the Midlands, the South-west and the North-west, and the declining share of Dublin city and the South-east. The figures presented earlier on the relative weight of tourism in the peripheral economies of the west also support this argument. However, this pattern of convergence is mitigated by two considerations; first, that many of the jobs in tourism—especially outside of Dublin—are seasonal and/or part-time; to some extent this is reflected in the fact that the share of Dublin in tourism revenue increased by one-fifth between 1976 and 1988, while the South-west and Mid-west just about held their shares, and the share of the North-west fell by about one-fifth. Secondly, visitor numbers after 1988 suggest that there is a new form of polarisation (Figure 4.4). The share of the South-west increased sharply, but so did that of the South-east and Dublin, reflecting the growth of new forms of tourism. A decline in the importance of return migrant tourism has also disadvantaged the peripheral regions.

The overall impact of tourism on the rich region versus poor region balance has therefore been complex. On the one hand it has had a positive impact on the poorer regions, but this has been selective. Tourism was one of the reasons why, in 1990, the South-west and the Mid-west regions had the second and third highest levels of per capita income in Ireland; they had index values of 100 and 95 respectively compared to 100 for the national average. However, many poor regions had not benefited to the same extent from tourism, and for this reason it is not surprising that the Midlands has the lowest per capita incomes in Ireland (index value of 85). At the same time, the strong competitive position of Dublin—especially—in the foreign market, has contributed to its well above average per capita incomes (112).

4.5   TOURISM AND POPULATION REDISTRIBUTION

Tourism contributes to population redistribution in three distinctive ways: via temporary flows for tourist purposes, via encouragement of labour migration, and via encouragement of permanent or semi-permanent non-employment migration especially in terms of second homes or retirement. Data on all these features are at best uneven and at worst anecdotal for both the UK and the Republic of Ireland.

The pattern of temporary population movements for the consumption of tourism is complex in detail, but at the interregional level tends to reflect movement from the more populated and prosperous South-east region to the more peripheral regions of the UK. This is illustrated, for example, by the West Country, which attracts 37% of all its visitors from London and the South-east. Comparable data are not available for the Republic of Ireland, but it can be suggested that the predominant flows are from Dublin to the traditional resorts of the South-east or to the western regions. These are particularly strong as almost one-third of the population of the Republic live in the greater Dublin region. Therefore, there is still a sense in which the geographical (and economic periphery) of the British Isles forms a pleasure periphery for the core economic regions. In the case of Ireland there is also a secondary core-periphery movement within the periphery, in the relationship between Dublin and the rest of the country. Similar patterns can also be found of course within the UK's regions, as for example in the annual influx into the Highlands region from Glasgow.

Tourism also generates seasonal or permanent immigration of labour migrants. Although an important feature of many tourist areas, this is a surprisingly under-researched topic. In Ireland, there is no way of separating out internal labour migration related to tourism from total inter-county migration data. Tourism-employment migration is likely to be limited with the exception of movements to the largest centres of tourism, mainly Dublin, Killarney and Galway/Salthill. However, Irish tourism is quite dispersed with individual centres and facilities being mostly small, and an absence of major mass tourism resorts. As there is a surplus of labour in almost all localities— national unemployment is 20%—this means that most labour needs can be met locally. There is no significant labour migration to work in Irish tourism. Data on the UK are equally problematic. There is, however, some anecdotal evidence to suggest that international migration is important in supplying labour in many areas of mass tourism such as London, the south coast resorts and the Channel Islands. There are also traditions of internal seasonal migration to jobs in holiday resorts and holiday camps. Mention can also be made here of a study of tourism entrepreneurs in Cornwall which showed that one-third of the owners of tourism businesses were from the South-east (Williams et al. 1989). The latter study confirmed that the attraction of a tourist area such as Cornwall to entrepreneurs is as much environmental/cultural as economic. This also applies in some measure to seasonal and permanent employees, and this no doubt is one of the ways in which costs are reduced through a form of self-exploitation. This contributes of course to the competitiveness of the tourism industry.

Tourism can also contribute to permanent or semi-permanent non-economic migration. This is especially marked in the UK, where there is a long tradition of investment in second homes in tourist regions such as Devon and the Lake District. This was given a further boost in the 1980s by the polarised increase in incomes among the middle classes and in the South-east region (Hudson and Williams 1989). Tourism is also likely to have influenced the streams of retirement migration from London and other large cities to rural and coastal regions (Warnes 1992). This is reflected in the distribution of elderly persons in the UK, with large concentrations along the south coast. There are no data on second homes or retirement migration for Ireland, but rates of both are low, especially of the latter. The main areas of second homes are probably Wicklow and the South-east coast (proximity to Dublin), the South-west (important to mainland European purchasers) and the West and Donegal (with an element of Northern Irish ownership in the latter). Retirement migration is limited but does exist on a small scale to coastal places such as Bray/Greystones near Dublin and to west Cork.

4.6   CONCLUSION

Mass tourism in the UK, and to a lesser extent Ireland, traditionally had a locational bias which favoured the poor regions. However, the pattern has shifted in favour of the rich regions in recent years, leastways in relative terms; again this applies particularly to the UK, but to some degree to Ireland. This shift is based on both the effects of internationalisation and the emergence of post-modernist tourism trends, as well as other factors such as the growth of business tourism. These new forms of tourism are less spatially polarised than traditional mass tourism. The regional shift calls into question the traditional view that tourism can be an important sector for bringing about regional convergence. However, it does not necessarily undermine the assertion that tourism is able to provide a basis for regional development in the poorer regions. The apparent contradiction is explained by the positive predictions of future tourism growth at different scales by the UK and Irish governments, the EU and the WTO. Given the increasing ubiquitousness of tourism attractions in the post-modernist era, there are prospects for tourism growth in all regions. But this chapter contends that internationalisation and the structure of the new domestic tourism markets are likely to favour the richer regions disproportionately in the UK. In Ireland, the outcome is more difficult to predict because Dublin is less dominant than London in the national tourist system, and because geographical distance is less of a barrier to movement within Ireland. The growth of ecotourism, which has been identified as one of four key strengths in the marketing strategy of Bord Fáilte (1992), is also likely to favour rural areas and, therefore, to advantage some of Ireland's poorer regions.

The changing form of tourism development in the British Isles raises a number of issues, many of which it shares with other European countries. Firstly, the new emphases on cultural, 'green' and rural tourism are placing unprecedented pressures on some of the most fragile urban and rural environments in the British Isles. In the UK, for example, it has been argued that changes in leisure behaviour, especially associated with the new middle class, have led to a danger of 'loving the countryside to death'. There are similar pressures in British cities such as Bath and Chester, and in Irish tourist areas such as Killarney and the Dingle peninsula. The challenge is to ensure that the very success of such areas in becoming tourist attractions does not mean that the resultant congestion and environmental costs do not result in a highly foreshortened product cycle.

Changes in the market for tourism, especially related to internationalisation, have meant that many of the traditional domestic resorts are ill equipped to meet the new forms of demand. As a result some resorts in the UK such as Southend and Torquay have experienced such high levels of unemployment that they have been included in the list of assisted areas eligible for regional policy assistance. In other words, they have been allocated a place in the (limited) state strategy for restructuring alongside some of the classic areas of manufacturing industry.

In both Ireland and the UK there has been an increasing tendency for the benefits of economic growth to become socially polarised. While, on the one hand, the more prosperous middle classes can afford two or three holidays a year, and perhaps purchase a second home, there is a large residual 'under-class' who are excluded from many of the resources and benefits of society including access to tourism. There are important questions here pertaining to need, entitlement and quality of life to which neither government has given adequate consideration.

5 Scandinavia: Tourism in Europe's Northern Periphery

LARS NYBERG
Mid-Sweden University, Sweden

5.1 THE NORDIC COUNTRIES

As a tourist destination, Scandinavia is looked upon as one region, at least in relation to overseas markets. Scandinavians, however, rarely use this concept. On the contrary, there are well-established links of cooperation between the Nordic countries, that is, Denmark (including the Faeroe Islands and Greenland), Finland, Iceland, Norway and Sweden. This cooperation takes place within the Nordic Council (since 1948). The agreements reached between the states include free movement of capital and labour, which means that both permanent and temporary migration is facilitated. Flows of investment and labour tend to mirror the particular economic situation in the receiving country relative to the sender(s). Sweden has traditionally been a receiving country, especially from Finland, but during the last decade Norway has attracted incoming flows of capital and labour, mainly to the larger cities.

No passport is needed to travel between the Nordic countries and this situation creates problems with travel statistics. There are considerable difficulties in establishing volumes of travel both for Nordic and non-Nordic tourists travelling across borders. Since these countries are visited mainly by private car, and with the purpose of seeing friends and relatives, it is likely that a large part of all tourist trips is not recorded in official statistics. Tourism in the Nordic countries is, therefore, difficult to measure, especially incoming tourism. The figures presented are rather crude estimates of flows which, most probably, are considerably larger than officially reported.

For the purposes of this chapter, Scandinavia is seen as the geographical region consisting of Denmark, Finland, Norway and Sweden (Table 5.1). Iceland will not be part of the discussion. There are great similarities, in many ways, between at least three of the countries; Denmark is the exception with her small area and southerly location, her membership of the EU since 1973, and not being linked by land to the Scandinavian peninsula. Finland is another exception, this time regarding language. While the other three countries use

European Tourism: Regions, Spaces and Restructuring. Edited by A. Montanari and A.M. Williams.
© 1995 European Science Foundation. Published in 1995 by John Wiley & Sons Ltd.

Table 5.1.   Population, area and income of the Scandinavian countries, 1989

Country	Inhabitants (million)	Area (sq.km)	Inhabitants per sq.km	GNP per inhabitant (US$)
Denmark	5.1	43 000	119	20 401
Finland	5.0	338 000	15	23 268
Norway	4.2	324 000	13	21 491
Sweden	8.5	450 000	19	22 303
(OECD				17 387)

Source: Statistics Sweden (1992).

almost the same written and spoken language, Finnish is completely different; 10% of the population in Finland speak Swedish, notably on the island of Åland in the Baltic, where it is the official language.

Historically the ties between the countries have been very close, so that Denmark–Norway and Sweden–Finland have been linked for several hundred years, quite apart from a period during the second part of the nineteenth century, when Norway and Sweden formed a union (until 1905). For over 100 years, until 1917, Finland was a part of the Russian Empire. Before that Sweden and Finland were one kingdom, as were Denmark and Norway. These ties still remain, in many ways, to make Scandinavia a rather homogeneous cultural region, as many visitors see it.

5.2   GEOGRAPHICAL ASPECTS OF SCANDINAVIAN TOURISM

Scandinavia is the northernmost part of Europe (see Figure 5.1). As parts of the region are sparsely populated and climatically subarctic, it displays a spectrum of regional problems. In relation to mainland Europe, Scandinavian countries are peripheral to the dominant markets, not least to the largest tourist markets.

Population distribution is very uneven. The coastal area, in the southern part of each country, is the location of both the capitals and the majority of the population. Northern Scandinavia, in particular the interior part, has extremely low levels of population, but is also an attractive tourist region. The North Calotte (north of the Arctic Circle) is increasingly growing in importance for tourism, with its natural focus on the North Cape in Norway. The growth in tourist demand in the peripheral areas puts a strain on the use of productive resources in general, and on infrastructure capacity in particular. This is of particular relevance when choosing a strategy for tourism development in relation to other forms of resource use (see Jenner and Smith 1992).

Tourism is growing in importance as an instrument to support regional development in the northern regions. However, this should not be exaggerated, for more traditional regional policy measures still dominate the use of state incentives to attract inward investment. Regional policy instruments are

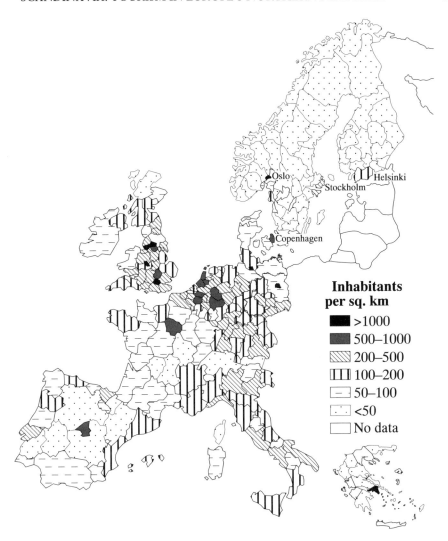

Figure 5.1.   Scandinavia in European context. Source: CEC (1994)

fairly similar for the three areally large countries, Finland, Norway and Sweden, because the problems they face are similar: large areas, long distances and small regional population bases. The most important goals have been to maintain the settlement patterns and to ensure long-term opportunities for employment and services (*NordRefo* 1991).

One important factor is that local and regional income taxes provide a resource base which allows communities to create their own development schemes. State subsidies have also, increasingly, been put at the disposal of regional authorities for decentralised decisions on the detailed use of these funds. This high level of local autonomy is underlined by the OECD which has shown that 40–50% of public expenditure in the Nordic countries is handled by local/regional authorities, while 10–30% is the level in other European countries (Veggeland and Hedegaard 1993).

Another important factor is that physical planning also takes place on the local level. National planning policies are carried out by financially strong local actors under local and regional control (Jorgensen and Lind 1988). This decentralised control over planning, resources and funds is one reason why interest has grown in tourism as a tool for local job creation and for the renewal of service provision. The background to this is that employment opportunities have been irrevocably lost in the traditional primary and secondary industries and many of the more severe regional problems concern, in general, this lack of jobs, especially for younger people (see Flakstad 1989).

The creation of jobs with an appeal to young women is seen as one of the most important tasks facing many small communities in the northern, interior parts of Scandinavia (Flakstad 1989). Problems in terms of lower standards of living or meagre educational opportunities do not enter the picture, for high living standards are very equitably distributed within Scandinavia. As a result, the reasons for migrating are, usually, not directly connected with any particular aspects of poverty. Migration is, however, seen as a solution when the lack of jobs and especially of suitable jobs is a long-term prospect. That is why tourism is looked upon as a possible solution to many of the problems of these small communities. Tourism can offer jobs which are attractive to young people and it can create a more modern atmosphere in an otherwise stagnating local environment. This belief has been very pronounced, during the last 10–15 years, in different parts of northern Scandinavia.

The underlying problem is one of accessibility, of developing the infrastructure to form better internal and external links of high capacity and quality. This is equally important to local inhabitants, industry and tourists. The distances involved are, sometimes, almost prohibitive for the development of an industry, such as tourism, which is dependent on physical accessibility. Time is a crucial factor in tourism. A visit to Scandinavia involves a longer time period for transport alone than when visiting more established destination countries, such as Spain. It is difficult to find package tours to Scandinavia. Therefore, most of the travellers from other parts of Europe, as well as intra-Scandinavian tourists, use private cars as their mode of transport. Denmark is the only Scandinavian country land-linked to Western Europe, in any practical respect. In the rest of Scandinavia, ferry (or air) transport is needed (see Peisley 1992).

One of the most critical tasks for the Scandinavian countries, therefore, has been to find solutions to the accessibility problem. This is not a 'tourism problem' as such. Better accessibility is essential for the integration of the Scandinavian economies within the European economic space and the anticipated larger EU.

⊂⊃ Areas impacted by West Link/Nordic Link

⋯ Areas impacted by Via Baltica

◯ Areas impacted by Scan Link I

⊏⊐ Areas impacted by Scan Link II

Figure 5.2. Transnational regions and the impact of major infrastructure development. Source: Veggeland and Hedegaard (1993, p. 18)

Figure 5.2 shows the main corridors/links that are under discussion. The Baltic Link (via Baltica) from northern Germany through Poland and the Baltic states to Finland and St Petersburg will open up the most remote part of Scandinavia to Western and Eastern Europe. The well-established ferry lines between Finland and Sweden will then be even more important to form a core area around the Baltic Sea (Veggeland and Hedegaard 1993). The West Link connects the north-west European continent and the UK with Jutland and, by better ferry connections, with Norway for a North Sea core area of great importance to the western parts of Norway and Denmark. The Channel Tunnel is an integrated part of this scheme.

A bridge between Denmark and Sweden has been discussed for several decades and is close to a final decision. Denmark has completed the connection by land between Zealand and Jutland, via Flyn, while the proposed bridge over Øresund, from Copenhagen to Malmö in Sweden, will give better accessibility to both the Swedish west coast and to Oslo in Norway. This Scandinavian Link I is completed by better road and ferry connections to central and eastern Sweden and Stockholm from northern Germany in a possible second link.

Within the individual countries, Sweden has decided to expand considerably investment in road and rapid train connections during the remainder of the 1990s. In Norway and Finland similar efforts are being or have already been made (see also Elling 1993). There are therefore good prospects for significant improvements in the external and internal links of Scandinavia, and these will have an impact on the region's tourism industry.

5.3 TOURISM AND TOURISM POLICY IN SCANDINAVIA

5.3.1 General background

Tourism statistics are not very accurate in the Scandinavian countries as they are mainly based on commercial accommodation figures. Since the larger part of tourism relies on non-commercial accommodation (visits to friends and relatives and stays in second homes) for foreign visitors and domestic travellers alike, the statistics will be rather misleading as the number of tourists cannot be registered in a true sense. As was mentioned previously, the Scandinavian countries do not have a passport or visa requirement for most visitors, which means that not even the number of non-Scandinavian visitors can be calculated in any accurate way. Table 5.2 shows some estimates of the number of commercial bed-nights for different markets in each of the four Scandinavian countries. Historic trends are difficult to establish, there being few statistical series which extend over more than 10–15 years, and these are based on varying definitions over time. Only the most recent figures are presented in Table 5.2. They are fairly representative of long-term proportions between countries and markets. Recent deviations are discussed in the text.

Table 5.2.   Commercial bed-nights in Scandinavia, 1993

Country	Domestic nights		Other Nordic nights		Other European nights		Other countries' nights	
	'000s	%	'000s	%	'000s	%	'000s	%
Denmark[a]	17650	35	4750	10	26550	53	1100	2
Finland[b]	9673	77	848	7	1590	13	362	3
Norway[c]	12609	67	2162	12	3323	18	598	3
Sweden[d]	24447	80	2088	7	3133	10	854	3

[a] Including second homes (44%) and private boats (3%) (Danish Tourist Board 1994).
[b] Hotels and similar establishments, holiday villages, camping and youth hostels (Finnish Tourist Board 1994 and NORTRA–Nor Travel Marketing).
[c] Hotels and camping, other forms of commercial accommodation partly included (NORTRA).
[d] Hotels, holiday villages, camping, youth hostels (Statistics Sweden).

As these figures only encompass a very small part of total tourism in each country, they must be considered only to provide indicators of the distribution between markets. Domestic tourism dominates all countries. The only exception is Denmark, where there are considerable numbers of German tourists and day visitors. In the remainder of this section we consider each country individually.

5.3.2   Denmark

Between 1987 and 1993 Denmark considerably expanded its efforts to support tourism in the country. The new policy was formulated in an Action Programme in 1987, wherein the case was put forward for tourism as an important source of export earnings and for the creation of new employment, not least in areas where other industries are facing problems (Ministeriet for Kommunikation og Turisme 1994).

Tourism policy is linked to general economic, social, environmental and cultural policies. Therefore, the instrument for almost doubling the number of guest-nights between 1987 and 1993 has been sustainable tourism in accordance with environmental protection objectives, developed through coordinating, network-oriented, regional tourism export groups. In total, 18 000 new jobs have been created, as estimated from turnover growth of 9 billion Danish kroner (DKr). Total employment in tourism is estimated at 107 000 (4% of the national total) and total turnover at 40 billion DKr, with 50% tourism exports in 1993. The goal is to achieve a 3.3% growth rate per year until the year 2000, creating another 17 000 jobs (Ministeriet for Kommunikation og Turisme 1994).

Tourists in Denmark consist of two very dominant groups: Danes with 35% and Germans with 48% of total bed-nights. Second homes, camping and hotels cover 95% of all accommodation. Hotels are, as in Scandinavia in general, mostly utilised by business travellers, due to the high price level in city hotels (Economist Intelligence Unit 1992).

Denmark is the Scandinavian country closest to the most populous part of the European continent, which is reflected in the large share of foreign visitors. Neighbouring Sweden and Norway are both important and traditional markets and destinations. The mutual tourist flows can be expected to grow with better and quicker transport links in the future, both by ferry and by the proposed bridge between Copenhagen and Malmö.

5.3.3. Finland

Finland has experienced a deep economic recession, which has influenced tourism in two ways. The rapid growth in unemployment affected domestic tourism negatively and the weak Finnish currency has made it more expensive for Finns to go abroad while, at the same time, making Finland more attractive to foreign visitors. This situation has replaced a pattern of steady growth in tourism consumption and new hotel capacity during the late 1970s and throughout the 1980s. The number of second homes grew by 80% in this period and charter trips abroad almost doubled between 1985 and 1990 alone, when the Finnish economy was at its height. Part of the explanation for the subsequent recession has been the loss of foreign (barter) trade with the former Soviet Union (Jenner and Smith 1992). Proximity to Russia and Estonia has created incoming flows of visitors from these markets, mainly to Helsinki. Russia was the third largest foreign market in 1993, after Sweden and Germany (in terms of number of visitors).

Finland is the most remote Scandinavian destination. Land borders with Sweden and Norway can be found only in the northernmost part of the country. These borders are open, while the Russian border is still difficult to pass and visas are required. For all other routes to Finland, ferries are necessary and Finland has a large number of direct links with Sweden, Estonia and Germany across the Baltic and, further north, the Gulf of Bothnia. Several million passengers are transported every year (Peisley 1992).

Ferry traffic is not only a large transport industry in Finland, but vitally important to accessibility. The completion of the Via Baltica, mentioned above (see Figure 5.2), and an economic recovery in Eastern Europe, are two factors which could create a new potential for Finnish incoming tourism.

5.3.4 Norway

As with the other Scandinavian countries, Norway relies heavily on domestic tourism and the travel account balance is markedly negative (–10.5 billion NKr in 1991). The tourism industry is small and predominantly small scale. Non-commercial accommodation is important and the number of hotels and campsites has remained almost static on a national basis. Occupancy rates are generally low (under 50%), rising slightly during the three summer months, when prices are lower (Economist Intelligence Unit 1993).

State policy for tourism in Norway aims at improving the industry's prof-itability as well as strengthening employment and services regionally, and enhancing recreational opportunities for Norwegians. This policy is to be carried out through intensified marketing of Norway abroad, by adopting a nationwide action plan for tourism development, and by putting more em-phasis on tourism education for young people going into the industry and for those already working there (Jean-Hansen and Haukeland 1993).

Norway has a long history as a destination for visitors from abroad. In the nineteenth century Britons already visited the Norwegian mountains and fjords for pleasure purposes and the UK has continued to be one of the main markets. Denmark, Sweden and (growing rapidly) Germany are most import-ant as generators of day visitors.

Norway has a long common border with Sweden and round-trips by car or chartered bus by foreign visitors tend to include both countries (via Denmark). The long north–south distances, and the very mountainous topography, make Norway rather difficult to travel by car. New investment in better roads with new tunnels and bridges, which are necessary improvements if this type of tourism is to expand, have gradually been undertaken during the 1990s. A dense network of airports exists, especially in northern Norway, and regular passenger ships travel along the North Sea coast all year round to increase accessibility (Brinchmann and Huse 1991).

5.3.5   Sweden

Sweden is the largest Scandinavian country, in terms of both population and area, and also has the largest share of domestic tourism. Since Sweden under-takes a regular household survey of travel habits (the Tourism and Travel Database, since 1989), it is interesting and possible to compare commercial and non-commercial accommodation figures. It would not be unrealistic to transfer these proportions to both the Norwegian and Finnish situations, which have very similar domestic tourism, although this is less so in the case of Denmark.

The total number of bed-nights spent within Sweden by Swedes was 162 million (leisure) and 18 million (business) in 1993. Of these only 55 million (30%) were in commercial accommodation. Another 87 million bed-nights were spent abroad and must be added to the total (figures from the Tourism and Travel Database 1993).

These figures indicate that 70% of all bed-nights are not registered in official statistics. A reason for this is that visits to friends and relatives (VFR-trips) and stays in second homes are so dominant. The large migratory movements from periphery to centre during the 1950s and 1960s have meant that most urban households have friends and relatives distributed all over the country. Second homes are very common; 40% of all Swedish households have access to a second home during their main summer holiday (National Atlas of Sweden 1993). This situation is similar in the neighbouring countries.

State tourism policy at present is relatively restricted to a view of tourism as an export industry. The Swedish Tourist Board was established in 1976 and issued with a rather wide set of responsibilities. It was replaced in 1992 by the industry-owned Swedish Travel and Tourism Council, supported by temporary state funds for marketing Sweden abroad.

The foreign markets are dominated by Germans and Norwegians. Together they account for almost half of the commercial bed-nights spent by visitors from abroad. The Nordic market has been almost halved during the turbulent years in the early 1990s, when Sweden introduced VAT for tourism services, most notably transport. The increase in tourism prices affected both Swedes and incoming visitors and, before the enforced devaluation of the Swedish currency in November 1992, tourism traffic declined by 20–30% in a few years. After the devaluation, foreign interest has grown and domestic demand is also expected to pick up (NUTEK 1993).

External accessibility is a problem and there are ferry connections to Denmark, Finland, Germany, the UK, the Netherlands, Estonia, Russia and Poland. Within this elongated country, where two-thirds of the area (central and northern Sweden) has 12% of the population, internal accessibility is equally important. Road distances are long, 1800 km north to south, and at a maximum, almost 400 km east to west. A good road, rail and airline network is essential for tourism. The private car is totally dominant as a mode of transport. It has an 80% share of all overnight leisure trips and 65% of business trips (1992), despite the long distances involved (the Tourism and Travel Databases).

5.3.6 Scandinavia: some similarities

Domestic tourism dominates Scandinavia, the exception being Denmark. Low external and internal accessibility is part of the explanation of this situation. Another possible answer, mainly in relation to foreign markets, is that all Nordic countries have a high standard of living and, consequently, they are high-cost countries as holiday destinations.

The high GNP per capita (see Table 5.1) also means that tourism is an important activity for the Nordic people. It is very common to travel abroad, out of Scandinavia, and Mediterranean destinations are particularly popular. Tourism imports exceed tourism exports by 100% in all countries except Denmark (Statistics Sweden 1992) and so makes a negative contribution to the current account.

However, Scandinavia as a tourist destination for other markets has grown in importance and, with present trends in demand towards ecotourism, less crowded destinations and better quality for money, the Scandinavian countries are expected to become more attractive in the future. The general policy has been to expand the role of the tourism industry in these post-industrial economies. Developing tourism as an employment generator, not least in declining areas, is a recognised goal in all four countries.

5.4 TOURIST PRODUCTS AND REGIONAL PRODUCTION

5.4.1 Image: a problem of social construction

Scandinavian countries have not, so far, been competitors for southbound European tourist flows. On the contrary, they are important contributors to these flows themselves. What kind of visitors then are going north? As has already been noted, Germans, Dutch, Britons and, from other parts of the world, Americans and Japanese, are the main non-Scandinavian visitors (various statistical sources). But these flows are mere trickles in the total ebb and flow of international tourism in Europe (*World Travel and Tourism Review* 1993).

A 1992 study in 10 European countries of the tourism image of Sweden gives some insight into the attitudes of the potential visitor. There are two negative expressions which are very significant—too expensive and too cold. Alongside the frequency of the comments of 'not interested' and 'prefer going south', these opinions are difficult to overlook. What the survey results say is that in the European population as a whole there are, indeed, strong motivations against going north and such a social construction of Scandinavian tourism is difficult to change (Styrelsen för Sverigebilden 1992).

On the positive side, there is one composite factor that Europeans associate with Sweden: unspoiled nature and beautiful scenery. 'Friendly people' and 'peaceful surroundings' complement the picture of a country with tourist products that should be attractive (Styrelsen för Sverigebilden 1992). The counterbalancing negative factors are, however, stronger and they are basically the same for all the Scandinavian countries (Economist Intelligence Unit 1986).

This is one reason why Scandinavia has never experienced large-scale tourism, unless of domestic origin and spatially concentrated in specific localities. Tourism has not been seen as an important industry nationally, only regionally, and then usually as a purely seasonal phenomenon.

The other reason is the relative remoteness of Scandinavia, both externally and internally. Domestic tourist flows tend to go south too, even within the individual countries. The population centres are located in the southern parts and remarkably few travel north, whether you look at Finland, Norway or Sweden. Denmark, as an areally much smaller country, follows other rules. The explanation is also inevitable—too expensive (to travel there) and too cold. Costs and climate are powerful factors in holiday destination decision-making (see Mill and Morrison 1992).

5.4.2 Seasonal aspects

The major summer holiday season is fairly short in Scandinavia; late June to the middle of August, with July as the peak month. Many small resorts, mainly located along the coasts, multiply their populations several times for 7–8 weeks and then they return to their normal anonymity thereafter. The economic base for those resorts to survive on tourism alone is simply not there. On the contrary, they will have to rely on imported seasonal labour to be able to supply the services required by the visitors (see Ericsson 1992).

Some of this labour will go to the winter resorts in the mountains during the winter tourist season: Christmas and New Year, late February and onwards over Easter until the season closes in April. The mountain resorts in southern and central Norway, along the Swedish–Norwegian border further up the Swedish side, and in northernmost Finland, are the Scandinavian equivalent of seaside resorts. These are small local communities, but tourism is particularly important because of a two-season flow of visitors (Aronsson 1989). Summer is the lower season, generally, with only 20–30% of total tourism in these resorts.

This very pronounced seasonality also means that weather conditions play a decisive role in the success of many resorts. Low summer temperatures or mild winters with poor snow conditions can easily disturb visitor flows, not only during the current season, but also in the following years. Scandinavians find their way easily to the Mediterranean or to the Alps if national alternatives fail to meet expectations. This underlines the internationalisation of the competitive framework for many forms of tourism, especially in high-income markets.

5.4.3 Distribution of tourist demand

The tourist demand pattern, as measured by commercial accommodation statistics and information on visits to friends and relatives, plus the location of second homes, seems to be remarkably stable. The tourist resort life-cycle (Butler 1980) seems to be a very long one in the Scandinavian countries. New destinations appear, but they also disappear due to having seasons too short to carry the capital investment needed to satisfy the quality-conscious visitors. Since tourism has been growing relatively slowly, there is not a great deal of new demand to be apportioned between prospective new destinations. In addition, the sharp downturn in tourist demand in Sweden and Finland in the early 1990s has caused grave problems for the tourism industry, especially where new investment had been made in the expectation of rising or, at least, stable, demand (see NUTEK 1993).

The capitals of all four countries are the single largest tourist destinations. Business visitors all year round (except in summer) and holiday travellers, peaking during the summer months, give the capitals a good tourism infrastructure. They have excellent accessibility and local/regional markets large enough to secure a diversified supply of attractions, events and activities. Cultural and historic interests can be satisfied as well as having ample shopping opportunities. Foreign visitors also tend to include the capitals in their agenda. Out of the top five attractions in Denmark, four are situated in Copenhagen (Economist Intelligence Unit 1993). Friends and relatives living in the capitals are important determinants of visits and overnight accommodation (the Tourism and Travel Database).

Self-catering in camping sites, holiday villages and, above all, in private second homes is the most widely used form of accommodation all over Scandinavia, even in winter. This results in a very scattered pattern of holiday destinations, with pockets of high densities of visitors along the coasts, around inland lakes and lake systems and (in winter) in the mountains.

In Denmark, central and northern Jutland is well endowed with second homes and camping sites, along both the western and eastern coastlines. The island of Bornholm in the Baltic is easily reached by ferry from several countries (Economist Intelligence Unit 1993). Norway and the Southern south-eastern valleys are the main destination areas for both summer and winter holidays. There are fashionable hotels in the mountain resorts and second homes and huts in the coastal areas. In northern Norway (above the Arctic Circle) fishing villages, which have now lost much of their traditional industry, are expanding their tourist activities. The North Cape and the Lofoten Islands receive 200 000–250 000 visitors in summer (Viken and Slettvold 1988). Many come from other countries in chartered transport or in their own cars, going through Sweden and/or Finland on the easier roads to and from their areas of origin (Viken 1991).

Sweden has over 600 000 second homes (National Atlas of Sweden 1993), mostly in coastal locations but also widely dispersed throughout the country. There is a tendency for second homes to be located relatively close to the owners' permanent homes, although there is a concentration along the west coast, north and south of Gothenburg, and in the Stockholm archipelago. Holiday villages can be found in popular destination regions together with camping sites, for example on the islands of Gotland and Öland in the Baltic. Camping is the single largest commercial accommodation form in Sweden (Statistics Sweden 1993). In mountain resorts, holiday villages are often condominiums sublet to visitors by agents. Time-share apartments are more difficult to find, as there is not a substantial market in Scandinavia for this type of accommodation.

The Finnish archipelago houses many second homes and harbours for pleasure boating. The lake district in the south-east is attractive for its many waterways (Finnish Tourist Board 1994). The coast along the Gulf of Bothnia, with its ferry connections to central and northern Sweden, receives a large number of visitors, both incoming and outgoing, centred on the town of Vaasa. Interestingly enough, Finland has been very successful in developing tourism in the northernmost part of Scandinavia. Finnish Lapland receives domestic and international visitors for most of the year. A large part of the international visitors are on their way to or from the North Cape, but domestic visitors favour the area as a winter destination (Viken 1991).

5.4.4 Regional production and population movements

The social, and to some extent the material, construction of tourism has passed through several distinct phases. Historically, Scandinavian destinations were visited by wealthy foreigners fishing salmon or hunting grouse in the remoter areas. Domestic tourism centred on seaside or mountain resorts, where participation in social (upper-class) life in pleasant and healthy surroundings was the main motive. During the railway era some of the resorts grew slowly when they became destinations for larger groups of visitors, not necessarily from the same social and economic background as the earlier groups of tourists. Traditional hotels, pensions and private summer villas from the late nineteenth and early twentieth centuries can still be found alongside more recent constructions in these, still popular, resorts (see National Atlas of Sweden 1993).

Development in the Nordic countries occurred in parallel with domestic tourism expansion in Western Europe. The introduction of paid holidays during the 1930s gave rise to longer trips by rail or, increasingly, by private car (Andolf 1989). The small populations of the Scandinavian countries, compared to the UK, Germany and France, did not, however, allow the same kind of development of large-scale resorts. A major characteristic of tourism in Scandinavia, therefore, is the dominance of many small destinations, with only a few larger resorts in each country. The main cities are also very popular, particularly for visitors from smaller towns or from the countryside. People living in the big cities generate reverse tourism flows. The pull of the city is well matched by the push from city life during the holiday periods (see Dann 1981). Tourist flows, therefore, are widely dispersed and as Scandinavians are generally accustomed to changing their habitats during their vacations, quite large temporary population movements take place.

Since second homes are so important and as they are, generally, located in less densely populated areas, there is a considerable relocation of people from towns and cities to countryside regions. If, as is common, the second home is located near the place where the owners and their families live permanently, the use of the second home over the year can be very high. A survey of second-home owners in the northern Stockholm archipelago, where the vast majority of owners live in Stockholm, showed that 75% of the owners lived less than 1.5 hours' drive away. On average they used their second homes 102 days a year (Back and Primeus 1988), that is mainly during the summer vacation and most spring, autumn and even winter weekends.

These regular flows contribute to supporting a high level of local services in many of these host communities, thereby providing benefits to the local inhabitants as well. One aspect, though, studied by Bohlin (1982) in Sweden, is that the users of second homes make most of their purchases at home, if they live near their cottage. They bring a stock of food and other equipment with them for their visit. Only in the case where the second home is a considerable distance away will the user take full advantage of local suppliers; however, the average number of user-days are then also considerably lower (Bohlin 1982).

The importance of second homes as a destination has been shown in a survey in the Roros region in eastern central Norway; Roros is a very attractive destination, which has been declared a world heritage site by UNESCO.

Flognfeldt (1993) calculated total annual bed-nights (1991) to be 620 000, with 110 000 in hotels, 40 000 in camping and 420 000 in second homes. The balance is made up by stays with friends and relatives and camping outside of regular sites. Day visitor numbers were estimated at 150 000.

A considerable amount of purchasing power is, thus, redistributed to destinations through second-home accommodation. This added income is often of decisive importance for the survival of local trade, since the 'normal' market of permanent residents is limited (see Aronsson 1989).

Second homes cause a semi-permanent redistribution of population from towns and cities to the countryside, which is of a major magnitude relative to total population. The redistribution will also be quite constant over the years, since these houses are used in a very regular way by the owners.

Another very common form of holidaying is to make a round-trip by car, with or without a mobile caravan, staying in camping sites, youth hostels, rented rooms or with friends and relatives. This kind of trip often includes short stays at several destinations (see Pearce 1987a), where certain destination regions are favoured and certain circuits more heavily used than others. Large numbers of visitors make occasional stops at popular places. In many parts of Scandinavia there are such 'summer cities', with mainly day visitors (see the Roros example above). It is in these spots that theme parks, events, attractions and shopping opportunities are developed to capitalise on the passing consumer market. In tourist marketing these places are often more conspicuous than destinations for staying visitors. Their attractiveness is based on mundane rather than exotic experiences and the local economy flourishes from a steady flow of very temporary visitors during the tourist high season. Such destinations may have a large number of temporary shops and other services that disappear at the end of the high season when the theme park closes and the events are over. Whether the local economy keeps the extra income generated or not is a matter of debate, and depends on external control and the pattern of inter-firm linkages (see, for example, Ryan 1991).

In several cases in Sweden where shopping opportunities are the attraction, shopping malls with ample parking spaces have been located on the outskirts of towns; these have gradually forced more centrally located shops to move out as well. The result has been that the city centre has lost many of the shopping functions otherwise typical of a central business district.

The transit routes, from origin to destination, are often long in Scandinavia. This gives rise to a rather particular type of tourist business, where strategically located areas develop catering and overnight facilities for the travelling tourist (see Pearce 1987a). Most major roads no longer pass through towns and cities, but have bypassed them. Roadside restaurants and modern hotels/motels with low-cost accommodation have expanded considerably over the last decade. These establishments are often part of larger chains operating in several Scandinavian countries. The location decisions taken on the optimum location of such services appear to display an acute understanding of the concept of spatial interaction and could well be used as textbook illustrations of geographical theories (see for example Lloyd and Dicken 1977; Haggett 1983). The long distances make traffic volume less important, but knowing the location of major origins and destinations makes it possible to calculate where the majority of the travellers will need to stop. In these locations, transient tourism often becomes a locally important industry.

5.5 TOURISM AND THE SCANDINAVIAN PERIPHERY

5.5.1 The role of tourism

Tourism in the Scandinavian countries is increasingly important to the periphery. Firstly, peripheral areas constitute large parts of each country. Again, Denmark is the exception, although many of the small Danish islands have some of the characteristics associated with a centre–periphery economy (see Healey and Ilbery 1991; Godvin 1988). Tourists—both domestic and international ones—tend to search for experiences of nature and scenery. They will travel to and stay in areas where the natural resources are most attractive. These areas are, in many instances, found in the periphery.

Secondly, the socio-economic profile of peripheral Scandinavia is largely well known: declining traditional industries, high unemployment, an ageing population and dependence on subsidies from central government. Unlike some other parts of peripheral Europe, there exists a relatively high standard of living in these areas as a result of substantial state interregional transfers. State subsidies aim to create better employment opportunities by offering grants and loans to existing or new businesses on beneficial terms (see Oscarsson 1989).

The areas marked on Figure 5.3 have three common features: they are peripheral, they have very low population densities and they are dependent on natural resources (Oscarsson 1989). In the case of northern Norway, fishing has been the traditional industry, in the Swedish areas forestry and mining, and in Finland forestry.

With the development of post-industrial society the service sector has also expanded in these areas. Tourists make use of the landscape assets and transport facilities of these areas. The public sector is geared towards stimulating modernisation and development, by providing higher education, investment in infrastructure and access to modern communication technologies. Tourism takes advantage of that and, today, these areas have expanded their share of tourism production considerably by catering for the demand for 'wilderness' experiences in rather comfortable and secure surroundings. The so-called 'new' tourist (Poon 1993), individualistic and environmentally conscious, can be offered well-designed activities and modern accommodation without feeling part of a mass-production process; this has proven to be attractive to a growing number of visitors.

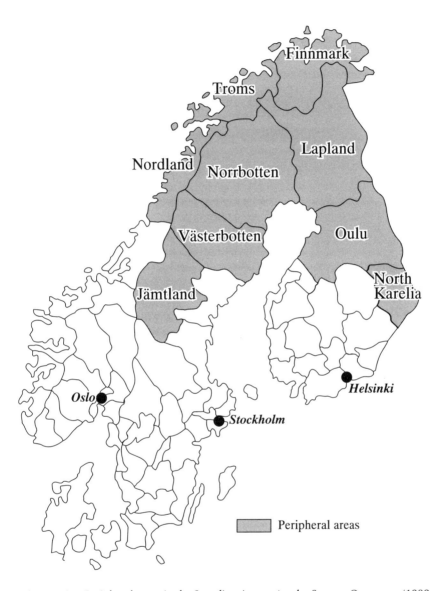

Figure 5.3. Peripheral areas in the Scandinavian peninsula. Source: Oscarsson (1989, p. 5)

The share of commercial bed-nights accounted for by the peripheral areas in 1993 was 27% in Finland and 13% in Sweden (Finnish Tourist Board 1994; Statistics Sweden 1993). The share of the total hotel and camping capacity of northern Norway is also 13% (Economist Intelligence Unit 1993). A survey of visitors arriving in private cars in Finnmark county in northernmost Norway in 1987 showed that the Norwegians accounted for only 20% of the total. Finnish tourists had the largest share (37%) and of the other visitors, Germans—with a 17% share—were the next major group of visitors (Viken and Slettvold 1988). Foreign visitors are, thus, very important for this northern region.

5.5.2 Some examples of tourism in a peripheral economy

In a recent survey in Norway, Ericsson (1992, p. 196) has concluded that:

- in those regions where the tourist market has a limited employment impact locally recruited employees in tourism account for a large share of the tourism labour force
- regions with a dominant tourist market have a less stable labour market
- regions with a large share of full-service accommodation (regardless of the size of the tourist market) have more professionally qualified personnel

These findings are interesting, because they give a snapshot of the general problem of tourism as a local industry, especially in areas with small local populations, which is the situation in most of northern Scandinavia.

In two comparative studies, in 1985 and 1991, in Åre commune in the county of Jämtland in western central Sweden, seasonal employment in a highly tourism-dependent commune was surveyed (Paulsson 1985; Johansson and Johansson 1991). The results showed that the composition of seasonal labour had changed in several ways between the two dates. The changes are summarised in Table 5.3. This table confirms the patterns noted by Ericsson. The local labour market in sparsely populated areas cannot support the ex-pansion of tourism without relying on temporarily imported labour. When tourism expands, local labour will have to be supplemented by recruitment from the more populous parts of the country. These additions to seasonal

Table 5.3.   Seasonal employment composition in Åre commune, 1985 and 1991

Recruitment area	1985	1991
Local, regional	66%	31%
Stockholm region	13%	25%
Northern Sweden	6%	10%
Southern and central Sweden	14%	34%
Other characteristics		
Single	67%	78%
Married/cohabiting	33%	22%
Formal tourism qualifications	20%	30%
Number of seasonally employed	800	1 500
Average age (years)	27.5	23.5

labour will be younger and better educated. They are also quite irreplaceable for the proper functioning of the local tourism industry.

The main problem for increasingly tourism-dependent regions is how to create year-round employment out of a seasonally variable industry. If that is not possible, tourism as a major industry will give little permanent additions to local or regional employment, and the area will not be much better off than before the tourism expansion. It can be argued that what the peripheral areas need most is a combination of work opportunities; tourism, especially in two-season areas, might be the major source of employment, but it cannot be the only one if the aim is permanent employment which helps to stabilise population levels in the community (Nyberg 1989).

The peripheral northern areas of Scandinavia are, more and more, looking towards tourism as a growth industry. There are two reasons for this. One is that the traditional sources of employment are rapidly drying up and that public sector jobs are less likely to dominate the labour market in the future, due to budgetary constraints. The second reason is more positive. Interest in the tourism products offered in these remote parts of Europe has been growing and is expected to grow further in the future (Jenner and Smith 1992).

This situation constitutes a dilemma. Tourism expansion cannot be on a seasonal basis alone, as that will give an unstable labour market where the centre will still be required to guarantee a temporary inflow of labour. This will also cause an outflow of income. The northern regions will have to find combinations of jobs, where tourism professionals can have access to other professional occupations or to other sources of income between the tourist seasons. Otherwise tourism will be just another kind of resource use where the major benefits accrue to the centres of these countries.

5.6 SCANDINAVIAN TOURISM IN TRANSITION

5.6.1 Three scenarios

In a recent report, Selstad (1993) analyses different scenarios for tourism development in Scandinavia from the perspective of European integration. The deregulation of transport, harmonisation of VAT rates and coordination of new investment in infrastructure will serve to influence tourist travel in several ways. However, there are other factors concerned with tourist motivation, product image and cultural integration/fragmentation that might hold more profound implications for tourists' future choices of destinations.

The first scenario shows a continuation of present trends with a growth of both traditional and non-traditional destinations. Economic factors lie behind this development. But Selstad also indicates a polarisation of tourist flows. At one pole there is increasing mass-production of tourist services in the urbanised resort complexes in southern Europe. At the other pole of the demand spectrum is the individual 'wanderlust' traveller (Gray 1970) who will prefer to use better and cheaper transport opportunities to visit new destinations. Business travel will increase due to a higher level of economic integration and the Scandinavian countries will be interested partners in the ongoing development of knowledge-based industries.

The scenario emphasises the extension of the existing pattern. The capitals, parts of southern and western Norway and northern Finland, will continue to be growing destinations in a European perspective.

The second scenario focuses on cultural regionalisation. Europeans will become more oriented towards their cultural home regions and growth of international travel will, according to this scenario, flatten out and partly be exchanged for intraregional travel. One interesting aspect is that Selstad (1993) visualises a situation wherein further development of large-scale resorts will be restricted in order to protect the natural and cultural environment. Common history and culture will influence demand and, hence, travel flows in such a scenario. In this scenario, northern Scandinavia is of relatively little interest, as it is too culturally unconnected outside its own region. It will continue to be peripheral. City-based tourism will grow and the capitals and larger cities in southern Scandinavia will become focal points of interest (see Figure 5.2).

In the third scenario, environmental considerations, wherein ecology and sustainability are key concepts, will influence travel flows considerably. Transport will be voluntarily restricted as it consumes natural resources and as it is recognised as an environmental hazard. The concept of carrying capacity (see, for example, Inskeep 1991) will be applied to a larger degree to destination development. Scandinavia, as Europe's 'green lung', will be contrasted to the environmental problems in the Mediterranean and Alpine regions. The potential for ecotourism to become a future major form of tourism has been questioned (see Wight 1993), but it is evident that environmental issues and debates on the consumption of non-renewable resources will become more prominent, both for industry in general, and for tourism.

Two factors, then, will be in favour of tourist expansion in Scandinavia. The first concerns the growing interest in nature-based tourism in environmentally clean and visually unspoilt surroundings. Increasing flows from continental Europe to such areas will benefit economically the Scandinavian peninsula and its northern and central parts in particular. The other factor focuses on the internal market and what will happen if travel from Scandinavia is exchanged for intra-Scandinavian tourism. As has been emphasised previously, the major flows have always been of domestic origin and partly out of Scandinavia. A redistribution of these flows to internal travel will be more important, as a whole, than a growth in incoming tourism. For Sweden alone, the number of outgoing (southbound) travellers is several times higher than incoming visitors from outside Scandinavia. Even a quite small redistribution will have a large impact on the domestic tourism industry, especially if this new demand is directed towards the northern, peripheral parts of the country.

5.6.2 Conclusions

The Scandinavian countries have not been very dependent on tourism in the past, with the exception of a few local destination regions. From a national point of view, tourism has been looked upon as a rather marginal industry, where employment and profitability figures are difficult to establish and therefore somewhat dubious. In recent years, however, attitudes towards this industry have become more positive. The relative autonomy of regional and local authorities over regional policy instruments has meant that support for tourism investment, directly and indirectly, has become more prominent in a growing number of regions. This is particularly the case in northern Scandinavia, where other industries have faltered.

The importance of tourism is likely to become stronger. The Olympic Winter Games in Lillehammer (Norway) in 1994 is seen as a long-term tourism investment (Economic Intelligence Unit 1993). There are ambitions to host both Olympic Summer and Winter Games in Sweden, for the same reason. Infrastructure has been improved throughout Scandinavia to offset some of the accessibility problems that are barriers to physical integration, internally and externally. This investment will, of course, also influence tourism potential. Eastern European countries are seen as important future partners in commerce and, increasingly, as interesting markets for incoming tourism.

Scandinavia will probably never have a mass market for its tourism products. Domestic visitors dominate and large-scale flows of visitors do not offer an appropriate way to exploit the specific landscape attractions that constitute the main reason for tourist interest in the Scandinavian countries.

Tourism might become more important for local labour markets, if flows grow. The problem of seasonality, which is endemic to the tourism industry, must be solved by methods other than expanding the season(s), so as to create robust labour markets in the peripheral regions. Other services, whether knowledge-based, or industries based on environmental/health care/quality-of-life advantages, are seen as possible complements to ensure year-round employment.

Part II

SPATIAL REORGANISATION OF TOURISM

6 Coastal Areas: Processes, Typologies and Prospects

MANUEL J. MARCHENA GÓMEZ
University of Seville, Spain
FERNANDO VERA REBOLLO
University of Alicante, Spain

6.1 INTRODUCTION: COASTAL TOURISM IN EUROPE

Mass tourism and the production of coastal tourism spaces, oriented towards the leisure needs of urban-industrial Europe, are some of the most characteristic social phenomena of the contemporary age.[1] This does not necessarily mean that coastal tourism is a new phenomenon, but it is a relatively recent one, leastways in its present form. European coastal tourism did not attain its present scale until the welfare state and Fordist production were both consolidated in Western Europe after the end of the Second World War.[2]

In fact the construction of the beach in Europe as a social product, whose value lies in its leisure, contemplative (gazing) and healing possibilities, took off in the mid eighteenth century. This was irreversibly consolidated by the 1870s, even though there were much earlier precedents for residential coastal tourism as at Campagne, to the north of the Gulf of Naples, at the peak of the Roman Empire. In the modern era, tourism made an uncertain and somewhat élitist start in an introspective phase which lasted until the end of the *ancien régime*, when the coast was largely valued for its therapeutic powers. Then spa towns began to appear, frequented by the bourgeois classes, from Swinemünde to San Sebastian, or Brighton to Scarborough, or Scheveningen to Dieppe (see Figure 6.1). Their nineteenth-century growth was intrinsically linked to the spread of the rail network (Corbin 1993).

At the beginning of the twentieth century the European coast, with its spas and leisure resorts, ceased to be viewed as purely a place of healing, and instead began to be considered a place of fashion and pleasure, primarily designed to satisfy the leisure requirements of the wealthier classes. The most obvious example of this social orientation, which originated around the middle of the eighteenth century, is the French Riviera, structured around the nodes of Nice, Cannes and Monte Carlo (Turner and Ash 1991).

European Tourism: Regions, Spaces and Restructuring. Edited by A. Montanari and A.M. Williams.
© 1995 European Science Foundation. Published in 1995 by John Wiley & Sons Ltd.

There is a clear difference between the coastal leisure areas which existed at the beginning of the twentieth century, and which established the positive image and much of the motivational force behind tourism growth, and the vastly transformed areas which have arisen during the second half of this century. This is based on three major factors:

1. The mass social character of the new tourist spaces which contrasts sharply with their former élitist profiles.
2. The spatial structure of the earlier period was dominated by specific discrete and clearly defined resorts, compared to the wider areal transformations of the present-day coast.
3. There has been a clear change of preference over time for the heliotropical climatic attractions of the more southerly latitudes.

Towards the end of the twentieth century, those European coastal areas offering both beaches and a warm sunny climate had become areas specialising in tourism, with the Mediterranean unquestionably being one of the leading world examples of this (Lozato-Giotart 1991). This has not, of course, prevented other more oceanic and more naturalist zones in northern Europe, with less favourable bathing conditions, from emerging as coastal tourism areas on the colder Atlantic face of Europe (Davidson 1992). In both cases, coastal tourism provides a clear demonstration of the social, economic and territorial changes experienced in Europe during the tourist discovery process (Marchena 1992).

The European tourist of the 1990s tends to be an experienced consumer and traveller who has been to several coastline destinations, especially southern ones, following a classic north–south migration pattern (Williams and Shaw 1991a). However, he or she also spends time in national or regional coastal areas closer to home, contributing to a second set of tourist flows on a more domestic scale, which complement the international movements.

Temporary holiday migration to the European coast is one of the most prominent phenomena of industrialised society, which has been reaffirmed by other features in the new post-Fordist production phase. While the summer continues to be the peak season for tourist flows to the coast (with seasonality being reinforced by the institutional constraints of school and work calendars), the form of mobility between coastal and urban centres is becoming more flexible, due to the growth of weekend breaks, second holidays, the purchase of holiday homes, etc. But it should be noted that although there have been changes in the form of coastal tourism, it remains a major object of tourism in both the Fordist and post-Fordist periods (Figure 6.1).

From a sociological perspective, there are few other social phenomena that have become accepted so widely, in virtually all demographic and economic segments of the population, as the perceived attractiveness of the coast as a place of leisure, fashion and 'natural' quality (Clary 1993). However, this social construction of the coast has generated its own contradictions. Not

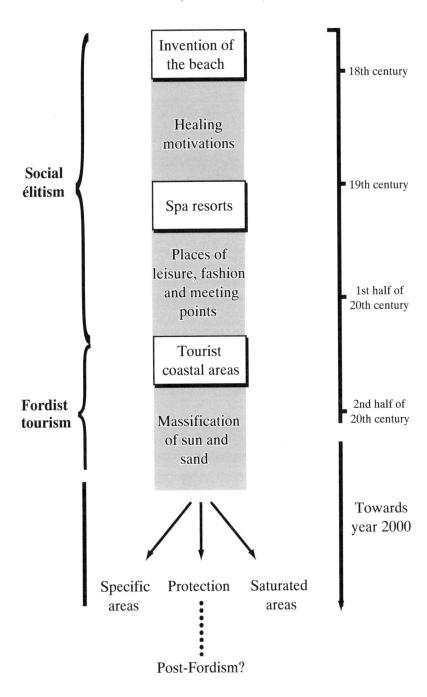

Figure 6.1.   Time sequence of European coastal tourism

least, the central issue today within tourist movements towards the coast is the problem of massification and environmental degradation, which mark the process of spatial reorganisation and the creation of the present-day tourist product. This raises the issue of the need to restructure mass coastal tourism. However, the fact that such restructuring is problematic is paralleled by the fact that tourist behavioural patterns are beginning to display a general weariness with the massed coastal products, especially the Mediterranean one, and with the negative environmental effects caused by conventional tourism (Montanari 1992).

In terms of economic contribution, the coastal product represents the crucial elements in the tourism industry. According to World Tourism Organisation (WTO) statistics, for example, 30% of all international tourism—or some 150 million arrivals each year—is directed towards the European Mediterranean (Ritchie and Hawkins 1992). As such, particularly for the southern states of the European Union (EU), it represents one of their main sources of exports and jobs (Williams 1993b). The experience of Spain highlights the contribution that tourism has made to particular economies; tourism revenue has grown from about $1 billion in 1955 to more than $50 billion in 1992 (Figure 6.2). The 'gap' between visitor numbers and revenue has also closed in the late 1990s as prices have risen and the growth in arrivals has slowed down.

The economic role of coastal tourism has come under scrutiny because the present phase of economic reorganisation of the European economy is characterised by technological supremacy, structural unemployment and economic

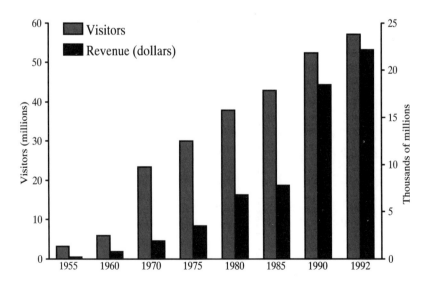

Figure 6.2. Spain: international visitor numbers and tourism revenue, 1955–92. Source: authors' calculations based on data provided by Secretaría General de Turismo TURESPAÑA

deregulation. Tourism is often highlighted as one of the most significant potential contributors to job generation in Europe. Yet it is clear that the vitality of coastal tourism is itself questionable. During recent years, the levels of consumption in Europe's coastal leisure economy have remained constant, rather than continuing to expand. However, this is put in context by the fact that this has occurred despite a relative fall in family incomes and in the consumption of durable goods across Western Europe, according to Eurostat. This means that tourist activities have assumed what can be termed structural weight or meaning in the decision-making of European consumers and, despite some faltering, these remain orientated to the coastline.[3]

For this reason, we believe that it is correct not to talk of saturation of coastal tourism, but rather to define the current situation in terms of the 'weariness' of demand, most notably in the areas of massed demand where the environmental impacts are most obvious. Moreover, it should be remembered that, quite apart from experienced Western European tourists who continue to be fascinated by the social construction of coastal tourism, the new outflows of tourists from the economies of Central and Eastern European will, in all probability, adhere to similar behavioural patterns. In this respect, it is perhaps significant that the first charter flight between Moscow and the Costa del Sol was opened in May 1994.

The territorial consequences of the phenomenon of coastal tourism are of vital importance. Indeed, it could be argued that the process of coastal tourism development represents one of the most significant urbanistic transformation processes, in terms of speed and voracity, to have taken place in contemporary Europe. It is not, of course, comparable to the urbanisation process inherent in the development of the conventional town or city, in terms of the quantity of space which has been transformed. However, the spatial concentration of tourist establishments along the beach line, followed by the development of traditional coastal settlements, which is especially prominent in the Mediterranean, does provide a process of territorial reorganisation which is unique in the history of Europe (for example, see Vera Rebollo 1987 and Marchena 1987).

The tourist coastal territory—whether massed or diffused—is, as we have suggested, a direct consequence of the Western style of economic development and of the resultant accompanying evolution of social motivations in different strata of the European population. These areas are now confronted with the need for structural reorganisation, partly because European tourists as consumers are demanding new quality standards in the coastal tourist product. It is, however, the territorial question which holds the key to reorganisation of the sector (Cazes 1992); in order for the new model of the coastal tourist product—an integrated, quality, environmentally sensitive product—to be introduced successfully, a notable reorganisation of space, as well as of the provision of services, is necessary in coastal tourism zones (WTO 1990).

6.2   MODELS OF COASTAL TOURISM DEVELOPMENT FROM THE LATE NINETEENTH CENTURY

In any attempt to systematise globally the processes of tourism involvement and development, it is possible to identify various types of areas, but among these coastal areas consistently stand out as being the most popular destination, in which a large proportion of overnights are concentrated. In these areas, the spatial impacts of tourism are associated, in an almost linear manner, with the processes of territorial reorganisation (generally informal or weakly structured) imposed by this activity in certain coastal areas. At the same time, the link of tourism with the raw materials of sun and sea is identified in such analyses. This focus on coastal tourism, however, does not preclude recognition of the recent emergence of new tourism products associated with other types of geographical areas, reflecting qualitative changes in demand.

Coastal tourist areas have been classified in a number of models, based on morphologies and time–space processes, usually studying developments from the supply side (Lozato-Giotart 1991; Boniface and Cooper 1994; Pearce 1989). The following typologies all share common features: those stressing time sequences in the development process (Miossec 1977); the transformation of pre-existing social and territorial structures (Peck and Lepie 1977); the spontaneous or planned character of areas, as well as their extensive or intensive implantation (Barbaza 1970); and even the relationship of such processes, from the wider European perspective, to the expansion of successive peripheries that are converted into new tourist destinations (Gormsen 1981). However, there are limitations to what are, in effect, supply-side models. It is difficult to undertake a global interpretation of the typologies of coastal tourism development if they do not take into account demand. The processes of configuration, consolidation and restructuring of these areas represent a response to changes which have occurred in social values and, more specifically, in the motivations, behaviour and practices of tourist consumers.

Butler (1980) provides one of the best known models of tourist development on a regional or local scale. This involves a systematic periodisation of space–time relationships, using the life-cycle concept, and it identifies the relationship between the rise in the number of visitors and the development of the receiving area. In this way the tourist destination is interpreted as a dynamic entity, subject to changes through time, whereby a hierarchy in terms of resorts is established according to their level of development, type of accommodation, degree of participation of economic agents and demand changes. Despite some constructive criticisms of the Butler model (Cooper 1990b; Debbage 1990; Haywood 1986; Agarwal 1994), its dynamic approach—from a demand and supply point of view—justifies the value of the model as a tool for both empirical analysis and for policy design and implementation in declining resorts.

A first approach to appraising tourism destinations within a global time–space framework allows us to differentiate between two models of tourism involvement in coastal areas, taking their historical shaping as a reference point:

1. Centres which developed as a result of traditional spa use, from the second half of the nineteenth century onwards, had specific and discrete locations, as opposed to the linear characteristics which typify the mass tourism territorial organisation model. Such centres were greatly influenced, if not determined, by their proximity and accessibility to transmitting urban centres (hence the key role played by the railways in their development). They were usually small towns with an élitist clientele (Nice, San Sebastián, Sorrento), although there were also more popular resorts (such as Blackpool and Morecambe in England, and Alicante on the Spanish Mediterranean coast), which represent the real precedents of current mass tourism (Vera Rebollo 1987). Tourist affluence and consumer power, while it did not attain a level comparable to the present in quantitative terms, represented a key to understanding the notable urbanistic transformations of this period whereby the social image of some of these towns was formed. Among their features were marine promenades and façades, hotels, piers, casinos and even the attitudes of the local population which had a predisposition to welcoming visitors. In any case, tourism—identified in almost all these places with the summer bathing season—appeared and imposed itself on the traditionally more enhanced urban industries, without becoming a clear factor in territorial planning.

2. The emergence of mass tourism in the 1950s, helped by the transformations which took place in transport and the growing custom (and expectation) among the working class of taking paid holidays, brought with it the growth of coastal resorts in the industrialised north European countries. Nevertheless, by the 1960s the internationalisation of the production of mass trips, together with the rise of sun and sea destinations, was directing tourist flows towards the Mediterranean coast, which was becoming the real leisure periphery of the European middle classes.

From the 1960s onwards, therefore, a dual process occurred as far as coastal tourist destinations were concerned. On the one hand, there was an overflow of tourists into the Mediterranean countries, where tourism became a basic factor in coastal territorial organisation and transformed local societies and existing economic bases. The linear model of urban-tourist development was established, thereby structuring a new territorial model in a quasi-spontaneous fashion, since tourist projects were usually implemented in the absence of a spatial planning framework. After the mid 1980s, these resorts suffered problems due to a fall in demand and were forced to face necessary restructuring (functional, environmental, sectoral and territorial), although the general process concealed contrasting realities according to the dynamics, the circumstances and the private and public initiatives in different localities. On the other hand, beach resorts such as Torbay, Ramsgate and Bournemouth in the UK, and similar resorts in other north-western European countries, such as the Netherlands, which had experienced rapid growth in the 1950s, entered a period of decline which intensified in the 1970s and the 1980s (Urry 1990). By the latter decade a serious crisis was emerging, leading to a debate over appropriate strategies for regenerating and reconverting these old coastal resorts.

6.2.1 Mediterranean mass tourism resorts: growth and crisis

The social reconstruction of coastal tourism, leading to the establishment of a specialised tourist and leisure area on the northern Mediterranean coast, provided the conditions for a spatial reorganisation with the territorial linking of tourist-transmitting and tourist-receiving areas. This is exemplified by the evolution of the European transport and communications infrastructure; for example, the Spanish A7 motorway linking Alicante with the French border near Gerona, and the motorway joining the French Côte d'Azur with the Italian Riviera. A new economic space has been created which, in turn, contributes to the regional dynamics of the coastal areas and, in certain cases, serves to sharpen the differences between coastal and inland regions. In this respect, the dualism of Spanish regions such as Catalonia, Valencia and Andalusia is notable, for the impact of coastal tourism has served to accentuate imbalances between a rural interior and a coastal fringe dedicated to the service sector, thereby consolidating a process of accumulative polarisation in terms of income and population. In recent years, in view of these regional disparities, the autonomous governments are seeking to channel tourism towards new products such as rural or ecotourism, in order to improve the regional economic balance.

There is no such thing as a single model of mass tourism development, even in the Mediterranean region. Instead the specific nature of mass tourism varies according to the existence of diverse development typologies, and the degree of overlap with regional structures. This is exemplified by the traditional spa resorts which, following a significant qualitative and quantitative transformation in terms of their functions, have been converted into mass-reception centres. New elements have also been incorporated into their make-up: new forms of accommodation, accompanied by real estate operations; infrastructures such as airports (as in the case of Alicante and Malaga); facilities related to modern tourism such as marinas; and commercial centres. In such cases, tourism has not become the dominant economic activity, but rather contributes one more round of investments in a complex local economy.

Where tourism has been introduced as a new activity, this is most likely to be in agricultural or forested areas, and the built environment is produced specifically for tourism. This spontaneous intensive model, which is singular in its indiscriminate occupation of ground space and a failure sometimes to use rationally natural resources, such as water, is the result of the real estate logic which directs supply processes. This is the model which most closely describes the current spatial organisation of the Mediterranean coast, whereby a substantial proportion of the coastal fringe is committed to tourism. In the case of the Costa Blanca, in Spain, for example, 95% of the coastline has been urbanised by tourism, penetrating inland by up to 20 km.

Since the 1980s, there have been important changes in Mediterranean tourism, which seems to have entered a new phase; this is the outcome of changes in the internationalisation of the economy, and of changes in the motivations which influence the demand for this product. But the critical change has occurred since the beginning of 1990s, when there was a decline in the life-cycle of a product based almost entirely on sun and sea, especially as its environmental consequences became clear. There was also the emergence of new competitor destinations in other areas—the southern Mediterranean, the Caribbean, and places in Asia—and of products offering alternative experiences to the coastal holiday. This crisis was manifested in a sharp fall in occupancy levels in many resorts. This was particularly acute in Spain where numbers fell in absolute terms in 1990 and stagnated between 1988 and 1993 (Figure 6.3).

The search for a solution led to policies such as a reduction in prices, which only contributed to further deterioration, both progressively and irreversibly, in the image of the tourist destination. This process of adjustment contains further impacts derived from the very contradictions produced by continued supply-side growth, especially in terms of ground occupation due to real estate urban ventures. Thus a redefinition of the entire system of the insertion of tourism in coastal areas has become necessary, involving a move towards the recomposition of congested areas, the need to implement policies which imply greater selectivity, and the inclusion of complementary accommodation provision capable of satisfying new trends in demand.

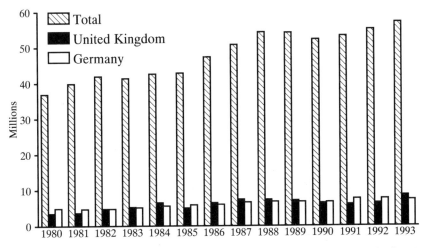

Figure 6.3. Spain: numbers of international visitors, 1980–93. Source: Authors' calculations based on data provided by the Secretaría General de Turismo, TURESPAÑA

It should not be forgotten, however, that in parallel with this decline, advances have been made such as improvements in access to urban centres and rising income levels in the domestic markets within the Mediterranean countries. These favour those tourist resorts which are considered by city-dwellers to provide accessible leisure areas. This is so in the case of Alicante and Madrid, thereby reaffirming a historical link, but now in the context of a more global conceptualisation of leisure and recreation rather than the traditional more seasonal model.

6.3   RESTRUCTURING POLICIES FOR COASTAL TOURISM

The decline and crisis in coastal resorts have led to a need to identify strategies, for both the public and private sectors, which could allow for the rejuvenation of destinations in terms of a product which offers new advantages and competitiveness. In this way, sectoral initiatives are seen as the key to relaunching and modernising tourism, taking advantage of its strong points and, at the same time, defining business objectives and commercialisation strategies which are better adapted to an area's competitive position and its regional setting. In short, it is clear that the orientation of new policies should be based on the strategic setting of the tourist industry.

In the Mediterranean region, an assessment of the improvements necessary has identified the need for a reorganisation of coastal tourism, with public and private investments being organised around one of two main policy lines:

1. Seeking improvements in the quality of existing mass tourism, by way of creating public infrastructures (urban planning, ecology, improved facilities). The objective here is to be attractive in the really large foreign markets in Europe, as well as the domestic market, by reorienting (mostly existing) facilities so as to meet the requirements of medium-income segments of demand; over the years, these had been progressively lost in favour of lower-income segments.
2. Creating high-quality areas which can function independently of—though being intertwined with—hegemonic mass tourism. Conditions necessary for the implementation of such actions include respect for the environment, high-quality infrastructures, and complementary service provision.

In spite of the obvious manifestation of the crisis in consolidated mass tourism areas (traditional sea and sand resorts), a wider discussion about new tourist policy orientations is being delayed, even though individual resorts have carried out improvements aimed at alleviating the symptoms of decline and at environmental enhancement. To some extent, the delay in implementing a more comprehensive policy response lies in the partial restoration of demand in some resorts in the mid 1990s, and their ability to attract a hard core of loyal repeat customers. In this sense, the traditional resorts can be 'victims of their own success'.

The actual degree and type of response at the level of local administrations depend on the structural conditions under which the tourist model operates and, to a large extent, on private sector initiatives and their effective coordination with public bodies. In all this it should not be forgotten that it is not actual tourist activity that is in crisis but, rather, changes in motivations, in demand and in the introduction of new dynamising elements. This means that old assumptions about the system will have to be reconsidered, as must its objectives and functioning, in order to face up to the decline in traditional areas.

6.3.1   Restructuring policies in the Mediterranean region

The implementation of new policies is always a complex process which involves different levels of organisation and has to confront problems of conflicting interests within the administration and between it and different economic agents. However, the framework for these is changing. State and autonomous government bodies are entering an era when, for tourism, there is an increased level of planning and interventionism. Even the EU is promoting actions in tourism which will affect coastal as well as other tourist areas. Particular attention should be paid to the Fifth Environmental Programme in which explicit reference is made to the relationship between tourism and protection of the environmental heritage (Montanari 1992). In the wake of widespread resort degradation, the stakes have been laid down for environmental quality to be one of the key elements in the determination of competitiveness in tourism in future.

Policies for restructuring and the modernisation of traditional receiver areas have more scope in those countries in which negative trends have been observed since the 1980s. Thus in the UK and other north-western European coastal areas, decline was detected as early as the 1970s, due to competition from foreign (Mediterranean) destinations and alternative forms of tourism (Goodall 1992; Williams and Shaw 1992). This can be seen in context of the shift away from Fordist production of mass tourism services to more recent post-modernist forms (Urry 1990). Experience suggests that there is no single model for ensuring survival. Instead, a variety of strategies are possible based on attracting new market segments and reviving existing ones.

Restructuring policies necessarily involve a continuous process depending on the size and importance of the destination. In life-cycle terms, they should constitute an intermediate phase between stagnation and post-stagnation, marked by a strategic approach which makes it possible to face the future by identifying key issues in the rejuvenation of the resort (Cooper 1992). There is a need to integrate innovation, technical change, rationalisation, changes in the labour market, in quality and in entrepreneurship (Urry 1987).

In the case of the West Country, which is the most important destination for domestic tourism in the UK, the negative trends during the last decade led to a regional Action Programme. This has three main strands: improvement in the region's competitive position, conservation of the environment and of cultural heritage, and the satisfaction of consumer needs. This set of proposals will have to be coordinated with, and complemented by, the initiatives of other organisations, especially those with coastal interests such as heritage coasts. Such proposals stress the importance of elaborating overall management plans which identify specific recreation models and define the organisation of land use and activities along the coast (Williams 1989).

The crisis of coastal tourism, resulting from the saturation of the mass tourism model, equally affects other regions in the sense that they are entering a new phase of structured tourist products, which should go beyond the Fordist style of organisation which characterised the cycle of mass tourism. This is the case in Portugal (Sirgado 1993), where the Algarve (destinations such as Albufeira, Portimâo and Loulè) is the outstanding tourism region. Here there is an overall regional strategy, concentrating on products and markets, on the one hand, and on promotion, on the other. The objectives are to improve the quality of supply and competitiveness, territorial planning, control, professionalisation, training and product image.

In the Mediterranean region[4] there are many examples of areas which, after being true paradigms of success in the mass supply of sun and sea tourism services in the 1980s, are now suffering from an evident loss in competitiveness, as well as aesthetic and environmental degradation. Spain has been one of the major recipients of both the positive and the negative trends in visitor movements. The signs of decline in the late 1980s and the 1990s (see Figure 6.1) have been such that the state has become involved in restructuring strategies, especially by means of its Plan Marco de Competitividad del Turismo Español (FUTURES). It is also coordinating its programmes with regional actions (in the case of Andalusia, for example, with the Plan DIA), and with municipal policies which play an essential role in the shaping of tourist resorts.

A special case of restructuring, on the municipal scale, is that of Torremolinos (Costa del Sol, Andalusia) in which all the characteristics related to sea and sand tourism and its degradation are evident: an inadequate supply given changes in demand, limited diversification, absence of innovation, a low level of professionalism, a price imbalance between the package and the services, inefficient infrastructures and facilities, and environmental deterioration.

In the context of the Plan FUTURES, a Pilot Plan of Recuperation for Tourist Areas is being undertaken, with the idea of maintaining a leading position in the tourist market for sea and sun holidays, by improving the quality of tourism infrastructures and adapting them to new market demands. Along these lines, and as an example of coordination between public administrations and the private sector, there is an attempt to redesign and improve the urban setting of Torremolinos and to preserve the environment while also respecting the aims of private businesses. The coordination of public and private actions is ensured by the creation of a consortium consisting of the state, autonomous and local administrations, as well as the private sector; this acts as a managing committee whose role is to follow up the propositions of the plan designed to overcome the deterioration of its image as a tourist product. As a whole, this is a tourism marketing plan which, at the same time, aims to form a new urban landscape and environment for tourism in relation to territorial and urban planning.

Other municipalities in the Spanish Mediterranean have undertaken restructuring of their tourist product by means of quality-oriented urban initiatives (e.g. Calvía in Majorca, and Sitges on the Costa Dorada). In other areas the restructuring has been based more on business strategies and commercialisation which, starting from an analysis of the scenery and of service provision, have been able to secure their competitive positions in the sun and sea market, with prospects for further success (as in the case of Benidorm).

6.4   THE FUTURE OF EUROPEAN COASTAL DEVELOPMENT

Coastal tourism has contributed to the reorganisation of the European space in so far as its development has reshaped popular perceptions of the coastal areas; these are now seen more positively, based on awareness of the alternative they offer to the stresses of everyday life, whereas historically they represented a hostile border zone.

By the 1990s, however, it has become clear that the European coastline is in need of reorganisation and improvement of its tourist supply, as it begins to fail to meet the holiday aspirations and expectations of the tourists themselves. Various momentary (structural, medium-term) variables are crucial in this respect:

1. Sensitivity regarding the prices of coastal tourist packages given the limited purchasing power of a large part of the lower-middle and working-class market in Europe for this product.
2. There has been an extraordinary increase in environmental awareness regarding tourist areas, whether these are polarised or dispersed, which has special relevance in terms of landscape consumption and the treatment of both fresh and sea water.
3. There is cyclical rediscovery of coasts in specific parts of the Mediterranean previously considered to be saturated by mass tourism, or the revaluation of old spa resorts (many of which have 'art nouveau' features), or of areas with little sunshine and almost bereft of tourist infrastructures.

Whatever changes are brought about by these structural variables, the tourist coastline is likely to continue to provide the prime destination for the largest flows of European tourists, in quantitative and even qualitative terms (Pompl and Lavery 1993). The experience of the mid 1990s confirms this for, despite new trends, there has been a strengthening of the tourist coastline, while the search for security has reinforced the position of known coastal resorts.[5]

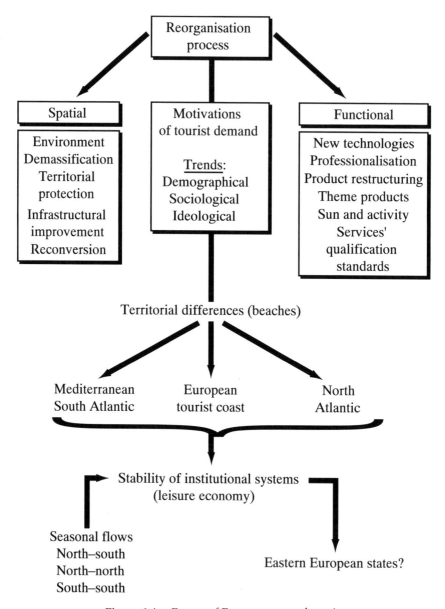

Figure 6.4. Future of European coastal tourism

The debate over spatial reorganisation is occurring, at the end of the twentieth century, in a context of recovery in demand, which to some degree confounds the prophecies of doom for the oversaturated, conventional sun and sea tourism model. This recovery is closely associated with the requalification of those coastal areas which have best been able to interpret the holiday market signs in the EU (Bote 1993). There has been a significant shift back to the classical mass tourist resorts of Europe for a number of reasons: the rise of so-called Islamic fundamentalism in the southern Mediterranean region, the disaster of Turkish tourism related to the violence of the Kurdish separatist movements, and a general weariness with exotic resorts such as the Caribbean. In addition, the Atlantic coastal resorts, with less extreme climates and less fragmented leisure economies, present another layer of complexity in the changing face of European coastal tourism (Vera Rebollo 1990).

The paradigm of quality—wrongly considered an end when really it is a means of obtaining better social, environmental and economic balances on the European coast (DIA 1993)—is the indisputable motor of the reorganisation of the linked functional and spatial attributes of the tourist sector. These changes, linked to the search for improved quality, are occurring against a background of social changes which have a strong impact on tourism markets: an ageing population, which is also increasingly travel-experienced, an underclass disadvantaged in terms of tourism, young people passing from unemployment to leisure (Racionero 1983) and, in the medium term, the daunting but uncertain challenge from the Eastern European countries.

Finally, the redefinition of the European coastal areas will depend on the ability to analyse the complex processes which are contributing to its reshaping (see Figure 6.4; CEC 1992). If this tourism sector is to satisfy the emerging pattern of needs, then investment is required in the general and the particular services demanded by tourists (involving more thematic and activity specialisation, and less reliance on the traditional sea and sun product), as well as in improved infrastructures to improve access to, and the maintenance of, the coastal tourist areas.

These requirements are particularly pressing within a leisure economy which is becoming more and more complex and structured with respect to the segments with consumption capacity in Europe, and where the coastal tourist product is following patterns similar to those in industries with tangible, manufactured goods (Nacher and Selma 1993). In the process of the 'tourism qualification' of coastal areas such as the Costa del Sol in Spain, an ageing and rejuvenation of territorial sectors—which were previously successful or rejected by demand—can be observed. The key difference with manufacturing is that the product cycle of coastal tourism refers essentially to combinations not only of functionally qualitative elements, but more basically to spatial and environmental ones.[6]

NOTES

1. A critical appraisal of this statement can be found in the following quote: 'What are the cohesion settings of modern-day man? Those areas in which each man knows he shares the same activity, or even the same passion, with the rest? Big department stores, motorways, sports stadiums, tourist resorts . . .' (Argullol and Trias 1992, pp. 51–52). (Literal translation of gender terms).

2. Data to verify this can be found in the 1950 series of statistics prepared by the WTO.

3. The annual reports produced by the Spanish Tourist Office abroad (London, Frankfurt, Paris, Rome, Brussels, etc.) are particularly significant in this analysis. They describe the tourism processes of the main transmitting markets. The main requirements of the demand continue to be environmental and coastal regions.

4. According to Montanari, the infrastructures of accommodation in the Mediterranean area of the EU are concentrated in a small number of resorts: Costa del Sol, Costa Blanca, Costa Dorada, Balearic Islands (Spain); Languedoc–Rousillon and Côte d'Azur (France); Versiglia, Costa Esmeralda, Peninsula Sorrentinga, Adriatic coast (Italy); Athens, Corfu and Crete (Greece).

5. This is verified by data on international tour operators' prices for coastal, especially Mediterranean destinations (see Bote and Sinclair 1991). Evidence can also be found in the annual statistics on competing sun and sea resorts by the Spanish government's General Secretary for Tourism.

6. In line with this, the Ministers of the EU in charge of the environment met in Santorini (Greece) in May 1994, and declared a need for a global *rapprochement* in order to combine the development of tourist programmes with the special attention being paid to the environment. It was even suggested that an 'eco-ticket' be introduced within the EU.

7 Rural Tourism: The Creation of New Tourist Spaces

CARMINDA CAVACO

University of Lisbon

7.1 INTRODUCTION: NEW TOURISM TRENDS

Tourism has grown considerably during recent decades in terms of pleasure trips spent away from home. Assessments of future prospects indicate the likelihood of further growth, at least in the developed countries. The preconditions for the realisation of this trend are an improvement in people's economic well-being and social security, stability in purchasing power, increased spatial mobility as motor cars and air travel are universalised, further entrenchment of the ingrained 'holiday cult', and the supply of reasonably priced holidays so that the mass tourist industry is able to capture hitherto economically marginalised market sectors. There is also a gender dimension: the fact that a growing number of women have joined the labour market and, therefore, also need and, moreover, are able to go on holiday, is relevant. It should further be remembered that there have been increases in annual leave entitlements as well as in the amount of leisure time available during the week. The deterioration in the quality of urban life, the increased pressures of the daily routine and the widespread feeling of professional frustration in many walks of life should also be taken into account.

There has been a recent tendency towards greater variation in the ways in which holidays are spent, and it has become increasingly popular to divide up annual leave into more and shorter segments. As a result, weekend and multi-seasonal tourism are more in demand and there is a greater variety of places to visit and activities to partake in: these include the call of wide open spaces, of the countryside and hilly areas, and of exotic settings—not to mention the coastal, urban and Alpine destinations. Far-off horizons, nature, ecology, landscape and culture—the authentic and the genuine—attract some tourists, while others are attracted to sun and sand, the city and its entertainment, or snow-scapes and winter sports. The objective of this chapter is to investigate the social construction, organisation and wider social ramifications of that form of tourism.

European Tourism: Regions, Spaces and Restructuring. Edited by A. Montanari and A.M. Williams.
© 1995 European Science Foundation. Published in 1995 by John Wiley & Sons Ltd.

7.2 THE RURAL SPACE AS A NEW TOURIST DESTINATION

When discussing rural tourism in this chapter, the term refers exclusively to farming country (reserved for crops, cattle, land clearance and forestry) either today or in the recent past. This sort of area is sufficiently distant from the coastline for its economic, social, landscape and functional dynamics not to be substantially affected by seaside tourism with its associated profusion of holiday homes and tourist villages spreading inwards from the coastal zones. They are also relatively removed from cities where periurban surroundings offer good conditions for recreational facilities for leisure-time activities and also accommodate second homes, usually for weekend occupation. In contrast, the rural areas considered here are, typically, inland hilly regions with different sorts of landscapes, with mostly peasant-type economies and societies, and a wealth of history and specific cultural traditions. However, the rural areas also include those suffering from serious problems of abandonment, relative poverty, isolation and desertification. Certain natural parks and reserves used to be, or still are, partly or fully occupied by mountainous farmland on which crops and livestock are raised, together with forestry and traditional fruit-gathering (wild fruit, mushrooms) or hunting. Such farms are included in rural tourism spaces.

In the evolution of new types of leisure activities, forms of specifically rural tourism, with strong environmental emphases, have become increasingly popular. It is in nature tourism that people can identify a multiple role in their environment, manifested in the humanising history of Europe's natural environments.

This kind of tourism is not really new. Over the centuries, a series of migrations have left their marks on town–country relationships; the old aristocratic families, with their country seats, gradually became more urbanised while the town bourgeoisie began to acquire country estates. For many people, rural tourism did not mean an interval in their working lives or a change in their daily routine in order to recharge their mental and physical batteries. Rather, it meant discovering or rediscovering a more relaxed change of air, atmosphere and daily routine. Their seasonal or periodic visits were quite important in terms of the rhythm of the agricultural year as they tended to fall around harvest-time, particularly when the grapes were being gathered, and also during the hunting season. Although this was important in supporting agricultural production, it did not, however, imply a significant increase in local trade. Neither did they cause any significant change in local socio-economic processes.

The landed estates were managed so that their recreational and social duties fitted in harmoniously with farming activities. The manor house—with its numerous rooms, gardens and park—was set apart from its resident population of farm-labourers, the vegetable gardens, orchards and stables. Although the manor house increasingly began to play a role as a second home, it always symbolised its roots in farming —although more in terms of income than active management. Many of these manor houses are still run on similar lines even today, despite the fact that their owners enjoy other life styles and other places to spend their holidays. However, it is also likely that more modern leisure-time installations such as swimming-pools, tennis courts, horse-riding and hunting have been provided.

In other cases, the rural areas were sought after and visited by convalescing patients, and those in ill health, owing to the exceptional quality of their environments and, more particularly, their climates. This demand helped to build up a thriving health tourism industry and the spa towns.

At a much later date, when the pressure of mass tourism was brought to bear on the summer-bathing season and it was recognised that there was a need to spread inland the potential benefits of economic and social development, tourism infrastructures were gradually introduced to generate new flows of holidaymakers, even if they were only on day visits or passing through on circular tours. A clear example of this was the policy of building the state-owned inns and hotels, the *paradores* in Spain and the *pousadas* in Portugal. This initially rather thin network of government inns was made denser by the appearance of private inns and of socially minded tourist accommodation (youth hostels, holiday places for underprivileged children, etc.) in the inland areas.

In the last 50 years demographic shifts have resulted in the growth of new forms of demand for tourism in the countryside, the mountainous areas and rural spaces traditionally located on city outskirts. As a result of the large-scale exodus from farms and rural areas to urban, industrialised regions—both at home and abroad—and following improvements in travelling (in the railway network and especially in the widening of car ownership), important currents of periodic but regular return visits have emerged; these mainly occur during the summer, coinciding with long school holidays, and working parents' annual leave. This sort of family tourism usually consists of people who were born in the rural areas and have relatively limited economic resources (they belong to the working or lower-middle classes). They normally stay with their extended families or with friends, or in the modest second homes they have inherited. They share in the largely self-subsistence economies typical of these local societies, and spend on or consume very few 'superfluous' (that is, non-basic) consumer goods. On the other hand, family tourism may also be composed of first-generation emigrants returning from abroad. The fact that they engage in conspicuous consumption while they are on holiday is rooted in the social and psychological complexes of return migrants, particularly with regard to countering the stigma of having been 'forced' to emigrate. This type of return tourism, mostly involving socio-economic groups with modest resources, has failed to make any significant or lasting impact on farms and the local economy, apart from benefiting the construction industry via expenditure to improve and repair farmhouses.

The 'urbanisation' of rural immigrants to the cities, and in particular of their urban-born children, has weakened links with the villages where their grandparents and extended families lived and perhaps still live. Family rights and duties are forgotten and their visits become more and more infrequent. At the same time, though, the improved material living conditions afforded by urban life allow them to take their holidays in what they perceive as being more high-status destinations, mainly by the sea. In consequence, in terms of traditional markets, rural areas have, increasingly, assumed a more residual function: they have been able to attract holidaymakers only if they are able to provide comfortable, pleasant accommodation at prices which fairly large urban families or young couples with small childen can afford. Personal relationships and blossoming friendships between the visiting family and their host families ensure the development of faithful clienteles and full, seasonal bookings. However, the problem of how to renew their clienteles in future, in the face of increasing competition and changing social customs, continues to be problematic for this type of tourism.

It is true that there are long-standing traditions of rural tourism in some countries. This is the case of Switzerland, Austria—in the Tyrol, Salzburg and Vovarlberg—as well as Sweden, where the link between the rural world of farming and tourism has always been marked. Tourism, especially the letting of rooms, has been one means for securing the survival of farming. In general, about one-fifth of Austrian, Swiss and Swedish farmers take in summer holidaymakers as against 8% of German and Dutch farmers, 4% of the French and 2% of Italian farmers (Requena and Aviles 1993, p. 115). However, in the case of Austria this supply is in decline as farmers have seen most of their main clientele—the Germans—enticed away not only by other destinations but by their competitors in the professional hotel industry. Tourists have been attracted by the more vivacious life of the hotels which depend on nearby shops and services (cafés, restaurants, handicraft shops, post offices, banks, etc.). In Germany itself, rural tourism has a long tradition. It has been a meeting place where rural culture encounters an urban culture that is extremely sensitive to nature and the bucolic, even if the price for this has been relatively less comfort and lower sanitary conditions for the tourists (although compensated for by comparatively low prices).

In recent decades tourist demand for rural spaces has undergone further changes and has become more diversified owing to its rediscovery by the medium, high and upper classes of urban society. These classes have already lost most of their rural heritage, and they no longer have any family connections in those areas which they visit. This is, in effect, a flight from the summer-holiday resorts of mass tourism and, instead, more middle-class tourists are choosing to visit rural areas. They are looking for alternatives to the sun and the beach and prefer isolation, privacy, rest, peace and quiet, personalised service, warm human relations, something that, above all, is different and special. In essence, they are looking for well-protected, 'pure', unspoilt nature; for grand, varied landscapes; for archaeological, historical, memorial and cultural heritage; for novel architecture with its roots in regional folklore; for festivals and feast days; for traditional music, dancing and folklore; and for traditional gastronomy. They are also looking for more active kinds of entertainment: discovery walks, bicycle rides, water-sports on lakes and rivers, horse-riding, hunting, fishing, learning the traditional arts and crafts, wild fruit-gathering in abandoned fields or working on host farms. In other words, they are giving new value to traditional destinations previously cast aside in the great summer stampede to the beach.

The market for this kind of tourism is not based on the neo-urban population. Rather, it attracts relatively well-off city-dwellers with no or few rural connections. These rural tourists have the individual travel freedom of their own cars, are educated, well-travelled and are demanding, critical consumers. They normally divide up their holiday and thus enjoy a series of shorter trips and stays which allow them to assemble combinations of journeys to exotic places, visits to the beach, activity holidays based on discovery and learning, and or taking restful vacations away from the stresses and pressures of work and home. And in addition to all this, they may also enjoy a holiday in a second home or a tourist villa.

7.3   TOURISTS AND THE RURAL WORLD

In the mid 1980s the EU undertook a survey of tourism behaviour in the member states which underlined the attraction of rural areas (Table 7.1). It also revealed the reasons for their preferences for these types of holidays (Table 7.2). In countries where rural tourism was important, over one-third of the population chose rural destinations for their holidays; this applied to Denmark, the Netherlands and Germany. Among the Dutch, 39% favoured rural spaces for their main holidays and 49% favoured them for their secondary

Table 7.1.   The EU: types of holiday destinations, at home and abroad, 1985[a]

Countries	Countryside[a]	Mountains	Cities	Seaside
Belgium	25	19	5	55
Denmark	35	14	40	42
Spain	27	19	27	53
France	29	27	18	52
Greece	8	11	20	70
Ireland	27	8	37	46
Italy	11[b]	24	19	58
Netherlands	39	32	21	36
Portugal	29	8	24	62
Germany	34	30	15	44
EU	25	23	19	52

[a] The term 'countryside' has different meanings in different countries, which partly explains the low numbers in Greece and Italy. [b] Excludes the lakes region.

Source: CEC General Directorate of Transport (1986).

Table 7.2. Holiday motivations in selected countries: principal attractive features (%), 1985[a]

Attractive features	Spain	Italy	Netherlands	Germany	EU
Natural attractions	52	63	66	47	56
Unspoilt landscape	17	37	42	43	37
Low cost of living	12	38	36	40	34
Monuments and museums	28	27	25	30	28
Complete rest	5	30	32	23	26
Comfortable hotels	14	24	22	22	26
Entertainment	19	22	17	21	23
Sports facilities	9	14	16	14	14

Source: See Table 7.1.

holidays, as against 34 and 39% respectively for the Germans. In England, three-quarters of the population visited the countryside at least once in 1991.

The principal reason why European tourists chose the rural world was its natural attractions and unspoilt landscape which, together with the type of services provided, give added value to both the countryside and the heritage of the past. Nevertheless, to counterbalance the emphasis given to rural tourism, it should be noted that, in the mid 1980s, 40–70% chose to spend their holidays at the coast.

The pattern of second holiday taking is particularly noteworthy; while 29% of EU inhabitants preferred the countryside for their secondary holidays, 29% preferred the seaside, 25% the cities and 23% the mountains. Given the tendency, already noted, for the educated and cultured, upper and middle classes to divide up their holidays into several smaller segments, the increasing flows to the countryside have to be interpreted more in terms of their tastes than of any need or wish to economise.

Surveys of the rural tourism markets in various countries allow us to identify their basic characteristics. In Germany (see Grolleau 1987) agrotourism deserves special attention due to the fact that, between 1970 and 1985, 1% of summer holidaymakers spent their vacations on farms, mainly the traditional, rustic farms in Bavaria. Their motivations stemmed from the feeling that they had lost contact with nature and, together with their families, wanted a change in routine and environment at prices which they could afford. They were mostly young married couples with small children, and adults over the age of 50, who lived in medium-sized and large cities, especially in their suburbs. They usually had medium and higher educational and socio-economic levels and were not necessarily from the neo-urban population segment. During their stay on the farm, they preferred spending their time sleeping, resting, going for walks, talking with other people, taking care of their children, swimming, sun-bathing, horse-riding, visiting natural parks and reserves, and even helping with the farm work.

In Italy, it is a well-known fact that in the 1980s (Cannata, cited in Grolleau 1987, pp. 125–127) agrotourism attracted several major market segments: the adult population (38% of the 30–40 age group and 23% of the 40–50s), those who were employed (45%), had liberal professions (17%) or were teachers (12%), and had medium (48%) and higher (31%) levels of education. They went on holiday with their families (60%) and friends (31%) and had half-board (52%) or self-catered (32%). They were attracted to the quiet life (48%), moderate prices (33%), contact with nature (32%) and cultural events (19.5%). Rural tourism was no longer reserved for neo-urban dwellers or the less wealthy. It has also been established that Italians chose rural tourism mainly because it offered them nature, scenery, peace and quiet, a return to tradition, and the likelihood of making new friendships. At the same time, agrotourism also implies a love of nature, an appreciation of the real and authentic, a desire for the quiet life, a love of novelty, adaptability, openness of spirit, and an interest in social relations. Moreover, it was thought that the ideal holiday should provide an opportunity for contact with nature, to feel free from job stresses, to enjoy the open air and sunshine with one's family, to change habits, to rest and to sleep one's fill, to meet other people, and to return to one's roots.

In Spain, official surveys show that its inland areas, including the cultivated countryside and the mountains, continue to be one of the major destinations for the domestic main holiday market. Spanish tourists set off in large numbers for the small towns or inland cities (19%), and for the hills and mountains (16%), although these are overshadowed by the attractive powers of the coast-line (54%). With regard to accommodation, a family or a friend's house is still predominant (32%), followed by second homes (16%), and rented chalets, apartments or condominiums (12%). Only 24.9% of Spanish holidaymakers stay in hotels, inns, apartment-hotels and boarding houses (chalets), while 9% go camping or caravanning and 2% stay in social accommodation.

With further reference to Spain, surveys undertaken by Bote (1993) in the 1980s provide evidence to conclude that 44% of the Spanish who went on holiday away from home were attracted to rural tourism. They belonged to the middle or lower-middle classes, were adults (51% in the 30–50 age group) and 52% had primary school education while 35% had secondary school education. They were also likely to be skilled workers (31%), retired or living on their pensions (16.6%), or they were small- and medium-scale entrepreneurs (10.5%), middle management and intermediate technicians (9%), and un-skilled wage-earners (9.6%). Furthermore, they travelled with their families (79%), in their own cars (70%), headed for inland villages (57%) and the mountains (32%) and stayed with family and friends (45%) or in their own houses in the village (22%). They rested (69%), went for walks (47%), met up with their extended families and friends (44%), went on excursions (22%) and regularly came back to the same place (71%) partly because it was economical to do so (17%) or because they had family duties to take care of (16%).

Official statistics for Portugal show that the inland regions attract about one-third of the population that spends its holidays away from home (35% in

1986; 34% in 1990). One-fifth make for the northern hinterland while very few go to the southern inland regions, but the coasts are the dominant desinations. These areas are visited by all the main socio-economic groups, although mainly by the lower-middle and lower classes, as well as the resident population of the areas themselves. In terms of the spatial framework used for collating tourism statistics, the mountains and plains, respectively, attract 10–15% and 6–7% of the domestic market, as against one-quarter to one-fifth of the Portuguese holidaymakers who are attracted to the Algarve. In 1990, the mountains in fact attracted about 10% of the population living in Greater Lisbon and 9% of the residents of Greater Oporto, while they attracted 40% of the people living in the northern hinterland. The plains attracted 10% of the Greater Lisbon inhabitants, 6% of the Greater Oporto inhabitants and 27% of the southern hinterland's regional population. The same official sources show that one-half of holidaymakers regularly visit the same favoured destination. This is due to the high cost of accommodation and transport and to personal or family economic constraints; more than one-half use their own motor cars (one-fifth go by coach or bus) and more than two-fifths stay with family and friends (about 1 in 10 rent a house or part of a house while an equal number stay at their holiday homes). In terms of area or regional preference, 30% chose the countryside in 1990 as against 8% going to the mountains. A large majority, however, still prefer going to the beach.

In Portugal, the countryside is gaining in importance because the supply of rural accommodation is growing and there is a new trend—especially among higher-income groups—to divide holiday time into two or more periods (even if 80% still take their holidays away from home in a single block). It is among these strata that are found the clientele of the new types of rural tourism based on more unusual common cultural and ecological patterns.

7.4   THE SUPPLY OF RURAL TOURIST ACCOMMODATION

The different demands made by tourism on rural spaces have been met by contrasting and specific forms of accommodation supply. The rural world of traditional tourism had never boasted a significant hotel industry or other form of commercial accommodation. The only supply was provided by small family units in the main settlements. They relied on family labour and provided fairly minimal facilities and services for their residential and transitory clientele. In the first phase, rooms were let in family residences which were not necessarily located on farms. The income generated had to be paid for, inevitably, through extra domestic labour and a considerable loss in the family's privacy. However, the seasonal injection of money did contribute to paying off the initial investment in tourism and to improving the bed and breakfast and other services on offer. In a later phase, unutilised old houses or farmhouses were reconverted into independent self-catering units with a small kitchen and bathroom adjoining the main building, or separate houses and apartments were built independently or grouped into holiday villages. Here and there the traditional type of hotel industry was resuscitated and small—mostly medium to upper-class—country hotels were built. In order to satisfy the demands of specific segments of the market, camping and caravan sites as well as permanent holiday camps were also built to accommodate mobile homes, tents and prefabricated holiday dwellings.

The exact sequence in the development of rural tourism has varied considerably from country to country. In France, for example, which had early (mid twentieth century) experience of modern rural tourism development, and acted as a model for other countries, the supply of accommodation is as follows: chambres d'hôtes, gîtes à la ferme, gîtes ruraux, gîtes d'enfants, gîtes d'étape, gîtes-relais, ferme-auberge, meublés de tourisme, tables d'hôtes, villages de vacances, auberge de jeunesse, hôtellerie, terrains de camping-caravaning, gîtes de nature, chalets de vacances, maison familiales de vacances. They are mostly socially oriented and/or second homes, that is, are in the non-commercial sector.

Investments were mostly endogenous, coming from the farmers themselves, the non-farming rural population and local government. Very few investments were exogenous and these were made with an eye on profits or were in socially minded tourism (holiday camps for underprivileged children, youth hostels, etc.). Active part-time or professional tourist entrepreneurs invested in complementary services, such as restaurants and bars (which might or might not be associated with accommodation), recreational and cultural events, sports and entertainments.

As particular rural areas gained impetus in their tourist 'vocation', then if they had access to natural and human resources and were also spatially accessible, there was a sharp increase in demand from city-dwellers for old houses to convert into second homes. Old houses were bought and renovated as second holiday homes, occupied at the weekends and/or during extended holiday periods. When the supply of available old houses had been exhausted, demand turned to small farms located near the main agglomerations, and later to more dispersed and isolated farms. These were usually subject to extensive renovation, but in a style which was sympathetic to traditional, regional architecture or in accordance with peasant architectural lines. Taken together with short-let commercial accommodation, these second homes have resulted in the attraction of further external investment in other services. They have also made general local infrastructures and social facilities more viable, and have helped to maintain minimum local living standards.

The spatial distribution of second homes is highly polarised, being influenced by a number of factors: the supply/price relationship, the quality of local social and cultural life, and the relative proximity of beaches, lakeside areas, natural parks and reserves, and protected environments. Factors such as distance and ease of accessibility from the owners' main residences are also important. This reflects the time and expense involved in each trip, and the way in which different social groups evaluate these costs and opportunities (see Shaw and Williams 1994).

7.5   RURAL TOURISM: CASE-STUDIES

This section examines the supply of rural tourism services in contrasting case studies of northern and southern Europe: Ireland and the Netherlands, Italy and Portugal, the UK and France. In terms of the EU as a whole, in 1987 30% of rural tourists stayed in country hotels, 21% with family or friends, 16% in camping parks, 16% in rented accommodation and 10% in second homes (Greffe 1992, p. 143). In Europe, medium to high population densities, high levels of owner occupation of land, and intensive farm production have led to conflicts between tourist access to rural space (with negative external consequences) and the use this land had for farming purposes. Thus, together with ecological and cultural limitations, social ceilings were imposed on the number of people who could be absorbed in the rural space.

In Ireland, in 1987, there were 2200 rooms in farmhouses (2% of the total) and 3370 rooms in country houses, together with 3400 beds in independent houses situated in holiday villages in the countryside (Grolleau 1987). There were two dozen camping and caravan parks offering almost 1500 places and some small village-inn hotels, as well as a number of old castles, manor houses and old hunting lodges which were luxuriously fitted out as manor-house hotels to host salmon fishing, hunting, golfers and horse-riding enthusiasts. Even at this date, about 20% of overnight accommodation was provided by country houses (located away from any sort of agglomeration) and farmhouses (on 20 or more acres of land). The official promotion of this kind of tourism came as a response to the need to satisfy quickly the ever-growing demand for quality accommodation (even if it was temporary) without, however, undermining the farmers' needs to supplement the income they derived from agriculture.

In the Netherlands, rural tourism mainly acted as an impetus to self-catering, especially camping—above all on farms—although it also promoted the business of letting rooms, apartments and furnished dwellings. In terms of agrotourism, this meant serving specialist groups, such as unaccompanied children, and promoting specialist recreation-oriented horse-farms and extensive restoration work on the farms. In the mid 1980s, Grolleau calculated that about 1200 farms—some 5–6% of the total—offered tourist accommodation. A similar proportion of farmers rented out spaces to campers, and a few dozen specialised in horse-riding. In 1991, it was estimated that in total there were 30 000 farms catering to tourists, providing 150 000 rooms and 250 000 beds (CEC 1991).

In Italy, rural tourism has maintained close links with the farming sector and has, therefore, been widely confused with agrotourism. In reality, the difference between rural tourism and agrotourism resides in the degree to which tourism plays a part in farming activity and income. In 1986, there was a 55 000-bed capacity in private rural tourism accommodation involving some 6000 farmers, of whom only 2000 considered that tourism was their secondary activity. The latter group is involved in agrotourism, defined by the fact that the income from tourism, and the amount of labour dedicated to it, is less than for more traditional farming activities (Grolleau 1987). As Scoullos (1992) argues, by definition agrotourism is a by-product of farming. It attracts tourists through its scenery which is bound to traditional systems, its livestock, its working and living conditions and by the way in which rural communities function in general. In other words, agrotourism is both complementary to and dependent on farming. In 1990, Italian agrotourism involved 6800 farms (2% of the total) and 9500 rural buildings, offering 90 000 beds (6.8 million overnight stays) (Velluti Zati 1992, p. 64); 1800 farms had been restored while there were 1500 camping parks and a similar number offered horse-riding. In terms of regional distribution, agrotourism was particularly important in restoring and adding further value added in areas such as: the Alto Adige/Bolsano (2500 farms), Tuscany (1200), Umbria (300) and Puglia in the Mezzogiorno (200).

In Portugal, the modern supply of rural tourism came into existence at the end of the 1970s. A heritage of great quality and historical value (palaces and large manor houses) situated in a rural environment (*turismo de habitaçâo*) and even on farms (leastways, the larger and prestigious farming estates) were put to tourism use after recovery, reconversion and restoration. This trend then spread to country houses with distinctive regional architecture (rural tourism) and farmhouses on the large profitable landed estates, such as the farms or *montes* of the Alentejo (for agrotourism and hunting). During most of the 1980s, the supply of rural tourism was modest, amounting to about 200 units with almost 2000 beds. Thereafter, the rate of development accelerated

Table 7.3. Progress in rural tourism in Portugal, 1989–94

Year	Working units				No. of beds
	Turismo de habitaçâo (palaces and manor houses)	Rural tourism (rustic and bourgeois village houses)	Agro-tourism	Total	
1989	95	90	20	205	1 617
1990	107	106	25	238	1 902
1991	118	118	40	276	2 314
1992	132	151	57	342[a]	3 051
1994[b]	148	174	67	389	3 557

[a] Includes two country hotels.
[b] February 1994.

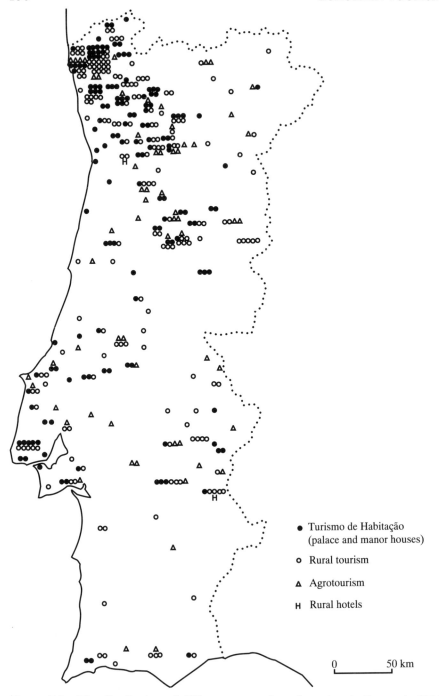

Figure 7.1. The distribution of different types of rural tourism in Portugal, 1994.
Source: Data provided by the Direcçâo Geral do Turismo, Lisbon

quite considerably and, in 1994, the supply stood at 389 units and 3500 beds (Table 7.3), with *turismo de habitaçâo* and rural tourism each accounting for approximately 40% of the supply of bed spaces. At the same time the supply has become more differentiated, with the growth of tourist villages and country hotels, together with new state- and privately owned inns, and it has also become more widely distributed spatially. Initially, the North-west was the dominant area and, in the 1980s, accounted for 40% of beds; Viana do Castelo district alone accounted for 17%, with the municipality of Ponte de Lima—the cradle of *turismo de habitaçâo*—being especially important. This regional dominance has gradually declined in favour of other areas (Figure 7.1), both in the adjacent hinterland (for example Viseu and Guarda, 17%) and in the southern inland areas (Santarém, Portalegre and Évora, 15%). The form this has taken is variable, including *turismo de habitaçâo* (in manor houses and historical landed estates) and country houses, the *montes* of the Alentejo, and solid, old bourgeois houses.

In the case of rural tourism in the UK, numbers for 1990 indicate that 20% of farms are involved in tourism; 9.5% in providing accommodation; 5.5% in leisure-time activities and 4.5% in horse-riding activities (quoted in Shaw and Williams 1994).

The case of France stands out as an example of rural tourist development owing to its wide range of supply and the size of its accommodation capacity. In 1987, France had a supply of about 4 million beds or places to stay (apart from 11 million second homes) even though tourist activity only involved 2% of farmers (supplying something like 20 000 bed spaces); the figure has since risen but still does not surpass 4% (Grolleau 1987). In 1987 there were 35 000 *gîtes*; apart from being situated along the coastline, there were major spatial concentrations in Auvergne, Poitou-Charente, Limousin and Alsace, where guest-houses (*chambres d'hôtes*) were also common. At the same time, there were numerous holiday villages (providing social tourism services), one-third of which were built in the country but which attracted less than one-fifth of the clientele normally seeking this sort of accommodation. The number of camping–caravan sites on farmland (1027) was also fairly significant, as were the large areas reserved for natural camping sites, mainly located in Poitou–Charente (53), Limousin (51) and Auvergne (50). The aim of the promoters, the Association of Tourism in Rural Spaces (TER), and its European organisation, EUROTER, has been to supply a diverse range of facilities of recognised quality which are integrated within the local environment.

7.6 RURAL TOURISM AND LOCAL DEVELOPMENT

Those rural spaces which are distant from the dynamic cities and are not integrated as parts of larger urban regions (in other words, are in what may be termed medium and deep country) are going through a depression in many parts of Europe: there has been a crisis in traditional non-farming activities and in farming. The result has been large-scale outmigration from farms and from rural areas. There is demographic ageing, villages are being depopulated and abandoned (a crisis in the social fabric), and there are ever-increasing expanses of uncultivated land, whose brambles and undergrowth provide a fertile feeding ground for forest fires.

The repsonse to this crisis has been a search for local development strategies which are considered to be sustainable and which include activities that capitalise on local resources, especially those related to the environment, the landscape and the human and cultural heritage. The search for ways to increase value added and income has also meant diversifying farming and non-farming activity, and stimulating complementary tertiary activities with their synergies, among which is tourism. Throughout much of rural Europe, there is now a belief that tourism will be able to provide a new source of income and jobs, even if these are traditional rather than modern or innovative, and will mainly involve female employment. There are also expectations that tourism will break down social isolation and will help to foster new social and cultural relationships. Tourism has the capacity to facilitate the repopulation of rural areas with younger people (even if this is, mostly, on a temporary basis), and revitalise semi-abandoned places (Cavaco 1993). It should be able to tap into new consumer groups and wealthy clienteles who want to buy specialised, high-quality farm foods as well as other types of goods, especially handicrafts. Furthermore, tourism should also generate service sector growth, including those segments which are traditionally tourism-oriented such as accommodation, recreation, sports and cultural activities. To a certain extent, the increasing priority given to rural tourism is understandable given its economic and social significance to rural areas, as well as the need to diversify away from mass tourism which is posing increasingly difficult challenges for planners.

For the most part, tourist consumption occurs at the tourist sites themselves but it does generate considerable multiplier effects throughout local societies and economies. However, these impacts are ultimately dependent on the numbers of incoming visitors and their purchasing power. Needless to say, this has tended to improve owing to the recomposition of the demand for rural tourism, as new market segments replace the traditional model of economic holidays for neo-urban families. The new models of rural tourism have different consumer behaviour profiles which vary with the kind and price of accommodation chosen and with the age of the visitors.

One of the key challenges is to ensure that there is higher additional spending on consumer services (going beyond the essential accommodation, food and transport). It is also essential that minimum quality standards are achieved in the industry; otherwise, the future of tourism in a locality will be at risk and this will jeopardise its potential role as a vector of development. Therefore, there have to be minimum levels of professionalism which, in turn, imply the training and adaptation of all those involved—including management, activity organisers, tourist guides and inspectors. It is also essential that there is investment in different types of installations/facilities and complementary services apart from providing accommodation, eating places and transport.

Tourist development should have considerable potential for attracting visitors to the rural environment in the future, because there is the capacity to provide a wide range of 'healthy' leisure-time activities: for example, swimming-pools, tennis courts, golf courses, fishing and hunting grounds, horse-riding, walking, bicycle rides, traditional handicrafts, nature-watching, learning how to farm and cook regional dishes, or learning about local customs and traditions. To be able to deliver these sorts of activities, usually implies some degree of collective organisation.

Further development of rural tourism raises the issue of whether initiatives should be spatially diffused or concentrated, even if such tourism spaces are not very densely developed. This, in turn, depends on the type of rural settlement and the amount and extent of genuinely high-quality natural and historical resources, and heritage links. It also depends on existing infrastructures which are the outcome of previous rounds of investment, the accessibility of places, the facilities available for tourism promotion, and the availability of consumer services—which should always be small and medium sized, and therefore suitably adapted to entrepreneurial capacities in a rural, farming environment. Even if this last condition is met, this does not invalidate the need for, and convenience of, setting up special associative organisations for hunting, fishing or horse-riding, or for marketing tourist products and services.

From a theoretical point of view, rural tourism could be expected to generate income and jobs in rural areas. This could either be from direct engagement in tourist activity or from being in work which has been induced and encouraged by the multiplier effects of tourist spending: the real estate markets, the building trade and public works, furnishing and decorating, gardening and domestic service, children's nannies, handicrafts, fishing nurseries and rearing animals for hunting. Unfortunately, there is a lack of detailed research available which would allow us to predict the employment effects with any degree of certainty. Nevertheless, there is some consensus in the literature that, in terms of accommodation, restaurants, shops and non-specialised services, tourism would mainly help to protect the number of jobs already available and to correct imbalances in underemployment. If such positive effects can be realised, then this would be one way to avoid fragmentation, and the functional and social isolation of a marginalised rural world.

The complementary relationship between direct and indirect jobs and incomes is equally applicable to farming and, in particular, to farmers' wives and other family members. It is precisely in the services which are additional to food and accommodation that more new jobs will become available, even if it means part-time, seasonal work. This last aspect is unlikely to change, for rural tourism is essentially seasonal in nature, even if this is not necessarily limited to the summer period. Another reservation is that these rural tourist units are very often economically unstable and tend to rely on unskilled or poorly trained, low-paid workers.

From an economic point of view, rural tourism is expected to create wealth for people living in the region, via both profits and wages. This is more likely to be facilitated when the business is endogenous, relatively small (and perhaps profit-sharing) and artisanal (with limited investment per employee). It is also easier when rural tourism is integrated in diversified entrepreneurial and family structures, where the norm is pluriactivity and there is diverse sourcing of income.

The Integrated Rural Tourism Development Programmes for Andalusia have demonstrated the advantages of an integrated approach to planning which respects the environment (Marchena et al. 1992, pp. 101–105). It should be stressed, however, that rural tourism should not be regarded as an economic panacea; instead, the potential of rural tourism should be objectively and realistically assessed. There is already sufficient experience of rural tourism in some areas to make it possible to attempt such an assessment. In Norway, rural tourism provides almost two-thirds of the GNP linked to tourism (Greffe 1992, p. 131).

The danger is that the tourist economy, therefore, may come to dominate over other economic sectors, giving rise to the problem of overloading the tourism carrying capacity, with environmental, social and cultural consequences. For example, in Wallonia there were 47 holiday villages in 1979, of which 47% were in Dutch, 27% in Flemish, 9% in Walloon and 3% in Brussels ownership. The capacity of two-thirds of these tourist complexes largely exceeded the number of inhabitants in the nearest village. Also of interest is a survey by Mamday (1992, p. 614) for Coltines, a small rural parish of Cantal, which did not boast any important or exceptional natural or historical attractions although it did have rural tourism which was developed in an integral way. This noted that the population of the area increased and its mean age dropped in relation to the intensity of rural tourism. The local heritage was also restored. Accommodation, holiday camps, leisure areas and ski resorts were built, and an enhanced associative life was encouraged by the recreational and other projects which were developed by the local council, associations and others, so as to attract visitors.

In other cases, the rural tourism ingredients have been even stronger, such as on the small island of Amargos in the Cyclades archipelago situated between Attica and Rhodes. The island measures 126 sq. km and had 1636 inhabitants in 1991, 330 of whom lived in the island's main settlement. The economy was traditional and semi-municipal; it was based on farming and herding, small-scale crops and some fishing. Emigration to Athens and abroad (the USA and Australia) was pronounced, as was the number of men enlisting in the merchant navy. Recently there has been rapid development of tourism, with a subsequent rise in building and tertiary activities. This has led people to leave their farms and to turn them into pasture land for sheep and goats. Tourism also brought about other changes. Until the mid 1960s, the island had a poorly developed infrastructure: its quayside was largely unusable by larger boats, and there was a lack of electricity, running water in each home, roads suitable for motor cars, telephones or a heliport. By the mid 1990s it had all of these; apart from making living conditions less harsh, these infrastructures have opened up the potential for tourist development. Today the island is populated by Greeks who regularly and faithfully return to their birthplaces and live in their (modest or middle-class) family homes. It is also visited by many touring foreigners who wish to view the fourteenth-century Benedictine monastery.

Demand triggered off real-estate investments as well as work to rebuild houses, new guest-rooms and outbuildings and to install new standards of domestic comfort. By 1987 the island offered 416 beds in 196 legally registered rooms let by some 37 families. This almost entirely depended on small companies and local initiatives, rather than real-estate investment from Athens. New cafés, restaurants and bars appeared alongside new tearooms, discotheques, specialised shops, handicraft shops (selling ceramics, woven cloths and woollen goods) and souvenir shops. Kolodny (1992, p. 668) concluded that renting real estate has undoubtedly brought economic benefits for the islanders. The boom in the building trade raised the price of land and ensured an almost 'permanent' supply of jobs for skilled and semi-skilled builders, carpenters and lorry-drivers. Rental income has been invested locally creating new jobs and opportunities, so that young people returning from Athens often see no reason why they should leave again. All this has happened despite the fact that there has been no coordination whatsoever of the development, no physical planning, no building regulations, and no formal organisation of tourism services.

It is important not to be deceived by the illusions of economic success. It is inevitably very difficult to integrate tourism with local, traditional and fatalistic societies which are in danger of remaining on the fringes of the new economic dynamics which have been activated by tourism. This has been the case of La Chaise-Dieu (Auvergne), where the Benedictine abbey has been revived by an internationally famous music festival attracting people from all over the world. It has also been the case of Margeride, with its eco-museum, that has a most pedagogical and cultural aim, and is interested in making economic use of the area's historical and ethnographical heritage. The local population, however, has always shown a marked lack of enthusiasm for, and been largely uninterested in, the project. Even in Périgord Noir, which has been particularly endowed with beautiful scenery, sites to visit and places of heritage, tourism is 'une chance de développement du Périgord, mais une parmi d'autres, pas plus (. . .) si précieux qu'il soit pour l'économie locale et n'est pas, bien sûr, facteur de croissance démographique (. . .). Le solde migratoire positif est surtout du à la venue de retraités. Et il est tourjours aussi difficile de trouver un emploi et de vivre au pays . . .' (Genty 1992, p. 580).

Apart from a certain amount of tourist development in Creuse (Trina, 1992), the region has continued to be a rural area suffering from economic difficulties. The rural population has left in large numbers, the population has aged and there seem to be no attractive, flexible alternative ways to diversify the local economy. Although it has a well-protected, natural environment that is peaceful, calm and restful, and although it is rich in waterside sites, such as fish-stocked streams, and boasts shady forested areas, varied landscapes and peasant architecture, tourist accommodation is sorely lacking in terms of both quality and geographical dispersion. Furthermore, the accommodation stock is not well adapted to housing large numbers of coach-borne tourists. In addition, its management is best described as primitive, there is no professional training available, and efficiency levels are barely mediocre. There has also been a failure to develop cooperative ventures to improve marketing or to stimulate and widen the range of tourist activities, so that the clientele is highly seasonal and traditional. Creuse lacks an original and distinctive image as a tourist centre, and it is not surprising that tourism intermediaries have failed to promote it more widely. This illustrates some of the problems of those rural tourism development policies which tend to have sectoral rather than local or regional perspectives.

In Portugal, rural tourism has only really been successful in the Minho, mostly in the area around Ponte de Lima. The dominance of *turismo de habitaçâo*, with its emphasis on quality accommodation and services, has assured it has a high status and select clientele. The formation of an effective association of proprietors, with a single central reservations office, has made it possible for tourists to visit and stay in a number of places in the region as well as in other parts of the country. Ponte de Lima is a typically rural area of Minho. It farms in the traditional Minho way, growing maize and grapes for wine and, at the same time, raises cattle and utilises the pine forests. At present, it is attracting considerable funding from both domestic and foreign investors who are interested in the region's tourism potential. Farms are only one of the types of accommodation available for tourists. Indeed, in many cases, tourism has been an instrument for families to finance the rehabilitation of grand old family manor houses. In order to obtain artificially low interest rate loans and non-reimbursable subsidies, the families owning the manor houses have been obliged to sign 10-year tourist-rights agreements.

In other cases, the aim has been more commercial, namely to increase the value added of family estates by adjusting them to new forms of increasingly popular thematic or adventure tourism. For example, in the USA, many farm- ... enterprises raise birds and animals, and derive rental income from the use of hunters, photographers capturing wildlife on tourists on organised expeditions (Greffe 1992, p. 137). ting is increasing in importance in all the inland areas of more particularly in the Alentejo. This is also the case in most important hunting grounds are located in Salamanca

In summary, it may be stated that:

- Rural tourism is playing an increasingly important and diversified role in local development, mainly in terms of revitalising and reorganising local economies, and improving the quality of life, even in rural areas which seem to have no agricultural prospects or which have been plunged into industrial crises.
- Tourist flows can be interpreted as generators of wealth, at least with respect to complementary earnings, in certain farming, artisanal and tertiary structures, where they are able to assure the basic conditions for survival.
- Rural tourism has made it possible to realise the economic value of specific, quality-based production of foodstuffs, as well as of unused and abandoned family real estate, unique scenery, spaces and culture, even if many of the consumer goods are bought in urban retail outlets in the towns that many of the tourists originate from.
- Inward investment and the number of new firms established are both limited owing to the nature of rural tourism which is restricted in extent, dispersed and offers low returns on economic investment. This is even in the case with country hotels, tourist villages or clienteles which enjoy considerable purchasing power. This explains why there are so many instances where rational development strategies end in confusion between the roles of domestic and entrepreneurial economies.
- Despite frequently being characterised by marked host–guest social differences, rural tourism opens up the possibility of new social contacts, thus breaking down some of the isolation and the solitude enforced on the elderly and on people living alone in rural areas. It brings about a cultural exchange which eventually leads to a reshaping of the social fabric, and changes mentalities and values.
- Rural tourism offers the prospects of a revaluation of heritage and its symbolic monuments, of the environment and also of the identity of villages, places and areas so that they can acquire social value, dignity and a certain mobility.
- Rural tourism development strategies should always be mindful of the need for environmental protection and the physical planning of space, so that it is able to maintain diverse activities and forms of production in an area.

The rural tourist seeks out and visually consumes landscapes (particularly if it is unusual), the environment and wildlife, as well as monuments and redundant old buildings such as windmills and water-mills which have intrinsic ecological and cultural values. Given these conditions, it is not surprising that rural tourism has attracted special attention from the recent EU LEADER programme for areas 1 and 5b (as defined in the reform of European Regional Policy), in which an integrated approach to rural development has been proposed at local level. The programme has attracted a wide range of measures proposed by local action groups. They include providing assistance to rural development, training

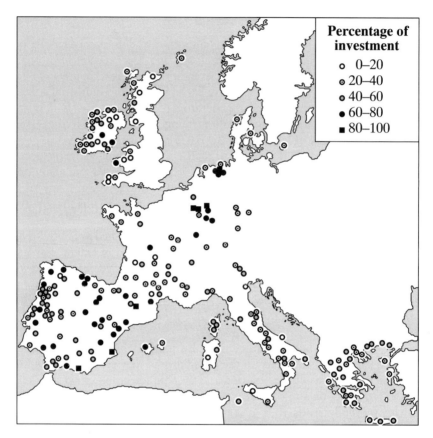

Figure 7.2. The EU's LEADER programme: proportion of investment in rural tourism.
Source: Commission of the European Union

measures, rural tourism, back-up for small and medium-sized firms, as well as
for the handicrafts industry, and improving the value added of farm produce.

The philosophy of the LEADER programme is based on fostering economic
diversification, and protecting both the natural and cultural environment and
the quality of rural life. It is not specifically a programme which is concerned
with tourism, but in 71 of the 271 LEADER areas investment in tourism has
been a leading activity. With respect to individual member states, more than
50% of investment was concentrated in Belgium, Germany and Portugal, as
against less than 35% in Italy, France or Denmark (see Figure 7.2). Nevertheless, rural tourism should not be viewed as the only, or necessarily the ideal,
solution to the problems of economic and social marginalisation in many
areas. It is merely one activity that should be undertaken in conjunction with
others, generating multiplier effects on modest, usually endogenous, investments, with care being taken not to unbalance overall development.

The limitations of the LEADER programme are evident if the projects of the LAGs (local action groups) in Portugal are analysed in detail, for many of these are merely plans for improving the face of local life: painting the façades of buildings, tidying up squares and public gardens, prettying up villages, restoring old wind- and water-mills for recreational purposes, building swimming-pools and leisure centres.

7.7   CONCLUSIONS

Higher average family incomes in the developed countries have led to the widespread adoption of the present Western European model of work–home–free time–holiday relationships. Despite some societal changes, the principal 'force' in most people's lives is still work; going on holiday provides a chance to break with daily routine and regain one's physical and mental strength. This period of renewed composure is therefore preparation for returning to work and to performing a job more effectively. While this generalisation has wide applicability, it is not the only source of motivation for holidays.

Once the reserve of the privileged few, holidays have now become a 'social victory'; holiday trips and summer spells at the seaside have been democratised and are available to the mass market. First, and even second, generation neo-urban dwellers in the lower-income brackets, who are unable to travel further afield, usually return to their 'home' villages at holiday time to meet up with their extended families or stay in the houses they have inherited; they have often restored and improved the latter, although not without considerable personal cost. Sometimes these houses have been completely rebuilt, as happens in the southern European countryside in areas where there has been heavy emigration. Less frequently, urban families with limited economic resources and/or small children, sometimes rent rooms or other sorts of rural accommodation. But whatever the form of this rural tourism, it remains the case that the seaside is still the principal and preferred objective of the tourist gaze of many of these people, even if high prices may oblige them to go camping or caravanning rather than stay in hotels or rented apartments.

During recent decades there has been a significant change in the urban population's systems of values and in their behavioural patterns. This has had repercussions on their life styles, especially their holidays: they place a higher value on quality, have a taste for living life more fully and for immediacy of consumption. This does not necessarily imply a heady commitment to materialist values, for many also appreciate nature more and place 'being' above 'having'.

One of the implications of these social trends is that, increasingly, tourists are seeking more sedentary holidays that favour communication and integration in the local communities they are visiting. This in turn leads to more harmonious, and more balanced economic, social and cultural relations. In effect, the outcome is a 'soft' version of tourism, wherein the number of visitors is adjusted to local and regional capacity, ensuring that the natural and social equilibrium is maintained. The outcome can be sustainable tourism, and holidays which are all the more savoured if they are divided up, spent in varied places, and motivated by diverse reasons that range from simply wanting to have a good rest, to wanting to immerse oneself in the environment, culture, sports or learning about traditional arts and crafts.

The new demand for new types of rural tourism mainly comes from a culturally urbanised population belonging to the upper-middle and upper strata of society. They are thoroughly versed in matters of geography, history and the environment and have the broader, wordly experience gained from urban living, from visiting cosmopolitan destinations and from many years of international travel. Visits to the countryside, therefore, enter into plans for personal portfolios of varied holidays which are divided up into sections/ weeks. These portfolios involve combinations of: distant, exotic journeys, spells at the beach or in the snow, sedentary stays in the countryside or, at least, tours around or overnight stops in the countryside.

As more holiday destinations appeared—chosen and promoted by the élite initially—then over time they inevitably became increasingly available to the masses. The élite would then move on to discover new sites that were less accessible, even if they were less comfortable, thus establishing new poles and tourist areas where the cycle would be repeated. We therefore have every reason to predict the beginning of a new cycle that favours the remotest rural areas, far away from the periurban fields and local/regional beaches primarily reserved for weekend leisure and second homes. However, this does beg the question of whether this new beginning, which is somewhat diffused or polarised into set spaces, displays the necessary conditions for long-term success.

The rural area has been reconstructed as a holiday space in view of various interacting factors: people's right to go on holiday; greater individual and collective ease of mobility; the idea that holidays should be spent away from home; the loss of the roots that many city-dwellers once had in the countryside; mass tourism promoting summer holidays at the seaside; the increasing demand for holidays for the elderly; the price competitivity of holidays in the countryside; and the demands made by the worldly and the experienced for high-quality and specialised services. All these changes call for marketing of rural areas and attempts to make them profitable, at several different levels.

These trends are occurring at the same time as many of the farms and nearby villages are in the process of being abandoned. These farms have lost out to more competitive farms in more productive areas. One particular outcome is that many farms, which have been included in natural parks and reserves or have been declared protected environments, are being deserted by their inhabitants. It is at this point that we can most clearly see the convergence of demand for rural and environmental tourism in these areas, and the importance of increasing the value added of tourism by means of developing a wide range of integrated rural tourism able to attract people to the locality.

The likelihood that tourism will be able to play a positive role in these processes depends upon many factors. They range from the independent nature of the initiatives taken and the way they are handled (sharing, training and controlling resources), to the scale on which such initiatives are carried out, the backing they receive in financial and legal terms, how they fit into the wider local framework, as well as the nature of the spaces in question and their localisation with regard to the clienteles interested in them.

It is a fact that people going to the countryside do so for only a few days (long weekends or a week) and that distance usually presents no problem in the cost of either air or car-travel time. Moreover, these types of new tourists are sensitive to safety issues and the humanisation of landscapes and accommodation. For this reason, it is important that the deep countryside, with vast areas classified and protected in terms of their environmental or landscape features, should not be demographically and culturally deserted areas, if they are to attract tourists. Investment will also be essential in order to ensure that they have the required basic infrastructures. In the intermediate countryside with its active farm-life, tourism ensures complementary incomes and activities and makes business ventures feasible in other types of trade and services.

Given the potential contribution of rural tourism to a wide variety of local economies, it is not surprising that, in many instances, the promotion of rural tourism has been integrated in territorial physical planning and development policies. Elsewhere, the impulse has come from farms seeking to become more profitable in terms of widening their range of activities and capitalising on their heritage, real estate and human and cultural spaces.

Rural tourism will not of course have a uniform impact on rural spaces. The urban exodus, involving the return of ageing or retired people to their villages and small towns in the deep country, will not spread out over space like an oil slick but, rather, will appear selectively. In the same way, the tourist potential of each area will be different and will work in favour of areas providing the best conditions for maintaining a minimum base of permanent residents. These are the areas that will most effectively be able to respond to the contemplative, cultural and active needs of their visitors.

This sort of tourism is classified as rural, owing to the destination that is chosen. However, the reasons behind the choice are many and varied. The tourist flees from the masses but also avoids the human desert. She or he seeks nature but also wants history, culture and social life. For this reason, rural tourism can never be considered a panacea or a miraculous solution for the deterioration and abandonment of vast rural areas.

8 Metropolitan Areas: Economic Globalisation and Urban Tourism

ARIE SHACHAR
The Hebrew University of Jerusalem, Israel

8.1 INTRODUCTION

Many cities in the Western world are undergoing a deep restructuring process of unparalleled dimensions and complexity. A few of these cities are emerging from this restructuring process to become 'world cities'—major nodes in a global control and management system, global financial centres and major attractions for businesspeople and visitors from all over the world. Examples of this new type of urban development are New York, London, Paris, Frankfurt and, in the Pacific realm, Tokyo and Los Angeles (Friedman 1986; Sassen 1991). In addition to these major metropolitan areas, some of the larger cities in North America, Europe and the Pacific Rim are acquiring economic roles which move them forward on the continuum of world cities' characteristics; eventually, they become world cities of a lower hierarchical level (Friedmann 1993; Shachar 1994).

Urban tourism is treated in this chapter as a major component in the process of globalisation of the economic bases of the emerging and fast crystallising world cities. The main thrust of this chapter will be to elaborate the role of urban tourism in the large metropolitan areas of the Western world, laying a strong emphasis on the economic, social and cultural roles of tourism in the globalisation processes of emerging world cities (Law 1994).

The major features of the urban restructuring processes which were dominant in the last generation are all related to a radical change in the economic base of these cities, a direct outcome of their massive deindustrialisation (Savitch 1988). The industrial base of many cities declined steadily due to two processes. The first was the closure of manufacturing plants, and the reduction of employment in warehousing and in heavy transportation. The decline in manufacturing activities was mainly the outcome of the new international division of labour which brought about a massive transfer of manufacturing activities to the countries of the European periphery and then to the newly industrialised countries, mainly in the western Pacific Rim. The second major

European Tourism: Regions, Spaces and Restructuring. Edited by A. Montanari and A.M. Williams.
© 1995 European Science Foundation. Published in 1995 by John Wiley & Sons Ltd.

process which led to the industrial decline of the big cities was the decentralisation of manufacturing activities out of their central areas and of the inner rings
of their metropolitan fringes, or just beyond these. There was relocation to
'greenfield' sites, completely separate from the metropolitan areas, or even to
national peripheries, stimulated by significant government incentives and support (Scott 1988).

The deindustrialisation process of the major cities brought about a massive
loss of jobs and increased unemployment, forcing the urban authorities to
search frantically for alternative sources of employment. These could only be
found in the service sector which, in the last generation, evolved as the leading
segment in the urban economy, having a higher than average growth rate and
income levels (Daniels 1991). Within the generally vital and expanding urban
service sector, tourism became a major component of the urban economic base
in many urban centres, providing new employment opportunities wherever it
developed into a major urban activity (Law 1992).

This chapter deals with one of the two main components of urban tourism,
namely its demand side. It does not examine the supply side, the production of
tourism services (but see Jansen-Verbeke 1988) and the commodification of
tourist attractions (Harvey 1989). This chapter is also not concerned with
another possible line of enquiry, the elaboration of the effects of tourism
consumption on the urban structure (Ashworth and Tunbridge 1990; Sorkin
1992). Instead, it deals with the main processes of a demographic and economic nature which influence the demand for urban tourism, focusing on the
impact of economic globalisation processes on the future evolution of urban
tourism.

8.2   METROPOLITAN TOURISM IN EUROPE: BASIC DATA

This section aims at providing the factual bases for the analysis of metropolitan tourism in Europe. It is a well-known truism that statistics of tourism,
especially urban tourism, are scarce, of dubious quality and inconsistent reli-
ability. Furthermore, due to the application of different definitions in different
countries, in most cases they are not comparable on an international basis. The
following brief review is based on a survey carried out by KPMG Consultants
(1993) on behalf of the VVV (the Tourist Agency) of the city of Amsterdam.
The main statistical results of this survey are presented in a new publication of
EURICUR, of the Erasmus University in Rotterdam (van den Berg et al. 1994).

The rank order of the major European cities in terms of tourism, in 1991, is
outlined in Table 8.1. This rank order, according to the number of nights
spent, is quite similar to that according to the number of arrivals. The one
exception is Rome, which is characterised (together with London) by a much
higher average length of stay than the other cities in this group.

The major European cities, ranked in terms of their level of attraction for
visitors, can clearly be divided into two groups: the first includes London and

Table 8.1.   Tourism in Europe's major metropolitan areas, 1991

	Arrivals	Nights spent	Average stay (days)
1. London	14 700 000	82 600 000	5.62
2. Paris	12 602 168	28 269 280	2.24
3. Munich	3 242 743	6 607 551	2.04
4. Rome	2 683 895	12 018 523	4.48
5. Vienna	2 637 572	6 717 752	2.55
6. Berlin	2 542 446	6 405 098	2.52
7. Milan	2 135 197	5 579 129	2.61
8. Brussels	2 045 800	3 035 000	1.48
9. Frankfurt	1 863 168	3 442 828	1.85
10. Barcelona	1 818 609	4 089 509	2.25

Source: van den Berg et al. (1994, p. 187).

Paris, which are cities of global attraction, with more than 12 million visitors per year; the second group includes the other cities in the list, which might be defined as European attractions, and these have approximately 2–3 million visitors each.

This two-level hierarchy, determined solely by the cities' attraction of visitors, corresponds quite well to the hierarchy of the European world cities, in which London and Paris are defined as the two cities with the highest levels in terms of the scale of world city characteristics (RECLUS/DATAR 1989; Parkinson et al. 1992). The identification of London and Paris as belonging to the upper level of the urban hierarchy of world cities, as well as the upper level of the urban hierarchy defined by the level of attraction to visitors, allows for a deeper exploration of the relationship between metropolitan tourism and the development of world cities.

A point of major importance in the economic role of urban tourism is the length of stay of visitors in a particular city. This is the most significant of all the variables affecting the economic benefits of urban tourism. Table 8.1 shows that, for most large European cities, the average stay is relatively uniform, ranging between 1.5 and 2.5 nights. The only obvious exceptions are London (average stay of 5.6 nights) and Rome (4.5 nights). Explanation of the much higher length of stay in London and Rome requires a specific study, but it is possible to speculate on the reasons for this singularity. For Rome, the longer stay can be related to the pilgrimage nature of the visits; for London, it can be attributed to the special combination of business and culture, for which that city is well known (HMSO 1991). From a policy point of view, any extension of stay in a particular city will produce considerable economic benefits and should therefore be encouraged by actions to improve existing tourist attractions and create new ones.

Metropolitan tourism is characterised by an inseparable combination of tourists and businesspeople both visiting a given destination. This is complicated even further by the fact that some of the business trips, such as participation in

Table 8.2. Leisure tourism as a proportion of domestic and foreign tourism market segments, 1991

| Cities | Total visitors | Leisure tourists as a percentage of: | |
		Domestic visitors	Foreign visitors
Antwerp	41	49	40
Barcelona	35	24	45
Berlin	41	33	65
Berne	60	33	75
Copenhagen	49	n.a.	n.a.
London	43	49	41
Milan	16	n.a.	40
Paris	40	n.a.	60
Rome	79	66	88
Salzburg	72	n.a.	90
Venice	65	n.a.	90

n.a. = not available.

Source: van den Berg et al. (1994, Annex II, p. 188).

conferences, turn into tourist trips after or before the conference. Many business travellers therefore contribute to the tourist industry by availing themselves of the cultural and entertainment facilities. Therefore, the segmentation of visitors between tourist and business trips, in the context of visits to the big cities, is not clear-cut and not very meaningful. Nevertheless, as some information on the breakdown of urban travel, according to the main purpose of the trip, is available (based on the KPMG survey 1993) for a few of the major European cities, this is presented here (Table 8.2).

On the basis of the data presented in Table 8.2, we can identify those cities in which the majority of visitors are holiday tourists: Rome, Salzburg, Venice and Berne. These are also cities where urban tourism is the backbone of the urban economy. In contrast, for most of the cities in this table, holiday tourists constitute between 40 and 50% of their visitors, and this is also true for the two European world cities, London and Paris. This distribution reflects a combination of business and vacation tourism as the two main attractions of these cities. Milan is singled out due to the very low proportion of holiday tourists among its visitors, reflecting the overwhelming business character of this city and the effective competition from other Italian cities for urban and cultural tourism.

All the big European cities attract visitors both from domestic and foreign markets. Almost invariably, the share of holiday tourists (as opposed to business tourists) is higher in the foreign than in the domestic market segment. This finding supports the notion of the international character of urban tourism, and emphasises that it has a strong export value. In this respect, international urban tourism can be seen to fit into the framework of the economic globalisation processes which currently are shaping the world economy.

The growth of the tourism market has been most pronounced since the early 1960s, making it one of the principal sectors of the world economy. The number of people crossing national borders for the purposes of visits, business, tourism and leisure can only be described as staggering, being estimated at about 400 million people a year at the beginning of the 1990s. The total economic output of these huge movements is estimated to be approximately $160 billion, which makes tourism the largest single sector of the world economy (van den Berg et al. 1994, p. 1).

The statistics on tourism are reasonably detailed and reliable in terms of the national origins and destinations of the tourists. But information on their specific destinations, in regional or urban terms, is incidental, of a poor standard and mostly unsuitable for comparative research. This may be the main reason for the very late recognition of an important major trend in world tourism: the rapid increase in the share of urban tourism in the total market for tourism in all the destinations. This is not to say that urban destinations only recently became important in European tourism. On the contrary, the 'Grand Tour' was composed of a glittering collection of urban places, big and small, old and new, which had to be visited along a predetermined and well-known itinerary. But these types of visits were quite exceptional and were reserved for a relatively few fortunate young men of means and talent. The destinations of the majority of tourists were resort areas on beaches, in mountains, in spas and, more generally, in nature, in open spaces, and in rural environments (Urry 1990). This trend fixed the image of tourism as being oriented towards the countryside, while urban centres—characterised as being crowded, noisy and filthy—were regarded only as the point of origin of the tourists.

8.3   FACTORS AFFECTING THE DEMAND FOR METROPOLITAN TOURISM

Urban tourism has become a major component of world tourism during the 1960s and the 1970s. The 'massification' of urban tourism was motivated by several factors, some of which pertain to the general rise of tourism while others are specific in enhancing its urban component (Williams and Shaw 1991c). The factors contributing to the general increase in tourism are well known and will, therefore, not be discussed here. But it is worth while to elaborate on the reasons for the recent increase in urban tourism.

A major factor affecting urban tourism is the changing age-structure of the European population (Shaw and Williams 1994, Chapter 3). With the 'greying' of Europe, the number of families with children is fast diminishing. While family tourism is mainly oriented towards areas of recreation, sport, beach and open space activities, more elderly couples and singles prefer urban settings and the forms of entertainment in an urban milieu. It is hypothesised that the smaller the number of children per family, then the larger will be the number of 'empty-nested' families, and the greater will be the market share of urban tourism.

The average expenditure on urban tourism (per person, per day) is higher than the unit revenue of recreational tourism in a non-urban location. This is the result of the fact that urban tourism includes a significant component of shopping, entertainment and cultural activities. Accommodation in cities, especially the metropolitan ones, is also more expensive than in the country-side and in small towns. This feature of urban tourism relates its demand to the level of income of the tourists. In Western Europe, the disposable income of households has been increasing steadily due to the rise in salaries and to a higher level of participation of women in the labour force. It is hypothesised that the demand for urban tourism has a positive elasticity of more than a unit and, therefore, an increase in disposable income will strongly affect the demand for urban tourism, increasing its market share of general tourism demand.

Another important reason for the rapid expansion of demand for urban tourism lies in the steady improvement in the level of education over the last generation in all parts of Europe. The higher the level of education, the deeper is what may be termed cultural curiosity and the eagerness to participate in the numerous cultural activities provided in major cities. It can be hypothesised that the more educated the tourists are, the more interested they will be in becoming acquainted with the historical and cultural heritage of their own and other countries, usually concentrated in capital cities and in a handful of other big cities (Ritchie and Zins 1978). Better education stimulates an interest in the arts, the theatre, music and opera, and in all types of entertainment and artistic performances. From the supply side, the economic threshold for most of these activities is very high, which means that they can operate successfully in only the largest cities which have national and international service hinterlands. This geographical patterning of the performing arts in the culture industries gives urban tourism a strong metropolitan character, with an emphasis on the world cities which occupy the highest level of the global urban hierarchy.

The demand for urban tourism has also grown because of the marked in-crease in leisure time, due to shorter working weeks and more flexible working schedules (WTO 1983, p. 16). These new patterns of work schedules allow for 'mini-breaks', usually short vacations of 2–3 days. Such a short break does not permit very long travel time. Therefore, preference is given to the big cities as tourist destinations, as these have much higher levels of accessibility by all modes of transportation (Pigram 1983, p. 25).

The demand for urban tourism is, of course, also affected by developments on the supply side. In particular, the new rapid ground transportation net-work, which is extending over many parts of Western Europe, will allow travel over much longer distances in a shorter travel time, thus opening a vast poten-tial market for metropolitan tourism. The spatial structure of these networks will enhance the accessibility and attractiveness of the major nodes of the urban system in air transport, continuing deregulation—and the ensuing competition between airlines—will lower the airfares to most destinations.

Furthermore, it will open new tourist opportunities for cheap packages to the major urban centres.

8.4 BUSINESS TRAVEL AND METROPOLITAN TOURISM

The demand for urban tourism has been strongly affected by the explosive increase in business travel. This increase has two main expressions: regular business travel needed for business meetings, consultations and management contacts; the other type is travelling to mass gatherings, in the form of conferences, conventions and trade fairs. Each of these is considered in further detail.

Regular business travel is the outcome of the need for face-to-face contact between businesspeople, mainly those in the upper echelons of their organisations. The more complex the business decisions, the stronger the need for interpersonal exchange (Castells 1989). It has become evident that recent technological breakthroughs in telecommunications are not a substitute for personal interaction but, on the contrary, give more importance and prevalence to such exchanges. This type of business travel strongly shapes the flows of businesspeople among the major urban centres, in which are located the headquarters of big corporations, of financial institutions, and a multitude of producer services (Amin and Thrift 1992). The figures available for some European cities on the division between business and leisure travel indicate that, in almost all cases, the share of business travel is much higher than that of leisure. Except for Edinburgh, which is unique in attracting large numbers of holiday tourists because of its famous festival, the other cities benefit mostly from business travellers who greatly outnumber the leisure tourists (Table 8.3).

The point which is emphasised here is that urban tourism is constituted not only of leisure travellers, but is also strongly influenced by business travellers, many of whom stay overnight in their urban destination, enjoying their cultural and entertainment facilities and even spending some time in the city's museums or visiting historical attractions (Law 1991). Many of the business travellers also indulge in shopping for specialised items of local character and

Table 8.3. Business and leisure tourism in selected cities, 1991

	Bed-nights in hotels (millions)	Percentage	
		Business	Leisure
Antwerp	n.a.	65	35
Copenhagen	2.9	62	38
Edinburgh	4.4	30	70
Glasgow	n.a.	75	25
Lyons	2.7	92	8

n.a. = not available.

Source: van den Berg et al. (1994, p. 161).

quality. We can thus conclude that the sharp distinction between business and leisure travellers is not very meaningful and that the marked increase in business travellers will cause a parallel increase in terms of urban leisure tourism, in many of its facets.

The recent growth in the importance of business travel in the development of urban tourism is a direct outcome of the internationalisation of the world economy. It is, of course, true that business travel to the major urban centres has been a well-established phenomenon since the early emergence of international trading. But only recently has this attained such a substantial share of the urban travel market. This is a result of the rapid pace of the internationalisation of the world economy which brought about a marked increase in the demand for business travel (Petersen and Belchambers 1990).

The business traveller contributes significantly to the urban economic base as his or her spending power is considerably higher than that of the leisure traveller. It has been estimated that a business traveller spends three times more per day than the leisure traveller (Lawson 1982). The fast pace of growth of business travel has given it a distinct share of the urban tourism market. The latest available figures indicate that, at the beginning of the 1990s, business travel accounted for about 30% of all international tourism (WTO 1991). The combination of the increased numbers of business travellers and their high spending capacity will make business travel the main stimulus in the future growth of urban tourism and its economic impact.

The spatial pattern of the main flows of business travel is composed of three components: travel among the world cities—the financial centres, and the command and control centres of the world economy; travel between the world cities and the regional headquarters of multinational corporations; and, thirdly, travel between them and the sites of production dispersed in many parts of the world, mainly in the newly industrialised countries of the world semi-periphery (Hymer 1975; Dicken 1992).

No detailed data are available on the magnitude of the flows of business travel between the three levels of management of the world economy. It is only possible to hypothesise that the largest stream will be among the world cities themselves (New York, London, Tokyo, Paris, Frankfurt and Los Angeles) and between the world cities and the regional headquarters of multinational corporations (Cohen 1981). As the world economy becomes increasingly integrated, the flows of travellers in these two types of business travel will tend to strengthen, which will also tend to augment the positions of the major metropolitan areas of the world.

Conference tourism represents the second facet of business travel of both national and international organisations. Across the world, and particularly in North America and Europe, conventions, congresses and fairs constitute a growth sector of urban tourism. The modern convention industry started in the USA and evolved into a major activity, spreading out to engulf Europe as well (Smith 1989). At the end of the 1980s, the number of meetings and conventions of all types in the USA went over the million mark per year, the value of the North American convention market being estimated at around $45 billion a year, and the number of delegates and participants as approximately 74 million (Smith 1990). The British conference market at the same period was estimated at about 700 000 meetings and conferences (Coopers Lybrand 1990).

There is considerable diversity in the conference market. Many corporate, associational and academic conferences are quite small, often comprising no more than 100 delegates or so, while the major associations, political parties and unions may convene thousands or even tens of thousands of participants at their conferences. Many of the big conferences are international in nature, attracting delegates and representatives of the mass media from all parts of the world. Some of the UN conferences, such as the Earth Summit in Rio de Janeiro (1992), or the Population and Development Conference in Cairo (1994), are truly global in nature, amassing tens of thousands of delegates from all the countries of the world. Another example of the size these gatherings can reach is the International Rotary Meeting convened at the International Exhibition Centre in Birmingham which was attended by 23 000 delegates. Because of the very large number of participants at international conferences, and the relatively long duration of the meetings, they are regarded as being of major economic benefit to the cities where they convene. As a result, cities compete fiercely to be the venue of these conferences (Var et al. 1985).

For a city to be a centre of international conferences, it has to fulfil several demanding requirements. To name the most important ones: a very high level of accessibility, especially in terms of air travel and, more recently, even in terms of very fast train networks; modern, spacious and well-equipped conference facilities; and a large stock of high-quality accommodation. A further feature is more elusive but of greater importance in attracting international conferences to a particular city: it is a positive urban image which will please not only the delegates but, more importantly, their 'accompanying persons' (Shaw and Williams 1994, p. 39).

Only a relatively few cities can offer the entire bundle of these requirements, giving the major European world cities—Paris and London—the leading edge in hosting international conferences. Trailing behind are capital cities, such as Madrid and Brussels, or cities with a strong international character, such as Geneva. As attendance at international conferences and conventions is becoming an integral part of the way of life in the growing business and professional world, urban tourism is likely to be strongly stimulated by this type of business travel in future.

8.5   CONCLUSION

In conclusion, this chapter has presented several hypotheses regarding the effects of demographic and economic processes on the demand for urban tourism. These hypotheses need to be tested and validated empirically. But it does not seem to be unreasonable to conclude that the 'greying' of the European population, on the one hand, combined with the growing globalisation of the economy, on the other, will tend to bring about a major increase in the volume of urban tourism in the future. This increase in demand from urban visitors and tourists will be strongly stimulated by major investments by public–private partnerships in the creation of new primary attractions, such as cultural and entertainment facilities, special events and festivities, and the physical and symbolic articulation of heritage areas. For the business and conference visitors, the secondary elements of hotels, restaurants and conference facilities might even assume the role of primary attractions. The consumption of urban tourism, combined with investment in the production of tourist services and of new tourist attractions, might propel urban tourism into becoming the major economic dynamism of post-industrial internationally oriented cities.

Part III

TRANSNATIONALISATION

9 Capital and the Transnationalisation of Tourism

ALLAN M. WILLIAMS
University of Exeter, UK

9.1 INTRODUCTION: SOME THEORETICAL ISSUES

Tourism has a highly dualistic industrial structure which is polarised between large numbers of small firms (typically in retailing, and accommodation services) and a small number of large companies (for example, in air transport). Over time this structure has been subject to change due to the transnationalisation of tourism activity. This is, in part, the outcome of an expansion of international travel in the post-war period, especially since the late 1950s, reflecting both the internationalisation of business travel (Hymer 1975) and the growth of mass leisure tourism (Shaw and Williams 1994, Chapter 10). The precise form of internationalisation has varied between sectors: business hotels and some of the niche markets for specialised tours have been subject to globalisation tendencies, while—until recently—the mass leisure tourism market has been subject to a Europeanisation of tourism activity. The process of internationalisation has been advanced by both merger and acquisition activity as well as by 'greenfield' investments. Examples of the former include Ladbroke's (UK) takeover of the Hilton International chain, ITT Sheraton's (USA) 1993 purchase of CIGA, the debt-laden Italian hotel chain, and Bass's (UK) purchase of the giant Holiday Inn group.

The internationalisation of tourism activity and investment has to be seen in context of the more general and increasingly rapid process of globalisation of international investment. For example, Julius (1990) reports that whereas total foreign direct investment (FDI) grew at twice the rate of GDP in the world economy in the 1960s, it was growing at four times this rate in the 1980s. Virtually all this FDI originates, and some three-quarters is located, in the developed countries. There are no precise data available on the tourism sector but the geographical pattern of FDI is likely to be broadly comparable. There are several reasons for the internationalisation of tourism FDI. In part it is related to the internationalisation of demand, which in turn is the outcome of the cultural redefinition of valued leisure time and activities (Urry 1990),

European Tourism: Regions, Spaces and Restructuring. Edited by A. Montanari and A.M. Williams.
© 1995 European Science Foundation. Published in 1995 by John Wiley & Sons Ltd.

as well as of the cost reductions in international travel. Tourism services have to be delivered in the form of face-to-face contacts at the tourist sites, so that there has been a strong market logic driving the internationalisation of FDI and tourist company activity.

In addition, tourism has been subject to some of the same internationalisation pressures as have other branches of economic activity. Porter (1985, 1986), writing on the global economy, argues that firms' competitive strategies are based on seeking cost leadership, product differentiation, and focusing on market niches; under certain circumstances these may dictate the internationalisation of tourist activity and investment. The same features can be seen to apply to tourist firms in Europe. For example, tour companies may seek cost leadership in the mass market by establishing holiday packages in leading low-cost destination countries, by focusing on product differentiation (holidays in the 'real' Spain, discovering the secrets of Portugal, etc.) and on niche markets (such as high valued added hunting or gastronomic holidays).

Dunning's (1977) eclectic theory of multinational activity can also be applied to explain the transnational activity in the tourism sector. According to this theory there are three main reasons for multinational activity: firms enter international markets for offensive and defensive purposes with respect to 'ownership' advantages such as a brand name; in order to reduce uncertainty by 'internalising' the use of ownership-specific advantages; and to seek out 'location-specific advantages' which are only available in particular sites. This theory provides an important conceptual peg for considering the transnationalisation of tourism activity, not least because Dunning and McQueen (1982) have already applied this theory to the hotel industry.

Care must be taken not to over-generalise concerning the transnationalisation of tourism capital. Transnational activity in the tourism sector is highly uneven between sectors in both its degree of penetration and in its form. This chapter uses Dunning's eclectic theory as a starting point to investigate some of these differences. Given the constraints of space, the discussion concentrates on three of the sectors in which multinationalisation of activity is more fully developed: air travel, hotels and tour companies. It should be emphasised, however, that these operate alongside several sectors where small firms dominate, such as leisure retailing, and some forms of self-catering accommodation.

9.2 INTERNATIONAL AIRLINES: TRUE TOURISM TRANSNATIONALS?

In 1992 there were an estimated 130 airlines in Western Europe providing jet services to the scheduled and the charter markets (McGowan 1994). There was, however, a high degree of concentration in the industry with only three airlines—Air France, Lufthansa and British Airways—flying more than 50 000

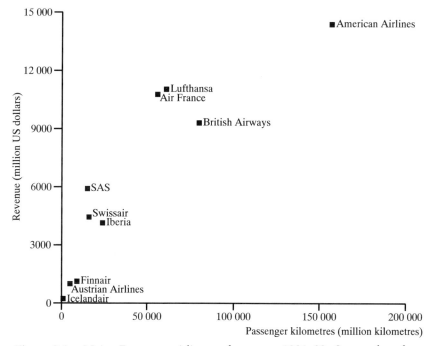

Figure 9.1. Major European airline performance, 1991–92. Source: based on data provided in McGowan (1994, p. 17)

passenger kilometres (Figure 9.1). Yet this is a tourism sector in which transnationalisation is extremely well developed.

One of the reasons for the high level of transnational activity in this sector is the massive investment required in a high technology product in order to operate in European markets. It was technological advances which led to a sharp real decline in unit operating costs in the 1950s through to the mid 1970s, and which facilitated the growth of airline services (Doganis 1985). The large capital outlay required to purchase aircraft and supporting installations, and to constantly update air fleets, also dictated the need for large and relatively secure markets so as to recover costs. The same logic applied to the introduction of computer reservation systems in the 1980s and 1990s; only the largest companies had sufficient resources to invest in the most sophisticated systems but these, in turn, provided the large carriers with significant marketing advantages.

Unlike the USA, the fragmentation of the European market into relatively small national market segments dictated far more strongly that major airlines would have to internationalise in order to secure enhanced market shares. In Europe this is potentially a very competitive business because short routes have relatively high costs per passenger kilometre compared to, say, transcontinental routes: this is due to the large amounts of fuel required for take-off, difficulties in maximising capital (the fleet) and labour (the crew) on short flights, and the charges associated with landing, ground handling and traffic control.

The large airline companies have responded to these and other pressures by seeking to benefit from what Dunning terms 'ownership' and 'internalisation' advantages. Multinationalisation has been essential to those airlines which have sought to capitalise on 'ownership' of a brand image, because there are significant economies of scale in branding, advertising and marketing, especially in the wake of developing computer reservation systems (McGowan 1994). There are also economies of scale involved in realising 'internalisation' advantages, and these again dictate the need for transnationalisation. This is most clearly seen in the way major airlines operate networks of systems of hubs and spokes. Typically, this allows airlines to carry passengers on one route (a spoke) to a central hub from where they can transfer to other spokes. Ensuring that all these journeys are taken on one company's flights—that is, internalisation—will both increase and help guarantee market share. In order to realise these internalisation advantages, however, the airlines have to invest in a relatively widespread system of spokes to a large network of countries. Incidentally, we can note that such a strategy implies '. . . significant sunk cost commitments for new entrants and considerable advantages to incumbent operators' (McGowan 1994, p. 3); that is, it is a difficult industry for new-comers to break into on any significant scale.

These essential reasons for the transnationalisation of airline activity have been reinforced in recent years by other pressures for concentration including the impact of recession on demand, fuel price increases, competition from charter airlines and chronic over-capacity in some market segments. This has led individual companies to seek out new alliances, mergers and acquisitions, and also new international 'greenfield' investments in order to enhance their competitiveness. Any one company may engage a combination of such mea-sures in order to strengthen its position in international markets, as is demon-strated by British Airways (Figure 9.2). By 1994 it had established a major presence in Russia, Denmark, the USA, Australia, France and Germany via its alliances and acquisitions which were in addition to the direct operations of the parent company in these and other countries.

While the need to secure economies of scale is important in the trans-nationalisation of airline activity, it should not be thought that this process has occurred in a competitive market. Instead, air transport '. . . has been shaped in the past by the combined forces of sovereignty, nationalism and protection-ism' (Wheatcroft 1990, p. 353). Most European countries have a 'national flag carrier' and many of these such as Aer Lingus (100%), Air France (90%), Alitalia (85%) and Iberia (100%) remain completely or largely in state owner-ship. Their competition is moderated by strict market bilateral sharing ar-rangements, which are designed to protect the positions of national carriers. This partly explains the existence of such large variations in efficiency among

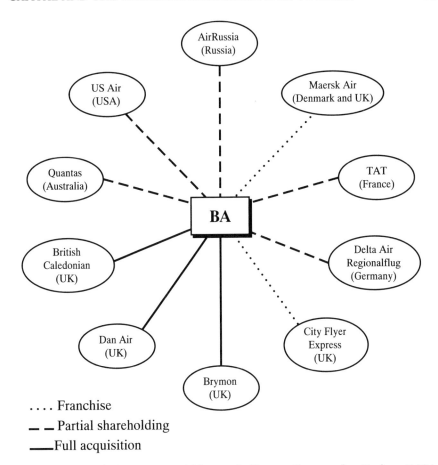

Figure 9.2. British Airways: acquisitions and alliances. Source: after Graham (1994, p. 94)

the main carriers, as is indicated by a crude comparison of their revenues and of the passenger kilometres flown (Figure 9.1).

Despite this highly regulated environment, the national airlines—which mostly operate in the scheduled market segment—have been experiencing increasing real competitive pressures from two main sources. Firstly, their market share is under pressure from the charter airline companies which operate in a far less regulated market segment. Since 1975 the latter have captured a larger proportion of the market by volume than have the scheduled companies; in 1990 this amounted to a 56% share of the total European market (Economist Intelligence Unit 1991). The second set of pressures emanates from the EU's declared intention to create a single aviation market by 1997, in which EU companies will be able to offer services between any two points within the Union irrespective of their nationalities. Even though it is likely that various means will be found to contravene the spirit of EU legislation (for example, a failure to license new services because of airport congestion), there is still likely to be a significant increase in the level of competition. This could bring about a major shake-out in the industry, and if the USA experience of deregulation is anything to go by—where the airlines collectively lost $10 billion, 1990–92 (*Financial Times* 18 June 1993)—then a series of bankruptcies and/or further concentration can be anticipated.

9.3   HOTELS: AN UNEVEN PATTERN OF TRANSNATIONALISATION

Dunning and McQueen (1982) have provided a detailed assessment of the relevance of the eclectic theory of multinationals to an analysis of the hotel sector. They argue that all three of the principal reasons for transnationalisation can apply. First, there is the 'ownership' factor whereby prestigious chains such as Hilton and Sheraton seek to capitalise on their brand images, which convey clear impressions of the quality and the range of services to be provided; this ensures that the services provided match the aspirations of their customers, which is one element in generating brand loyalty. It is proprietary rights over a differentiated product which essentially creates the ownership conditions for transnationalisation in this sector. Secondly, they seek to internalise transactions within the corporation and, therefore, prefer a direct presence in foreign markets rather than subcontracting (except where this is carried out via franchising). Thirdly, they seek to capitalise on locational advantages which in the case of hotels means having a presence in most of the principal locations that their regular customers are likely to visit.

The extent of the transnationalisation tendencies is evident in Table 9.1 which lists the 10 largest quoted hotel companies in the EU. This 'league table' is dominated by French and UK capital; these are also the two countries which have the largest hotel sectors in Europe. However, the tendency to increasing

Table 9.1.   Top 10 quoted hotel companies in the EU, 1992

Chain	Nationality	Total no. of hotel rooms
Accor	France	112810
Forte	UK	36750
Louvre	France	25576
Queens Moat Houses	UK	21123
Ladbroke	UK	15164
BIL Mont Charlotte	New Zealand	14170
Bass	UK	11944
Saison	Japan	9530
ITT	USA	8038
Rank	UK	6939

Source: After Slattery and Johnson (1993, p. 68).

globalisation of hotel capital is also reflected in the presence of Japanese-, New Zealand- and US-owned companies. Furthermore, this is not a one-way flow of inward investment, for there have also been purchases of American chains by European companies; Bass's purchase of Holiday Inn and Ladbroke's of the Hilton International chain both exemplify this. The exact model of transnationalisation can assume one of several forms, not least because there can be an economic rationale for firms to separate the ownership of the hotel as a property asset from the business of providing tourism services. Thus hotels may be owned outright, but they may also be franchised (common to Holiday Inn for example) or be run under management contracts (as is favoured by Resorts Hotels of the UK).

The conditions for the multinationalisation of hotel activity identified by Dunning and McQueen are in fact peculiar to the international business

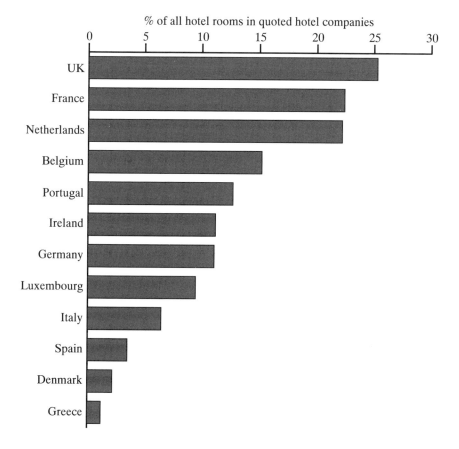

Figure 9.3.   Concentration of hotel rooms in quoted hotel companies in the EU, 1992. Source: based on Kleinwort and Benson Securities data quoted in Slattery and Johnson (1993, p. 67)

tourism market segment. This is certainly an important market segment. It has been estimated, for example, that total business travel (domestic and international) is valued annually at more than $94 billion in Germany, France and the UK (*Financial Times* 9 November 1993). Nevertheless, this is only one market segment, which explains why most hotels are not in transnational ownership, or even in national chains, but are instead independently owned. There is a lack of reliable data on the transnational structures of the European hotel industry, but we do have some data on corporate structures. In particular, data have been collated on the proportions of the hotel rooms in Europe which belong to quoted companies (Figure 9.3); only in the UK, France and the Netherlands do the figures exceed 20%. While non-quoted status does not necessarily indicate either smallness or independent ownership, it is at least indicative that most of the hotel sector is not in transnational ownership.

The reasons for the limited corporate ownership—let alone transnational ownership—can be explained by two factors. First, small firms are particularly adept at surviving. They do so via two possible strategies. Either they reduce their costs substantially through self-exploitation of their own and their families' labour (working long hours for poor returns), or they emphasise the quality of the highly personalised services that they provide, for which they are able to charge a premium over and above that pertaining to the range and quantity of services and facilities that they offer. Secondly, in the mass tourism market, the conditions of production favour the operations of tour companies which traditionally subcontract to local hotel owners rather than being direct investors in accommodation services. This latter feature is examined in more detail in the following section.

9.4   THE ROLE OF THE INTERNATIONAL TOUR COMPANIES: VERTICAL AND HORIZONTAL LINKAGES

Until recently, there has been surprisingly little FDI in the mass tourism industry. For example, in Spain—the principal European example of a mass destination country—the leading 65 hotel groups (not identical with the quoted companies discussed earlier) own 31% of all hotel capacity; however, only one in four have any foreign capital participation and in only one in eight groups does this exceed 50% of their total capital (Estudios Turísticos 1988). This can be explained in terms of the overall structure of the international mass tourism industry, which is dominated by tour companies, and in terms of Dunning and McQueen's eclectic theory of multinationals.

There are some 'ownership' advantages in the mass tourism industry and these have been cornered by the tour companies which have the resources to finance mass advertising and marketing costs, including the printing of brochures in runs of tens of thousands or, for the largest companies, in runs of hundreds of thousands or even millions. The enormous costs involved can only be recouped by the tour companies which have the potential to realise economies of scale from selling massive numbers of holidays in a wide range of resorts in large numbers of destination countries. Hotels and airlines are not in a position to compete in these markets. However, while there are some 'owner-ship' advantages in branding for the tour companies, especially in terms of building up customer loyalty, this does not inevitably lead to their investing in foreign hotels. Similarly, there are no clear 'locational' or 'internalisation' reasons why tour companies have to invest in foreign hotels.

The reasons for the non-applicability of the eclectic theory to the inter-national tour companies are to be found in the very nature of the mass tourism product—a standardised holiday product, socially constructed around the attractions of either sunshine, sea and sand or of snow and skiing. There is relatively little product differentiation between resorts and coun-tries, and the main competition has tended to be in terms of price differen-tials. There is, therefore, no imperative for tour companies to own their own hotels. All that is required, as a minimum, is that the tour company can deliver certain levels of (sometimes minimal) services at relatively low prices in the resorts for which there is effective demand. The most efficient means of achieving this, in terms of prices, is via a system of subcontracting to locally owned hotel groups. This yields oligopsonistic powers (Storper 1985) to the tour companies: they have the advantages of large-scale purchasing power set against a supply dominated by a relatively large number of undifferentiated, small-scale hotel companies.

These market advantages are reinforced by the increased flexibility that has been acquired by the tour companies; by virtue of their limited fixed invest-ment in any particular location, they are relatively free to change suppliers, or even resorts or countries, in response to either fluctuations in demand or variation in prices. This strategy of subcontracting is the logical outcome of the needs of the tour companies to minimise costs and reduce uncertainty in rela-tively volatile markets (Gomez and Sinclair 1991). In effect this is achieved by passing on to the hotel owners as much of the risk and the downwards press-ures on costs and prices as is feasible. Not all the risk, however, can be passed on in this way, as is evident from a number of spectacular bankruptcies in the highly competitive UK tour sector. The most recent and one of the largest was the collapse in the early 1990s of the UK's second largest international air tour company, the International Leisure Group.

This analysis of tour companies does, to some extent, represent a traditional perspective on the tour companies. That is not to say that the tour company sector has become extensively transnationalised, or that they have widespread foreign investments in hotels. The only European tour company which has truly global reach is France's Club Méditerranée which has 24% of its bed capacity outside of Europe and has a US subsidiary to handle its American and Asian business, while only 33% of its clients are French (Bywater 1992, p. 17). In contrast, most European tour companies have been used to operating al-most exclusively in terms of national market segments, but there are some

Table 9.2. Europe's top 10 package tour companies: turnover and business strategies, 1991–92

Company	Nationality	Turnover (million ECU)	Investment in			
			Accom-modation	Airline	Travel agency	Tour selling in other country
TUI	Germany	2 590	Yes	No	No	Yes
Thomson	UK	1 623	No	Yes	Yes	No
NUR	Germany	1 220	Yes	No	Yes	Yes
LTU	Germany	1 206	Yes	Yes	No	Yes
Kuoni	Switzerland	1 190	No[a]	No	Yes	Yes
Club Méd.	France	1 122	Yes	Yes	Yes	Yes
DER	Germany	1 056	No	No	Yes	Yes
NRT Nordisk	Sweden	1 019	Yes	Yes	Yes	Yes
ITS	Germany	963	Yes	No	Yes	Yes
Owners Abroad	UK	916	No[a]	Yes	No	No

[a] Some non-strategic investment.

Source: After Bywater (1992, pp. 12 and 27).

indicators that this traditional pattern is breaking down. The actual picture, however, varies from country to country in respect not only of target markets, but also in the types of vertical and horizontal integration and FDI strategies pursued. The considerable variations in the structures of the leading companies are summarised in Table 9.2.

Tour company strategies have been evolving relatively rapidly in recent years. This is evident in three principal ways. Firstly, German companies have grown more rapidly than British ones, traditionally their main rivals in terms of size. German companies now dominate the rankings, shown in Table 9.2, in terms of turnover. This reflects their involvement in transnational marketing, something which the UK tour companies have largely ignored. The second and third features of company strategies are that there are major differences according to the nationality of the parent company, and that there has been growing vertical and horizontal integration of activities; these are now considered in further detail.

National differences in business strategies are most polarised in the case of the British and the German tour companies, which are by far the most important in Europe in terms of the volumes of tourists carried. German companies are now significantly larger than all their European competitors, with the exception of Thomson of the UK, which still holds the number two position. The German companies have the advantages of serving the largest domestic market in Europe, and also—unlike the British companies which specialise in using a single transport mode—being multi-modal. Furthermore, they have extended their market reach by extensive investment abroad, principally through acquisitions. As a result, some 30% of TUI sales are now outside of Germany, as are more than 50% of the sales of ITS. The most fertile new market areas for German companies have been the Netherlands and Belgium. They have been particularly successful in the latter, where NUR alone now accounts for more than 50% of all-inclusive holidays sold. In addition, the German companies have been active in developing vertical linkages, particularly in the hotel sector.

In contrast, the three largest UK tour companies—Thomson, Owners Abroad and Airtours (ranked sixteenth in Europe in terms of turnover)—have had very different business strategies. They have specialised in unimodal holidays, that is in all-inclusive air package holidays, and they have concentrated virtually exclusively on the UK market. To some extent, they have compensated for the relative limitation of market size by forcing down prices so as to extend purchasing access to package holidays to relatively low-income families. There are, however, signs that the major UK tour companies in recent years have sought to diversify both their marketing and their product. For example, in 1994 Airtours purchased the Scandinavian Leisure Group, thereby establishing a market presence outside of the UK; it also hoped to realise economies of scale in its operations by combining their two separate sets of resort offices. Perhaps even more significant was the 1994 decision by Thomson, for long the market leader in air package holidays, to purchase Marrhigh, the UK's largest domestic holiday cottage letting agency with some 6000 properties on its books. This reflects both a desire to diversify and to enter one of the high-growth sectors in the UK tourist industry. British companies, like their German counterparts, have also engaged in vertical integration strategies, but they differ in that they have mainly concentrated on owning airlines and travel agencies, and have shown little or no interest in purchasing hotels. While we have only concentrated here on German and British tour companies, most of the other majors are located somewhere on a continuum between these two poles.

This discussion of the broadening pattern of linkages and international activities raises the question of how they relate to Dunning's eclectic theory. Firstly, the issue of 'ownership' can be examined in terms of tour companies' hotel ownership. The debate on hotel ownership has become increasingly polarised in recent years. Bywater (1992, p. 56) summarises the positions as follows. Non-ownership allows you to negotiate rock bottom prices when the hotels are going through a bad patch, while securing quality standards via tight contract specifications. In contrast, '. . . those who support having hotels—whether owned, managed or leased—and incoming agencies argue that it guarantees them brand uniformity, quality control and, in the case of hotels, assures them of rooms at all times'. The latter argument indicates that Dunning's 'ownership' advantage does seem to have some weight for some international tour companies, a change which has largely been brought about by the increasing emphasis on quality in the mass tourism market. However, the argument is not entirely convincing, for many of these foreign-owned hotels do not operate directly under the brand names of their owners.

Secondly, there is of course clear evidence from the pattern of linkages that 'internalisation' is an important feature of tour company strategies, but the implications of this are less clear in terms of transnational ownership. As already observed, UK companies have developed upwards and downwards linkages to travel agencies and airlines; Thomson, for example, owns the Lunn Poly agency and Britannia Airways. Such a strategy allows them to internalise the commissions and profits that are realised in both marketing and delivering their holiday packages. They have not, however, sought to internalise their purchases of accommodation services. As a result, their internalisation strategies have not led them to major investments in foreign subsidiaries. In contrast, most of the other leading tour companies (see Table 9.2) have developed an interest in accommodation services, and this has led them to FDIs. Examples include TUI's investments in the Iberotel and Rui groups which provide it with 25 000 beds in Spain and which, together, constitute Spain's second largest hotel group (Bywater 1992, pp. 79–80). The extent of TUI's hotel ownership abroad is, however, exceptional. Most tour companies still do not own more than a small proportion of the hotels they use in particular resorts. NUR, for example, owns only 3% of its accommodation requirements in the Balearics, and 10% in the Canaries, even though these are its two most important destinations (Estudios Turísticos 1988). The logic of 'internalisation' has therefore led to some transnational investments in hotels—and there are also some foreign-owned travel agencies—but thus far this is still outweighed by the advantages of subcontracting.

Finally, with regards to 'locational' factors, these do dictate that the major tour companies should be able to offer holidays in all the more (culturally defined) popular destination countries and resorts. However, as there are many organisational and ownership forms for achieving this, as we have already noted, it does not necessarily lead to substantial transnational investments.

In summary, then, the international tour companies are becoming more diversified and internationalised. Thus far, the latter feature is more evident in the attempt to capture market share in northern European countries via acquisition of established tour companies than in large-scale investments in the destination countries.

9.5 TRANSNATIONALISATION AND TOURISM SPACES

International tourism has become a transnational business in that growth of the international market segment has consistently outstripped that of the domestic one since the 1960s, with there being an estimated 460 million international tourists in 1992 according to the World Tourism Organisations (WTO). In contrast, the transnationalisation of the production and delivery of tourism services has been limited, even though—as this chapter emphasises—

there are now rapid moves in this direction. The largest European hotel, airline and tour companies have increased their presence in other countries for a number of reasons. One important factor is the need to spread the company's business across different markets so as to reduce risk and to even out the impact of the business cycle (the timing of which tends to vary across Europe). There are also advantages to be secured from establishing vertical linkages so as to internalise the economic benefits of downstream and upstream purchases and sales. Increasingly, this involves companies in greenfield investments, mergers or acquisitions across international boundaries.

The net effects of these changes are twofold: there is an increase in the level of external control in response to growth in foreign tourism numbers and foreign investment in the tourism industry, and the form of external control is changing in response to new patterns of international linkages and ownership. As a result, increasing numbers of localities are subject to external decision-making (with regards to investments, marketing and types of tourism products to be developed). This may have a profound effect on the trajectories of local economic development, and therefore on employment, income and local cultural systems. In addition, internationalisation has meant that tourism-dependent local economies have become more susceptible to changes in the international economic environment. Hence recessionary impacts on consumer spending in Germany or the UK can quickly be transmitted, by an increasingly dense network of international linkages, into reductions in bookings and sales in particular localities across Europe.

The increasingly close relationships between the local and global economy are not limited to mass tourism. Internationalisation is increasingly the dominant force shaping tourism in many different formats: business tourism, mega-events such as the Olympics, or cultural tourism at major sites whether in Venice's churches and museums or the running of the bulls in Pamplona.

There is, in a sense, a self-reinforcing circle of relationships: increased foreign tourism makes it more attractive for multinational capital to participate in tourism, which in turn facilitates a further increase in foreign visitors. But the transnationalisation of tourism capital is not just dictated by cultural changes in tourism practices and 'gazes' (Urry 1990) and by technological changes in transport and telecommunications. Instead, tourism is also favoured by international capital because it provides opportunities to realise returns on investments over relatively short time periods (Britton 1991). Tourism also provides opportunities for multinational non-tourism capital to diversify into a growth sector: classic examples of such strategies include ITT's acquisition of Sheraton Hotels, and Bass's purchase of the Holiday Inn group. This underlines an important point: the analysis of tourism cannot be isolated from an understanding of the broader processes of restructuring in the economy at large. It also means that tourism, as an industry, has become increasingly vulnerable to the greater volatility and turbulence that have come to characterise the world economy since the mid 1970s, and especially in the late 1980s and early 1990s.

Transnationalisation has also been accompanied by the increasing flexibility and mobility of capital. This is linked to an overall tendency for investment and technological change to bring about a shortening of the product cycle. This in itself would lead to increasingly rapid changes in the objects of the tourist gaze (Urry 1990), illustrated by the construction of 'high-tech' pleasure parks (such as Futuroscope, in northern France), in the form of tourism (for example, new types of hotel and mobile accommodation), as well as in the destinations that become accessible due to changes in the speed and costs of transport. However, the effects of such changes on the mobility of capital are magnified by the essential features of large transnational companies (Dicken 1992): they control economic activities in more than one country, they can take advantage of geographical differences between countries and regions in terms of their factor endowments, and they have considerable geographical flexibility in their ability to shift resources and operations between locations at the global scale. This is all part of the global scan for profits. The implications are that localities may be subject to an increasingly rapid build-up of investment, as well as equally rapid disinvestment. This applies as much to investment in theme parks, such as Disneyland Paris, as to Mediterranean resorts.

The transnationalisation of tourism capital, while still at a relatively early stage compared to the changes experienced in sectors such as financial services, has nevertheless had an important impact upon local economies and the ability of the latter to control their own economic destinies. In addition new tensions are being generated in the regulation of the tourism sector. While this is still predominantly a preserve of national governments, the pressures of European economic integration as well as the very process of the internationalisation of capital, are calling into question the viability of the nation-state as a regulatory force. Thus far, EU action in this field has been relatively restricted (Williams and Shaw 1994), but the significance of the EU's tourism policy, and more fundamentally of its Social Agreement, its structural and transport investments, and its burgeoning environmental policies are all likely to have a profound effect on both the shape and content of the European tourism space and of European competitiveness in the global tourism space.

10 Tourism, Labour and International Migration

RUSSELL KING
University of Sussex, UK

10.1 INTRODUCTION

The aim of this chapter is to examine the internationalisation of the labour market in the tourism industry through the links between the industry and international migration. The account will be in three parts. First, the main aggregate flows of international labour migrations into Europe will be described, paying particular attention to their changing character during the post-Fordist era of the last 20 years. Second, it will be pointed out that the tourism and hospitality industry is a major source of jobs for immigrants. This is a well-known fact but unfortunately there are few data to support the assertion. Part of the reason for the paucity of information is the limited nature of cross-tabulated data on immigrant employment by sector, but data limitations also derive from the importance of the informal labour market in tourism, meaning that the immigrant presence is often unrecorded. These data limitations will be side-stepped by a more qualitative description of the roles that immigrants play in the tourist industry. While it is generally the case that immigrants occupy the lowest echelons of the tourist labour market, it is also true that the industry offers a number of settings for immigrant advancement and enterprise. The third and final part of the chapter will examine the impact of international return migration on the development of tourism in the home countries of the migrants. Once again, the information base is imperfect and the stress will be on case-studies.

10.2 THE CHANGING ROLE OF INTERNATIONAL MIGRATION IN EUROPE

The great European labour migrations of the 1950s and 1960s are fast becoming a distant memory. In retrospect, they can be seen as the demographic component of Fordism: mass migration from peripheral to core regions of the European economy provided a readily available, homogeneous and cheap

European Tourism: Regions, Spaces and Restructuring. Edited by A. Montanari and A.M. Williams.
© 1995 European Science Foundation. Published in 1995 by John Wiley & Sons Ltd.

supply of labour for the post-war industries of mass production (Fielding 1993). Millions of foreign workers migrated into the big cities and industrial heartlands of north-west Europe, later to be joined by other members of their families. Their origins were the poorer countries of Europe such as Ireland, Spain, Portugal, Italy and Greece, with additional flows developing from Algeria to France, Turkey to West Germany and Morocco to Belgium and the Netherlands. The former imperial powers also absorbed major migration flows from their colonies and ex-colonies in Africa, South Asia and the Caribbean.

Much has been written about these mass migrations, and from many points of view. Castles and Kosack (1973) produced the most thorough analysis and attributed to European capitalism a peculiar hunger for cheap foreign labour. The Marxian 'reserve army' thesis favoured by Castles and Kosack and endorsed by other influential writers such as Piore (1979) and Cohen (1987) was usually framed within the context of industrial labour, but it is important to point out that the mass labour migrations of the pre-oil crisis era were also partially directed to a range of service sector activities. While some of these were related to the specific needs of the labour market of the host country (the UK's recruitment of hospital and transport workers from the Caribbean is a case in point), other tertiary employment was created by the needs of the ethnic groups themselves. Shops and restaurants were established, catering initially for the local ethnic communities and then widening their appeal to the larger population's taste for the exotic as well as the cheap. In the UK the involvement of several ethnic groups in specific niches of the catering industry is a well-known facet of everyday life for those who patronise Chinese take-aways, Indian restaurants, Cypriot fish-and-chip shops or Italian pizzerias. Some of these specialisms also exist in other European countries (e.g. Chinese restaurants, Italian pizzerias) but these other countries also have their own ethnic catering industries which reflect their particular histories and source areas of migration—North African in France, Turkish in Germany, Indonesian in the Netherlands for example. Not all of these involvements of migrants in catering result from the Fordist migrations of the early post-war decades: some are much older, and others more recent.[1]

After the hiatus of the 1970s, when the oil crises stifled labour migration within and into Europe, new migration flows developed in the 1980s within the context of the increasing internationalisation of the global labour market. In this 'new age' of migration (Castles and Miller 1993) the links and interdependencies between different parts of the world are so extensive and highly ramified that migration can develop without cultural, geographical or colonial ties between sending and receiving countries and without there being any particularly strong demand for new labour from the receptor countries. The weight of non-economic factors, such as social, demographic and political variables, in determining migration flows has increased. Also important are the increasingly refined information links established between very distant areas of the 'global village' (Golini et al. 1993).

Castles and Miller (1993) and Salt et al. (1994) have explored the key dimensions of the new migrations affecting Europe in the 1980s and 1990s during the recent period of economic and political restructuring. Sources, mechanisms and types of migration have all changed. First, there is the economic and labour market context. Changing global investment patterns have removed much European manufacturing industry to production bases in the Third World where labour is cheap and flexible. Together with the micro-electronic revolution, which has reduced the demand for manual workers in manufacturing, this has eroded the base for traditional industrial jobs, and therefore one of the bases for traditional labour migrants. Instead the European labour market has seen a strong expansion in the service sector, parts of which—notably the tourism and hospitality industry—have become dominated by 'informal' practices. As far as the labour market and the demand for migrant workers are concerned, this means the casualistaion of employment, with increasingly insecure conditions of employment and growth in part-time and seasonal work. It also means an increasing differentiation of workers on the basis of gender, age and ethnicity: hence many women, young people and immigrants are pushed into casual and low-paid employment. Much of this labour market segmentation is found in the tourist sector in big cities and mass tourism destinations.

The insecure status of many of these members of the informal or secondary labour market is reinforced by their precarious position as illegal immigrants. Illegal migration is by definition a product of laws passed to control immigration. Since the clampdown in migrant recruitment in the 1970s, there has been a great deal of clandestine entry into Western Europe. Migrants from the developing world and newly liberated countries of Eastern Europe have entered Western Europe by stealth, arriving on tourist visas, quickly finding work and then not returning at the end of their permitted stay. Much of this clandestine entry has taken place into southern Europe where immigrant entry controls are lax and difficult to tighten because of long borders and coastlines and the impossibility of separating economic migrants from the ebb and flow of the tourist trade. I shall look at the specifically touristic character of migrant employment in countries such as Italy and Spain in the next section.

Despite a regime of mounting immigration control, the number of migrant workers in Western Europe has risen quite sharply during the 1980s and 1990s. The reasons for this apparent contradiction are complex, but some key elements include the rising pressure for emigration from the source regions (poverty, demographic increase, political instability, environmental degradation) and the increasing skill of migrants and agents in penetrating Europe's external barriers. During 1980–90 the stock of foreign labour rose by nearly a half in Luxembourg, by one-third in Austria, Switzerland and the UK, by 10% in Sweden, by around 6–7% in France and the Netherlands and by 3% in Belgium. Only in (West) Germany, of the major traditional immigration countries, was there a decline—of about 4%—although there was a rise in the total foreign population of nearly 18% over the same 1980–90 period (SOPEMI 1992).

For the most part these figures refer to officially registered and admitted workers and exclude various other categories such as seasonal workers, asylum-seekers and illegal immigrants, although the statistical accounting practices vary between countries. What is perhaps more important to appreciate is the growing variety of types and mechanisms of migration into Europe (Salt et al. 1994, pp. 160–162). Foremost among these are asylum-seekers whose numbers have risen dramatically since the mid 1980s. Many enter the labour market unofficially while their claims are being processed, and then stay on to work illegally if their applications for asylum are rejected. Another growing type of migrant, symptomatic of the blurring of the distinctions surrounding migration and other forms of mobility, is made up of student workers. Many students take foreign 'working holidays' for a few weeks in seasonal occupations. They are both tourists and migrant workers; moreover their work will often be in the tourist industry! In a similar vein, students who are studying abroad may work part-time, or stay on to work after completing their courses. In Eastern Europe, 'labour tourism' has become a common phenomenon. This occurs when people move across borders (typically from East to West) as visitors or tourists but with the express intention of picking up temporary work. Their aims are both to experience the freedom of being able to sample life in the West, and to earn hard currency to support themselves or finance their studies when they return to their own countries.

The above changes in the character of migration have fitted in well with the changing labour requirements of the tourism industry, as the next section shows. Tourism employment, in turn, has to be viewed within the context of these new forms of international migration within and into Europe.

10.3 IMMIGRANT EMPLOYMENT IN THE TOURIST INDUSTRY

Although tourism has been contributing an increasingly significant share of national employment in most European countries, and although this fact is recognised in most states, the lack of a proper statistical apparatus remains a serious obstacle to a clear evaluation of tourism's employment-creating effects. Following the World Tourism Organisation's (WTO) *Economic Review*, there are at least three main branches of tourist sector employment (WTO 1986, pp. 66–67). The traditional and most obvious branch of employment associated with tourism is that of hotels and other accommodation establishments (apartments, hostels, camping-grounds, etc.), along with restaurants and other catering enterprises. Such establishments are usually considered as 'touristic' if more than half of their production and custom is with tourists and travellers. The second branch of employment which may qualify as touristic is that of passenger transport. Using the 50% criterion, most transport outside of dedicated commuter lines and other short-distance links probably falls into the tourist category, and therefore transport employees must be regarded as part of the touristic workforce. More obviously connected with tourism are travel agency personnel associated with the distribution and marketing of the tourism product—tour operators, representatives, guides and reception staff. This is the third category of touristic employment, and it may also include employees responsible for organising leisure-time and recreational activities for tourists.

In addition to the three categories listed above, which all relate to the direct operation of the tourist and travel sector, there are a number of ancillary employment sectors concerned with the supply and maintenance of allied services and inputs. Accordingly a proportion of employment in the building industry and its ancillary trades can be considered as tourism-related.

The question now to be considered is the extent to which these various subsectors of touristic employment are attractive to migrants. A first point to make is that because international tourism is by definition a transnational business, the movement of tourism industry personnel from one country to another is inevitable. These movements will be at various levels according to the corporate hierarchy of the business. Thus there will be a 'high-skill' migration of managers, agents and marketing personnel connected with the international package holiday trade and with national attempts to promote the tourism market. At the next step down the occupational hierarchy and still thinking of international package tourism, there will be a need for agency representatives and guides: typically these are females with middle-level educational qualifications and some language and interpersonal skills who may be highly mobile from one resort to another. This mobility reflects the fact that tour companies make limited fixed capital investments in resorts and try to follow market changes by shifting both capital and labour from place to place over time. The mobility of this type of labour also reflects interlocking patterns of seasonality: winter seasons in the Canaries or the Caribbean, summer in the Balearics or the Italian rivieras.

At lower levels in the employment hierarchy of the tourism industry, the key point is that tourism is an industry which demands labour market flexibility. This is true whether the industry is organised on 'Fordist' lines of large-scale mass movements of tourists staying in large hotels providing a standardised product, or fragmented into many small accommodation and service units. The spatial and temporal polarisation of demand for tourist services poses considerable challenges for firms operating in the sector and they have responded to these via both numerical labour market flexibility involving seasonal, part-time, occasional and family workers and functional flexibility whereby workers tackle a diversity of jobs (see Shaw and Williams 1994). This labour market flexbility is also linked to specific gender divisions of labour as well as to systems of internal and international labour migration. Seasonality is the dominant factor in the tourist labour market in many countries in Europe. In Spain and Greece about half of all employment in hotels is seasonal; this proportion rises to 80% in regions like the Costa del Sol and the Balearic Islands where the holiday trade is dominated by summer visitors from northern Europe (Valenzuela 1988, p. 52).

Tourism's demand for seasonal and short-term labour fits well with many migrants' desires to work abroad for short periods, keeping their bases in their home countries. This is not to excuse the low wages and poor working conditions usually endured by the lower-status employees in the tourism industry; but it is true that short-term summer or other seasonal work is particularly suited to students and to temporary migrant visitors from Eastern Europe, North Africa and other less prosperous parts of the world.

Unfortunately there are very few data to measure the reliance of the tourism and hospitality industry on migrant labour, or to measure the penetration of that labour into various subsectors of the overall industry. Few countries keep accurate records on this, and only a few aggregate figures are available. For example, in the mid 1980s the proportion of total labour employed in hotels and restaurants that was made up of immigrant workers was estimated to be 38% in Switzerland, 24% in West Germany and 18% in Sweden (figures quoted in Williams and Shaw 1991d, p. 35). Figure 10.1 shows a somewhat more complete and up-to-date set of national data drawn from Eurostat. Based on the standard employment classification of the EU (with Swiss data regrouped to correspond to this), it shows the foreigner 'penetration' into the employment structure of each category. Since touristic employment is not a single category, the three categories most closely associated with tourism (distributive trades, hotels and catering; transport and communications; 'other services') are highlighted on the graphs. Foreign workers are particularly well represented in the tourist-related sectors in Switzerland and Luxembourg, much less so in the Netherlands and the UK, with France, Belgium and Germany occupying intermediate situations in this regard. A breakdown of these data over time shows that for most countries categories 60 (hotels, catering, distribution) and 90B (other services) are those with growing foreigner penetration and also the highest percentages of female workers present (SOPEMI 1992, pp. 23–26). This last fact implies a gendered division of labour within the migrant workforce.

Several qualifying points need to be made about these figures. The penetration index of foreigners in the various employment sectors should be distinguished from data which show the percentage distribution of foreign workers among the various employment categories. In Belgium, for example, the hotel and catering industry employs the greatest number of foreign workers, even though they account for less than 10% of this sector's total workforce. In the southern European countries of more recent immigration, the domination of the tourist sector in patterns of immigrant employment is likely to be even higher than those countries portrayed in Figure 10.1, although supporting data for this assertion are deficient. In Spain, for instance, 73% of immigrants with a valid work permit in 1990 were employed in services

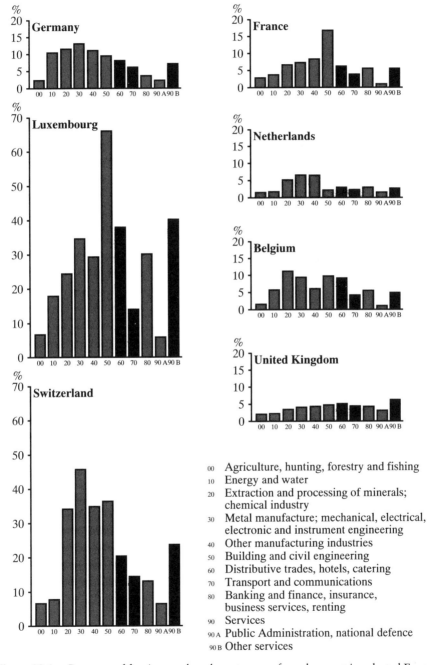

00 Agriculture, hunting, forestry and fishing
10 Energy and water
20 Extraction and processing of minerals;
    chemical industry
30 Metal manufacture; mechanical, electrical,
    electronic and instrument engineering
40 Other manufacturing industries
50 Building and civil engineering
60 Distributive trades, hotels, catering
70 Transport and communications
80 Banking and finance, insurance,
    business services, renting
90 Services
90 A Public Administration, national defence
90 B Other services

Figure 10.1.   Presence of foreign workers by category of employment in selected European countries, 1989–90. Source: SOPEMI (1992, pp. 24–25)

(cf. 15% in industry, 7% in construction and 4% in agriculture); however these figures (from Charmes et al. 1993, p. 33) refer to only a fraction of all the immigrants actually working in Spain. Because of its demand for large numbers of seasonal workers, Spanish tourism is able to tap into the large pool of unregistered immigrants.[2] Much the same probably happens in Portugal, Italy, Greece and southern France.

By far the most important caveat about 'official' data on migrant employment in tourism concerns the relevance of the informal or black economy. In fact in southern European countries where tourism is highly developed—Spain, Portugal, Italy, Greece and, to a certain extent, also France—it is precisely the tourism sector where the encounter between the black economy and immigrant workers is most sharply demonstrated. In Italy and Spain a significant part, probably the majority, of labour in the tourism industry consists of *lavoro nero* or 'black work', much of it made up of immigrants. Although quantitative information is practically non-existent since illegal immigrants are by definition unrecorded, Venturini (1992) has estimated that more than one-half, and perhaps as much as 80%, of immigrants in Italy are employed in the informal sector. In the recent literature on the new migrations from the Third World to southern Europe there are many references to the employment of immigrants in hotels and catering and to their self-employment as pedlars in towns and tourist resorts (see, for example, Bel Adell 1989; Bonifazi 1994; King and Rybaczuk 1993; Montanari and Cortese 1993a; Muñoz-Pérez and Izquierdo-Escribano 1989). Many of these tourist-related jobs in the informal labour market are gender- and nationality-specific. In both Spain and Italy, chambermaids and cleaners from the Philippines and some Latin American countries are widespread in hotels and apartment complexes. Hotels in big cities in Italy, especially Rome, employ kitchen and portering staff from many Third World countries such as Somalia, Eritrea, India and Morocco. Street-hawkers, a highly visible component of the street scene and beach life of Mediterranean tourist resorts, are mainly from Senegal and other West African countries. They migrate via kinship and tribal networks which they maintain abroad in order both to preserve their culture and facilitate access to housing and jobs.

National figures on immigrant employment in tourism are subject to local and regional variations according to the scale of tourism, the types of jobs available, the supplies of migrant workers on hand, and the labour market alternatives. Overall, tourism is one of the economic sectors which has a low-skill, low-entry threshold which therefore makes it very 'open' to immigrants. But circumstances do vary from place to place. In the mass tourism seaside resorts of the Mediterranean and in major touristic cities like Paris, London and Rome, exhaustion of the supply of local labour makes immigrants very important in the tourist and catering industries. The high figures for foreign employment in the Swiss tourist industry noted above are at least partly due to the fact that most Swiss will not work in the hotel and catering sectors because of the low pay and seasonality involved. Only one-third of the immigrant workers in the Swiss tourist industry have permanent jobs (Gilg 1991, p. 141). On the other hand, in rural areas of Europe small-scale diffuse tourism is based much more on local labour resources such as female and part-time workers released from agriculture (Clout 1984).

Employment of migrant workers may have other effects, depressing overall wages in the tourist industry, making such jobs unattractive to local people, but also making the industry competitive and profitable. Price competitivity is important in mass tourism where, because of lack of product differentiation, most competition is at the level of price minimisation. The mass concentration of tourists in certain locations such as densely packed beach resorts and tourist cities may act as a magnet to peripatetic migrants who try to create livelihoods for themselves on the fringes of the tourist economy as guides, money-changers and street-traders. In recent years there has been a proliferation of African pedlars patrolling the most popular beaches of southern Europe selling sun-glasses, leather goods, watches and various tourist trinkets. The vibrant retail-ing economy of many tourist towns, driven by a constantly rotating supply of tourists renewed every week or fortnight, may attract other more settled migrant groups who trade off the tourists' particular type of high spending power. The colonies of Indian jewellers who have settled in many Spanish coastal resorts are a case in point. Or there may be a market for a kind of expatriate labour which matches the nationality and tastes of the tourists: the involvement of British people in running bars and 'English' restaurants in Spanish resorts is a good example of this.

While this last example of the interaction between tourism, migration and gastronomic tastes is a result of tourists' conservatism—preferring their own food abroad to local dishes—it also happens that tourists develop a taste for the local cuisine which they want to repeat after they return home. Hence, a visit to an Italian or a Greek restaurant in their home city in northern Europe reminds them of happy times on holiday in Rimini or Rhodes. Zelinsky (1985) suggests that such an evening out can be regarded as a kind of surrogate touristic experience which the interior ambience of the ethnic restaurant, with its décor, pictures, artefacts and music, not to mention the costumes and behaviour of the staff, does much to reinforce. In this way the participation of increasing numbers of Europeans in international tourism creates a demand for ethnically diverse cuisines in restaurants run by a variety of immigrant groups. In the UK the dominant ethnic cuisines, in terms of numbers of restaur-ants, are Italian, Chinese and Indian, but others are developing—Greek, Span-ish, Caribbean, Mexican, Lebanese and many more. Not all of these build on patrons' specific touristic experiences, but tourism's broader transcultural in-fluences undoubtedly contribute to a growing desire to sample a diversity of ethnic cuisines. This demand offers entrepreneurial opportunities to estab-lished immigrant groups and encourages new migratory links. Zelinsky's (1985) fascinating exploration of the triangular relationship between tourism, ethnic restaurants and the transnationalisation of culture in North America invites a similar analysis of the European situation.

10.4   RETURN MIGRATION AND TOURIST DEVELOPMENT

Although international labour migration has generated a substantial number of permanently settled ethnic communities in north-west Europe, particularly as a result of the migration waves of the 1950s and 1960s, return migration has been an ever-present process. Return to the home country is the natural outcome of temporary migration, and such a return was anticipated both by the governments of the countries involved and by the migrants themselves for whom the home country functioned as an emotional base. Pressures for return mounted in the 1970s and 1980s as a result of the decline of the Fordist production systems for which many migrants had been recruited in preceding decades. These pressures were reinforced by official policies favouring return, both from the governments of the host countries, notably France in the 1970s and West Germany in the early 1980s, and from the migrants' own countries which tried to create conditions favouring a rapid reintegration of returnees. Finally, there were life-cycle factors: many migrants who left as young men and women in the 1950s and 1960s wanted to return because they had worked abroad long enough and wished to resettle in their home countries for the latter stages of their lives.

Therefore many peripheral regions of Europe which had been important sources of emigration during the earlier period, switched to net inmigration in the early 1970s. This brought back large backflows of migrants to countries such as Ireland, Portugal, Spain and Greece. Although some returning migrants were 'failures', others returned with foreign work experience, capital accumulated while abroad, and certain skills and attitudes such as language abilities and a broadened cultural horizon. All of these, it could be argued, are assets with potential for the development of tourism in these countries.

A proper evaluation of the impact of return migration on the development of tourism is gravely hampered by the availability of so little information. Some general trends are clear, however, and these can be enlivened by reference to case-studies. Ardittis (1988, p. 25) notes that returning migrants have three main employment characteristics. First there is a strong reluctance to return to farming. Most emigrants left to escape the rigours, low status and poor financial rewards of farming; therefore on their return they are looking for something better. Often this improved status is found in the tertiary sector—the second major trend. Thus the geographical cycle of emigration and return involves a sequence of employment moves from agriculture before departure to industry abroad and then to the service sector upon return. Post-return tertiary sector jobs are rarely found in public employment but in the variegated arena of private services. The third trend noted by Ardittis is the sharp increase in self-employment after return. Typically this independence is found within the service sector which offers a number of opportunities for small-scale entrepreneurship.

The extent to which this dual predilection for service sector activity and for self-employment is linked to the tourist industry varies from place to place. The unattractiveness and inefficiency of agriculture and the absence of industrial development in many migration source areas mean that the tourist industry has been one of the poles of attraction for returning migrants in regions like southern Europe and the west of Ireland. Return migrants' investment in tourism can also be seen as a mechanism for a significant if fragmented international transfer of capital into tourism. In the absence of any systematic data, three case-studies will be presented to illustrate these processes.

The first illustration is Mendonsa's (1982) study of the impact of migration on the fishing town and tourist resort of Nazaré, 60 km north of Lisbon. Comparing returnees from abroad with non-migrants and with townspeople who had migrated within Portugal, Mendonsa found that the international returnees were the most successful. This was largely because they had earned sufficient capital abroad to invest in the growing local tourist economy. Curiously, emigrants' involvement with the local tourist economy often started the moment they emigrated, for many would rent their vacant dwellings to visitors. Emigrants then capitalised further on tourist activities when they returned by investing in small hotels, accommodation to be rented to tourists, cafés, restaurants and other commercial establishments. According to Mendonsa's sample data, 78% of returned migrants rented property to tourists compared to only 41% of non-migrants. In spite of the fact that emigrants started from a lower socio-economic base than the other groups, after migration they were wealthier and had more capital and consumer goods. Comparing returnees from abroad with non-migrants, respective monthly incomes were $196 and $106. This differential was partly because of income saved abroad, and partly because of the profitability of investing some of that income in the local tourist economy. The Nazaré case-study illustrates a healthy symbiosis between tourist development and return migrants' investments: each one facilitates the other.

A second example, with many similarities to the first, comes from a study by King et al. (1984) on the tourist town of Amantea in Calabria, southern Italy. The authors interviewed a random sample of 79 returned migrants and found that the largest group—38%—had returned to create, or to find a job in, commercial and service sector activities, chiefly those linked to the touristic development of this beautiful stretch of coast. Returnee enterprises ranged from those obviously linked to tourism such as hotels, apartments and tourist gift shops, to those which were partially or seasonally linked to the summer influx of visitors such as food shops, bars and garages. The most active returnees commercially were those who had been in Venezuela (the majority destination for the town's emigrants), where many had already accumulated experiences of working in the service sector before return. A survey of the total stock of tourist facilities (14 hotels, 23 bars, 12 restaurants, 6 pizzerias, 6 discos and 6000 beds in private homes and apartments for rent to tourists) revealed that most had been set up using migrant capital. Ignoring the 6000 private beds, these enterprises had generated 310 jobs—a considerable impact on a small town.

Our third illustration is provided by studies of return migrant economic behaviour in former Yugoslavia. Already by the late 1960s a shift in the spatial distribution of returnee investment was taking place. The opening-up of small catering establishments in the interior had saturated areas such as the Dalmation hinterland and western Hercegovina with cafés, pubs and restaurants; as coastal tourism started to develop returnees switched their attention to the Dalmation littoral, specialising in small hotels and rooms for rent (Baučić 1972, p. 36). A study of the Croatian island of Brac revealed the critical importance of return migration and foreign-earned capital to the development of the island's tourist economy (Bennett 1979). Returnees were investing heavily in restaurants, *gostione* (guest-houses) and other tourist facilities: such investments had strong economic multiplier effects in the rest of the local economy. Domestic and foreign tourists brought consumer purchasing power demands, and local entrepreneurs bought construction materials and restaurant supplies, to the benefit of the local building industry and the island's farmers. A common pattern was for the younger generation of returned migrants to assume an entrepreneurial role developing new tourist accommodation businesses, while their parents remained in the background following traditional agricultural pursuits. The wars which accompanied the break-up of Yugoslavia disrupted this tourist boom, although Slovenia and the northern Croatian coastlands are now recovering.

Finally, there is another way in which international return migration relates to tourist development. As Cavaco (1993) points out in her study of return migration and rural change in Portugal, the systematic return of emigrants to their native villages for their summer holidays can be likened to a touristic migration. The village thus becomes a holiday resort for its migrants who, during the month or so that they stay, spend money lavishly and breathe life into local businesses, many of which will have been set up by returned migrants who have settled for good. Cavaco suggests that this kind of migration-led embryonic rural tourism could progress to other forms of tourism such as agritourism, camping and country clubs. Emigrant families, accustomed to dealing with foreigners and speaking other languages, may find a lucrative vocation in developing these kinds of rural tourism catering mainly for foreigners, which have been so successful in regions like Tuscany and the Dordogne. Of course not all regions of past emigration have the necessary combination of fine landscape, cultural attractions and benevolent climate as rural Portugal, so this kind of development is likely to be spatially restricted. It is also important to realise that most returned migrants have little entrepreneurial experience and relatively small amounts of capital to invest. Their primary goal may be the limited one of setting up a modest business to live from in a semi-retired state, rather than gamble hard-earned capital in larger-scale and more risky ventures such as large hotels, theme parks or country clubs.

The case-studies reviewed in this section are examples of processes which are undoubtedly widespread, particularly in coastal areas of Mediterranean Europe where the proliferation of small service establishments and the growth of tourist-related infrastructure have done so much to modify the landscape and settlement patterns, often in a disorganised fashion. There remains a need for more comparative studies to improve our knowledge of the roles of returning migrants in developing tourism and allied activities (Williams 1993a). In particular, the case-studies reviewed above are selective in that none refers to the impact of returned migrants on the more traditional areas of mass tourism such as the Adriatic Riviera or the Costa del Sol. Another linked question concerns the role of tourism in stimulating the rural–urban migration of returnees: to what extent, for example, do returnees who originally departed from a rural district of their country resettle in urban or touristic locations in order to maximise the returns on their investments?

10.5 CONCLUSION

This chapter has made a preliminary assessment of the internationalisation of European tourism through its involvement with transnational migratory movements. The main focus has been on the labour market where tourism's need, as an industry, is for flexible labour supplies. This tends to make it unattractive to local people, who want permanent jobs, except in poor regions where unemployment is high or where local people are able to integrate part-time and seasonal work in both farming (or some other sector like construction) and tourism. Seasonal migrants, labour tourists and students seeking holiday work are therefore often more attractive to employers who are able to exploit these workers' desires for short-term employment and reward them with low wages and no social security benefits. A high proportion of this kind of employment takes place as part of the informal sector. Where the migrant workers are defined as illegal by the host country, their wages may be less. Some migrants try to fashion a living for themselves in niches on the fringe of the tourist economy by peddling goods to tourists.

The relationship between international migration and mass tourism is partly reciprocal. Certainly mass and urban tourism do help to generate international migration. But the latter also help to shape the former. Cheap foreign labour can contribute to the tourist industry by perpetuating low-cost mass tourism and thereby postponing more fundamental reorganisation.

Other interactions between tourism and migration can also be envisaged. The cultural and economic impact of tourism on a backward region may provoke emigration by a kind of demonstration effect of the wealth and ways of urban society. Although tourists' behaviour while on holiday may give a false impression of this wealthy urban culture, it may nevertheless act to dislodge young people from their peripheral regions and induce them to become international migrants. Tourism and migration also provide a range of settings for entrepreneurship—Italian, Spanish and Greek restaurants in northern Europe, British pubs and German beer-halls in southern European tourist spots, and hotels and other touristic initiatives set up by return migrants when they repatriate themselves to regions which, since they departed as emigrants, have started to develop touristically.

All the processes identified in this chapter can be observed by the traveller and the fieldworker; but there is a great need both for quantitative data to document the scale of the phenomena under discussion, and for on-the-spot research to bring out the qualitative aspects of the processes involved and to differentiate impacts on mass tourism regions and areas of rural tourism.

NOTES

1. In the UK, for example, the Italian involvement with the hotel and catering industries is quite old and can be traced to the specialised immigration of ice-cream sellers at the end of the nineteenth century. Today Italians control thousands of catering establishments providing a variety of services the length and breadth of the country: ice-cream vans and shops, snack-bars, coffee-shops, pizzerias, restaurants and hotels. Their hard work and entrepreneurial talent have enabled them to follow market trends closely. In recent years, for instance, the Costa coffee bars have become part of the scene at airports and major railway stations, while many an English country pub restaurant is run by an Italian family, perhaps of second-generation immigrants. Some, like Lord Charles Forte, have risen to the very top—head of Europe's largest hotel and catering empire. Forte was born in a small village in southern Italy and migrated to Scotland as a young boy to join family interests in ice-cream and cafés which had already been established by the turn of the century (Forte 1986). The Berni catering group had similarly humble origins in Italian-owned ice-cream and temperance bars in turn-of-the-century South Wales (Hughes 1991).
2. Traditionally Spanish tourism relied for its seasonal workers on powerful currents of internal migration from interior regions to the coast and from southern regions (Andalusia, Murcia) to the Costa Brava and the Balearic Islands.

Part IV

NEW TOURISM PRODUCTS
AND SOCIAL CHANGE

11 Mega-events: Local Strategies and Global Tourist Attractions

CARLES CARRERAS I VERDAGUER
University of Barcelona

11.1 INTRODUCTION

This chapter presents some reflections on the role of place in the development of new tourist activities, and draws mainly on the recent experiences of the city of Barcelona. These reflections are rooted, in particular, in a long tradition in urban analysis (Carreras 1988, 1992, 1993), in which tourist activities have been analysed mostly as having only a secondary role although they have also been viewed as an almost unique form of economic crisis solution in city life in recent years. Yet, such tourist development, with more than a century of tradition behind it in the case of Barcelona, has been closely related to the process of the internationalisation of the city.

First, the author analyses the role of place in the restructuring of the economic system and its territorial organisation, and the consequences for new tourist activities, focusing on mega-events organisation. Second, some local strategies of tourism development, based on the case of Barcelona, are analysed. Finally, some theoretical issues are presented as a conclusion to these reflections.

11.2 PLACE AND INTERNATIONAL ECONOMIC ACTIVITIES: THE NEW GLOBAL–LOCAL CONFLICT

Locality has been one of the most relevant scales in the development of tourist activities. The local capacity to attract foreign visitors and consumers appears in very diversified forms. Some specific features of natural environments (such as sandy beaches, abrupt mountains, picturesque landscapes or wild forests), or other more abstract characteristics (such as calm, beauty, sunshine, strength of local culture, artistic or architectural wealth), or even more practical ones (such as low prices or a high level of tourism facilities), or a special combination of some of these, are locally based tourist resources. This local attractiveness is the first and one of the most powerful elements for the organisation of

European Tourism: Regions, Spaces and Restructuring. Edited by A. Montanari and A.M. Williams.
© 1995 European Science Foundation. Published in 1995 by John Wiley & Sons Ltd.

the economic circuit of tourism, even at the global scale (McIntosh 1977; Goodall and Ashworth 1990).

Despite the importance of this fact, during the 1960s and the 1970s many tourist developments were able to exploit, almost to the point of destruction, the basis of their local attractiveness, that is their principal 'own' resource. This has been the infamous case of the so-called balearisation[1] of many coastal or mountain tourist destinations.[2] Thus, locality attracts tourism, but tourism can completely change, over-occupy or even destroy its local attraction. This is a very common aspect of the relevant and contradictory relationship between tourism activities and place.

The process of globalisation of the general economy, which has accelerated since the 1973–74 oil crisis (Dicken 1992), did not diminish the relevance of the local scale. Thus, the role of place has been reinforced in at least two relatively different ways. On the one hand, the homogenisation process, which emanated from the internationalisation related to globalisation, which was especially strong in the case of the largest tour operator companies,[3] has favoured the factors of diversity; local differences, exceptional features, the spirit of adventure, and exoticism have become more and more the new attractive factors for increasing tourist flows. Place appears as a substrate hosting the new, but resisting changes throughout its material and cultural heritage (Santos et al. 1993). On the other hand, recent changes, even the crisis of the classical concept of the nation-state,[4] give a new relevance to the regional and local scales as a means of achieving connections with many new, different, international flows. In this regard, the flexibilisation of the economy and the restructuring process of capitalism (Lash and Urry 1987) facilitate the implementation of many different types of local and regional initiatives.

In addition to this, since the 1973–74 crisis, deindustrialisation has been accelerated, making service activities, in general, especially tourism-related ones, the most realistic economic alternatives—if not the only ones—for the majority of places, especially for the largest cities, with a certain tradition of internationalisation. The major cities, traditionally, were the principal generators of tourist flows, because of the high position of urban areas in the hierarchy of the welfare state, with its paid and guaranteed holidays. For this same reason, cities normally could also become massive tourist attractions. The current diffusion of a new global consumption culture, at a spatial level, reinforces the role of cities as a major stage for this universal custom. Franchising and other forms of transnational commercial activities transform differentiated urban areas into similar urban landscapes in a fragmented and dispersed but unique city, where international tourists can comfortably circulate (Carreras 1994).

In this general context, cities, as specific places, have a considerable potential for developing different strategies for the attraction of tourist flows. The main factors of this attraction can be summarised as:

1. Current urban communications infrastructures, such as airports, highways, high-speed trains and others;
2. Accommodation and commercial facilities, such as hotels, camping and car parks, shopping centres and commercial areas, stores and shops, popular and ethnic markets;
3. Urban cultural wealth, with historical or architectural monuments, romantic or popular landscapes, and major cultural facilities.

Today, all these factors have been added to by new ones such as fairs, exhibitions, congresses, sporting and cultural events and many others, all of which occupy an international arena.

The historical features of many urban places, especially European cities, play a very important role in this kind of attraction (Ashworth and Tunbridge 1990). In fact, many cities are currently in the process of selling themselves as tourist products in a global or, at least, an international market. This new fact implies the specifically urban development of the majority of the characteristics of what is generally considered to constitute the marketing process (Ashworth and Voogd 1990). Some cities even try to develop special strategies related to their natural or cultural location facilities; a sunbelt localisation, or new artistic or leisure pilgrimages[5] can become new factors of international attraction in this context.

Other leisure places, and not only urban ones, have also become more and more internationalised. This is exemplified by the development of world famous leisure parks, which have created new 'magic lands' such as Disneyland in the urban areas of Los Angeles or Paris, or Disneyworld in Orlando, or, more recently, the Tibigardens in Tarragona (Findlay 1992). These untrue but living cities sometimes become more permanent and alive than the ephemeral ones built for universal exhibitions (Canogar 1992).

11.3 THE ROLE OF MEGA-EVENTS

The so-called mega-events constitute one of the definitive points for reinforcing these international urban and local strategies (Spezia 1992). The term 'mega-events' implies a very great diversity of events requiring major investments, international marketing, media diffusion and tourist mass attraction. International fairs and major congresses (especially the institutionalised international exhibitions) or some cultural and religious events, or many sports competitions (especially the Olympics), provide the most relevant examples. Many different cities and states compete every year, and at many different levels, to organise these kinds of mega-events.

The usual definition of an 'event' is of something worthy of remark, because of its uniqueness, and 'mega' refers not only to its scale but also to the international diffusion of the event, especially on international TV networks. Nevertheless, although many localities, cities and regions currently are the stage of many different events, only a few of them ever obtain the qualitative dimensions of a mega-event. The end objective of the organisation of such mega-events is to reinforce local economic activities; so as to mark the position of each locality on the world map, in order to attract foreign capital, foreign investors and foreign visitors. Local strategies are designed to try and extend temporally what would otherwise be the purely momentary effects of such mega-events. It would be very difficult to try to delimit the boundary between mega, medium and small events more precisely than this. From a geographical point of view, however, it would be possible to outline a vague territorial delimitation based on the different range of each event, indicated by the furthest distance the population is willing to travel in order to attend such an event at a specific place. In this regard, they are special fairs or festivals at local, regional or national level, but only a few of them ever become international, and the reasons for this are varied and very unpredictable.

The organisation of mega-events has become an important scenario in place–state competition. The International Olympic Committee, in Lausanne, from 1894, and the Bureau International des Expositions, in Paris, from 1931, are unique examples of international institutions created with a remit to regulate this type of international competition, at the local and state level. Other international organisations also take 'local' decisions in order to organise important events, such as congresses and conferences, as is the case with the United Nations (Stockholm 1970 or Rio 1992), the GATT (numerous conferences in different places in the last Uruguay Round), the International Monetary Fund (currently in Washington, but every three years in other cities, mainly political capitals, such as Berlin 1988, Bangkok 1991 or Madrid 1994) or the EU (which every year nominates a different European cultural capital, such as Madrid 1992, Antwerp 1993 or Lisbon 1994).

From the point of view of the state, the successful bid for, and organisation of, a mega-event could appear as some kind of sign of international political or economic recognition; this explains the interest of many authoritarian or underdeveloped states in the organisation of Olympics or exhibitions. Arguably, this was the case of the Berlin Olympics in 1936, or Moscow in 1980 or Seoul in 1988. The same reasons could explain the frustration of China when Beijing did not succeed in winning the Olympics for the year 2000, losing out to Sydney. Such strategies tend to favour the political capitals, in order to reinforce the role of the state.

From the point of view of urban places, mega-events can become focal points in local strategies for internationalisation. This has been the case of the majority of the Olympic Games, like Saint Louis in 1904, or Los Angeles in 1932 and 1984, Barcelona in 1992, Atlanta in 1996 or Sydney in the year 2000. The case of the Olympics is especially relevant with 27 summer events having been organised, usually every four years, from 1896 to 2000 (Figure 11.1). A general indicator of the local relevance of hosting the Olympic event can be inferred from the fact that in Athens, in 1896, there were only 9 sports,

197

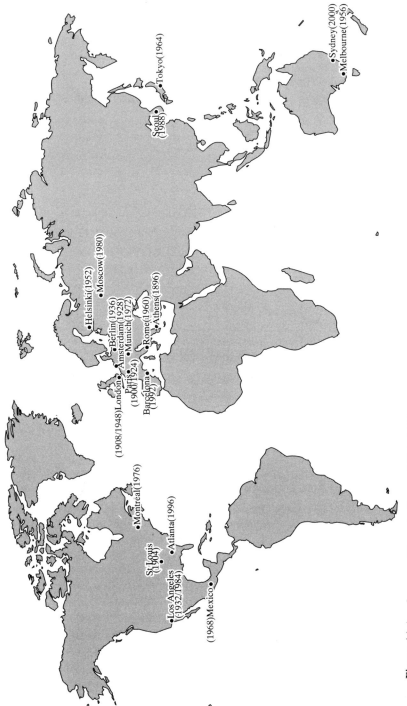

Figure 11.1. Summer Olympic Games 1896–2000

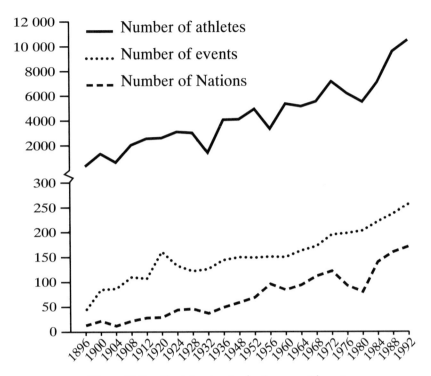

Figure 11.2.   Participation in the Summer Olympics

43 events, 13 states and 311 athletes participating (Figure 11.2); in the last Olympics in Barcelona, in 1992, there were 171 states, 10 500 athletes, 11 000 journalists, and an estimated television audience of 3500 million people.

The Winter Olymics constitute an even more spectacular example of the local–global contradiction, because the natural conditions needed for their organisation imply a very specific, generally mountainous, location. Oslo 1962, Sapporo 1972 or Sarajevo 1984 could be considered as exceptions to this rule. Nevertheless, the last Winter Games, organised in Lillehammer in 1994, provides a good example. The little Norwegian village normally has 22 000 inhabitants and 85 policemen, but during the Olympics a safety infrastructure of 3000 policemen (a 35-fold increase) received 40 000 accredited people, plus tourists, and national and international day visitors.

Other sports events, especially the more popular ones, can also become mega-events, because of their international status or general powers of attraction. World or continental championships, international and some national leagues or special sports festivals sometimes attain this status.

Universal exhibitions could be considered to be the modern culmination of the traditional industrial and commercial fairs. Thirty universal exhibitions have been organised from London, in 1851, to Lisbon, in 1998, with very

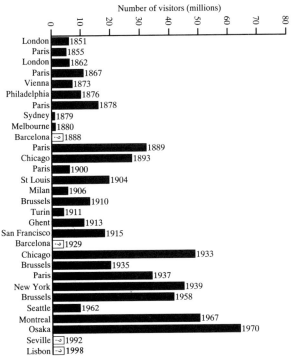

Figure 11.3.   Visitors to the Universal Exhibitions, 1851–1998

different rhythms and local relevance (Figures 11.3 and 11.4). Thanks to the records ofticket sales, it is possible to obtain statistical information on the numbers of visitors to the universal exhibitions in order to evaluate their potential tourism significance. The principal trend is indicated by the following figures: 64 million visitors in Osaka, in 1970; 50.3 in Montreal, in 1967; 48.7 in Chicago, in 1933; 44.9 in New York, in 1939; 41.4 in Brussels, in 1958; and 32.2 in Paris, in 1937. Every large city today organises many different commercial fairs, but only a few of these, generally with very specialised functions, secure a genuinely international audience generating major tourist flows. Frankfurt provides one such example. In 1991, the European ranking of cities in terms of the numbers of international fairs hosted was: Birmingham, 60; Milan, 57; Amsterdam, 31; Barcelona, 26; and Stuttgart, 24 (Bonneville et al. 1992).

Many cultural events also attain international powers of attraction, sometimes related to a local connection with an important personality. This is exemplified by the case of the annual drama festivals organised in Stratford-upon-Avon, the birthplace of William Shakespeare, or the musicals of Bayreuth, based on the connection with Richard Wagner, or of Salzburg, associated with Wolfgang Amadeus Mozart. Some places benefit from direct, even casual, connections with famous personalities, originating international pilgrimages, which constitute

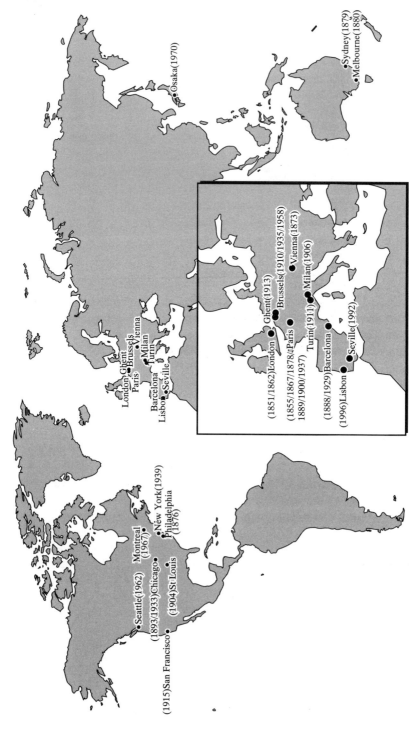

Figure 11.4. Universal exhibitions 1851–1996

major tourist flows. Other cities without this kind of connection are also able to organise cultural events, like the drama festivals of Avignon, the films of Cannes or Berlin, the music of Vienna or of the Isle of Man, or the carnivals of Venice and of Rio de Janeiro. A study of the international cultural influence of the biggest European cities has clearly demonstrated the role of the main capital cities, like London, Paris, Athens, Rome, Madrid or Vienna, as well as of some non-capital cities, like Milan or Barcelona (Reclus 1989).

Major opera theatres allow a small number of cities to maintain long seasons of festivals, thereby creating an international network, with a few strong points like La Scala in Milan, Covent Garden in London, l'Opéra in Paris, the Liceu in Barcelona,[6] the Bolshoi Theatre in Moscow, the Metropolitan Opera House in New York, and some others. Significant religious traditions also explain the international attraction of particular places like Benares, Rome, Salt Lake City, Lourdes, Santiago de Compostela or Fatima, or of the special tours and visits of the Roman Catholic Pope or the Dalai Lama.

It is very difficult to undertake an exhaustive survey of all the different possible mega-events. The discussion is therefore advanced via a deeper local case-study of the Barcelona '92 Olympics.

11.4 BARCELONA: MODEL OR ANTI-MODEL?

The city of Barcelona is very well located in the general processes discussed with more than a century of international policy at the local level (Carreras 1988). The special place of Barcelona within the Spanish urban system as a secondary city, particularly due to the late development of capitalism from 1850 onwards, forced the city to find its own economic way. The manufacturing basis, until 1973 at least, and the later specialisation in services, have permitted the development of local strategies in order to attract international flows. A clear sunbelt position, a rich architectural heritage, strong local and international culture, and a relatively developed socio-economic level are all major features which support these strategies. A special agreement among economic, cultural and political élites, periodically changing their leadership, has allowed continuity in recent years in the implementation of this realistic and traditional policy.

The establishment of a local tourist organisation in 1908, and of a commercial fair from 1920, both organised with a mixed pattern of private and public participation, have provided the material basis for Barcelona's long policy of international attraction. The existence of this tradition is very important in order to understand the recent success of Barcelona in mega-events organisation. Internationalisation has been more of a local urban policy than an occasional strategy; consequently, Barcelona's current policy cannot be automatically applied as a universal recipe for all large cities.

Economic and geopolitical reasons explain what can be termed 'the international century' of the city. The economic reasons lie in the fact that, since the beginning of the eighteenth century, the industrialisation process has been based on manufacturing which utilised a foreign raw material, which had to be imported, that is cotton. This explains why, for more than 150 years, Barcelona has reckoned with an international trade infrastructure connected to its harbour (18.3 million tonnes in 1992). This infrastructure implies the availability of information, skills and knowledge, and an international tradition. But geopolitical reasons are also important because, as capital of Catalonia, a nation with no state since medieval times, Barcelona—especially its local élites—is accustomed to looking at the international stage as a means of reinforcing its national position.

Some figures summarise the economic process. In 1733, the first cotton-weaving factory was established; in 1832, the first steam-powered factory began operating, again in cotton manufacturing; in 1841, a gas supply was installed in the city; in 1848, the first passenger railway was inaugurated, connecting Barcelona and the northern provincial city of Mataró; in 1854, it was the location of the first working-class general strike, which particularly affected the textile workers of the Barcelona area; and, in 1860, it adopted its first urban plan, which was characterised by a very deep technological approach.

The interaction of the economic, social and cultural consequences of these main features of the industrialisation process has found continuity in the development of a conscious and systematic internationalisation policy at local level. This policy has been implemented by combining the action of public and private influences, and there are some specific dates in the organisation of major events which are noteworthy.

On the one hand, 1888 was the year of the first universal exhibition in Barcelona. The main result of this exhibition was the affirmation of Barcelona as the second city in Spain, and the opening of its first urban park (Carreras 1988). Forty years later, in 1929, it organised a second international exhibition; the international crisis tarnished the economic relevance of this industrial fair, but the city succeeded in gaining a second urban park, with many different cultural infrastructures, and also a new architectural impulse, with the influence of the Bauhaus. The plans for a third universal exhibition in 1980 failed because of the political centralisation of the previous Francoist regime.

On the other hand, 1936 marked the beginning of the Spanish Civil War, and also the first Barcelona bid for the Olympic Games, which failed in favour of Berlin. In spite of this, some enthusiastic and democratic world athletes assembled in the so-called Popular Games of Barcelona, held in the Olympic stadium; this constituted the first core of the International Brigades against Fascism. Of lesser significance was the 1952 International Eucharistic Congress which was held in Barcelona. It was the first international event developed in Francoist Spain and permitted some renovation of the local urban plans. The political situation in Spain hindered the national nomination for the Olympic Games in 1960.

Finally, in 1992, Barcelona succeeded in its third and definitive bid to organise the Olympic Games, the main statistics relating to which have already been quoted. Economic and urban plans based on the image of Barcelona '92 have secured local agreement and, led by the mayor of the city, have been presented to international audiences. The tertiarisation of the city has been completed, international capital has provided strong collaboration, acting as new agents of attraction, and Barcelona reached a secondary ranking within the European urban hierarchy, below London, Paris and Milan, but alongside Madrid, Munich, Frankfurt, Rome, Brussels and Amsterdam, according to the Reclus (1989) report published three years before the Olympics.

As a clear consequence of this process, foreign visitors to the city have increased in number during recent years. In 1993, the year after the Games, Barcelona attracted more than 6 million international visitors, two-thirds of them arriving by plane,[7] while 57% lodged in the renewed and enlarged hotel infrastructure. The majority of visitors spent less than 2 days in the city, mainly (47.4%) came for tourist purposes, and were predominantly from Italy, the USA, France and Germany (53.4%). According to official tourist surveys, family tourism is increasing (36%), the majority being couples with no children, to the detriment of more traditional organised groups coming for the typical beach tourism.

Despite the extinguishing of Olympic enthusiasm, the urban policy of Barcelona is being further advanced. After 1992, more hotels have opened, as well as new shopping centres and other cultural facilities, like the National Theatre and the Auditorium; new projects in urban planning are also being implemented in order to increase the fluidity of traffic and improve the connection of the city with its sea border. The strategic plan Barcelona-2000[8] is the result of a new institutional and social agreement developing service and commercial activities, especially with the construction of new office centres in the core of the city and in its metropolitan surroundings. Barcelona bid for but failed to secure the headquarters of the Central European Bank, and the Pharmaceutical Patents Office, in October 1993, but is continuing to seek to enhance its international dimension.

The external echo of Barcelona's initiatives and events is always greater than the local, for positive reasons as well as for negative ones;[9] it constitutes a strong basis for further tourist development. But Barcelona is presented not as a model but as a case-study, because some general effects of globalisation do connect with its local tradition of internationalisation. In this regard, the Barcelona process is not only an example of the global trends, but also a contradictory example of the resisting force of place (Santos et al. 1993). Obviously, in some ways it is not a unique example; Barcelona could be included among other non-capital European cities, like Milan, Birmingham, Frankfurt, Lyons or Toulouse, and many others.[10]

11.5   FIRST CONCLUSIONS

It is difficult to set out any real conclusions from these first reflections on tourism, from the point of view of other cities organising mega-events.

Nevertheless, the theoretical complexity of the different fields involved in these, mainly urban and tourism, studies obliges us to point out some different principles, whose generality allows them to be considered as first conclusions.

The first point is related to the pertinacious capacity of cities to survive the majority of changes and crises, since the beginning of urban civilisation until the present. According to the well-known theory of Jane Jacobs, the largest urban regions have proven that they are able to implement many kinds of initiatives or strategies in order to develop their life even over the worst conjunctures; therefore, urban inhabitants and urban regions always appear richer and more dynamic than other parts of the territory (Jacobs 1984). Megaevents could be considered, in this sense, one of the most visible elements of the current local strategies for survival.

A second point refers to contemporary spatial restructuring processes. The contradictory globalisation and flexibilisation process of the economic system, and of the world territory, pushes some local places to develop international strategies. Big cities mainly benefit from this dynamic process of globalisation and fragmentation, because of the inertia of their historical investments and their political weight. However, the case of Barcelona shows the complexity and the length of the route to be followed by local places if they are to succeed to have connections at the international level. Their urban facilities appear to be an effective resource, but not all cities have been able to develop these satisfactorily.

Finally, a third point arises regarding the important role of tourist activities in the tertiarisation of cities. Tourist flows today are changing from their orientation to mass resorts, to favour more selective destinations instead, with clear thematic specialisation. So, cities are becoming more and more a stage, if not a final destination, as a cultural resource, alongside other new destinations, like ecological or adventure experiences, as well as the traditional products, like sun, sand and sex.

NOTES

1. This adjective, a dramatic one for the author because of his Balearic origin, refers to the massive and rapid urbanisation process of the main natural reserves of Majorca and Ibiza.
2. The organisation of the Winter Olympics in Lillehammer, in Norway, in February 1994, is a very good example of the intention to combine nature conservation and mega-event development.
3. The film, *If it is Tuesday, it's Belgium*, caricatures this homogenisation process very effectively.
4. It is necessary to stress that crisis does not mean disappearance, but significant change.
5. In France, Avignon with its theatre fair, or Paris with Disneyland Paris provide excellent examples of this fact.
6. The fire at the Liceu in February 1994 has been as international as the terrorist outrages because of the fame of the 1992 Olympics.
7. Passenger traffic at Barcelona Airport was: 1990, 9.0 million (37.4% international); 1991, 8.9 million (36.3% international); 1992, 10.0 million (38.9%

international); and 1993, 9.7 million (41.4% international). Figures come from the City Council review *Barcelona Economica*, No. 20, fourth quarter 1993, Ajuntament de Barcelona.

8. The strategic Plan Barcelona-2000 implies the cooperation of more than 200 public and private institutions operating in a very flexible form (Tello 1992).

9. The fire at the Liceu, and ETA (Basque terrorist organisation) bombs, must unfortunately be included in this international diffusion process.

10. For this reason, the urban study group in the Barcelona Department is now working in the field of international comparisons, especially with French (Lyons and Toulouse) and Brazilian cities (São Paulo and Rio de Janeiro) (Villes et Territoires 1992).

12 Tourism and the Environment

CHRISTOPH BECKER
University of Trier, Germany

12.1 TOURISM AND THE ENVIRONMENT: A CHANGING FRAMEWORK OF VALUES

While the Western world was characterised by euphoric growth in the 1960s, the 1970s witnessed a new social consciousness as the 'limits of growth' appeared to have been reached (Meadows et al. 1972). This was signalled not only by economic recession and social crises (a decrease in authoritarian structures), but also a growing awareness that the environment was being dangerously overburdened by large-scale technical changes, traffic and settlement developments. The strains, stresses and contradictions were observable in daily life, because important resources were and are being consumed in a finite manner.

A change of values has occurred with respect to development, with a shift away from massive projects and greater emphasis on qualitative growth. The importance of work as the focal point of life has also declined, while leisure time has attracted a higher priority in the life styles of the majority of the population. Linked to this qualitative change in social aspirations with respect to standards of living, there has been a growing awareness of the role of the environment.

While increased tourism is, in one sense, an expression of the new life styles, it also contributes to the environmental crises. Tourism has reached such an extent, with the growth of excursions and holiday trips, that the damage inflicted on the environment can no longer be overlooked. The work of Krippendorf has been particularly important in highlighting the relationship between tourism and the environment. In 1975 Krippendorf's book *Die Landschaftsfresser* (The landscape eaters) succeeded in arousing the sensibilities of a large sector of the Central European public to the ecological damage caused by tourism. Also important was the work of Jungk who in 1980 established 16 pairs of opposites describing 'hard' and 'soft' tourism. This was important in popularising the expression 'soft' tourism in German-speaking regions. In order to understand 'soft' tourism, an adequate regional tourism development strategy, such as that suggested by Krippendorf et al.

European Tourism: Regions, Spaces and Restructuring. Edited by A. Montanari and A.M. Williams.
© 1995 European Science Foundation. Published in 1995 by John Wiley & Sons Ltd.

Table 12.1.   Strategies of tourism development: selected elements

Hard tourism	Soft tourism
Development without planning	First planning, then development
Each community plans for itself	Planning for larger areas
Widespread and scattered construction	Concentrated construction so as to save land
Construction for indefinite need	Determining limits of final extension
Tourism in the hands of non-local promoters	Local population participates and makes decisions
Develop all facilities to their maximum capacity	Develop all facilities for average capacity

Source: Prepared by the author on the basis of Krippendorf et al. (1982, p. 379).

(1982), is also important (Table 12.1). It must be stressed, however, that both of these idealised descriptions of soft tourism are not to be understood as offering complete conceptualisations of new forms of tourism, but rather as providing more of a specific perspective on overall travel behaviour and a comprehensive general framework for analysis.

By the end of the 1980s the term 'sustainability' or, rather, 'sustainable development' had appeared in both political and scientific discussions. The Brundtland Report (World Commission on Environment and Development 1987) and the Rio Declaration (1992) were particularly decisive in popularising this debate. Perhaps of even greater significance in this respect was the UN Conference on the Environment and Development (UNCED or Eco '92). This debate has spilled over into the field of tourism. The language—and conceptualisation—of the debate has shifted from soft, green or ecotourism to sustainable tourism. This has crystallised into a concern with three equally important goals; economic development, social and environmental sustainability. Nevertheless, it has to be emphasised that the criteria required to operationalise these goals are still missing from the policy sphere.

These debates have attained the status of global issues. This was underlined by the fact that the World Tourism Organisation (WTO) presented a first study on sustainable tourism in 1992. The EU has also seized on activities in this field. Since 1992 DGXXIII (Directorate General of the European Union) has had an Action Plan for Tourism which gives a high profile to environmental issues. The overall budget for this programme is limited, but a number of small pilot projects have been supported, with a prize for excellence in the tourism and environment field to be awarded at the end of 1994. The pursuit of qualitative growth has also been taken up at the national level. One of the earliest exponents was Switzerland which in 1979 instigated a special commission to consider tourism–environment relationships (Beratende Kommission für Fremdenverkehr des Bundesrates 1979). This has been followed—at some distance—by a number of initiatives in other countries. For example, in Germany it was as late as 1993 before the Ministry of Economics issued a report on tourism and the environment. In the UK a *Journal of Sustainable Tourism* has been published since 1993.

One of the greatest obstacles to implementing 'soft' tourism strategies is that there is no commonly accepted model and also no stringent principles. There are some indicative models, but the optimum soft tourism solution is likely to be highly contingent, depending on the characteristics of particular situations and of particular sites (see below). Perhaps the most important limitation to the soft tourism approach is its limited applicability to places and areas of mass tourism; can these be converted 'softly' to 'soft tourism'? In these areas, it is no doubt possible to limit or modify the impact of tourism on the environment, but the sheer mass of visitors remains a major obstacle to developing a permanent 'soft' form of tourism, especially in a format which would sustain previous employment and business levels.

With the move towards 'soft', environmentally friendly tourism, there has been a wider paradigmatic shift. Until well into the 1970s, for example, there was widespread research on landscape evaluation processes with the aim, among others, of identifying suitable areas for the further development of tourism (Bonertz 1981). Due to the fact that, since the 1980s, attention has shifted away from the development of new tourist regions, the focus of research and public interest has become the care of the environment.

Linked to this shift, it has become popular to argue that tourism provides an ideal field of learning for environmentally conscious behaviour in general. It is true that there is often a limited willingness to learn during a holiday—perhaps because people are away from everyday stresses—and perhaps the damage to the environment in another country is more obvious than it is at home. However, it is also true that among tourists there is often a lack of self-criticism, which prevents them from recognising the damage caused by tourism. At the same time, and in spite of the societal shift in values, the truth is that probably only a small number of holidaymakers would be consciously willing to forgo personal comforts on the grounds of preserving the environment or even concerning themselves with the problems arising from tourism. After all, when on holiday most people wish to free themselves from the straitjacket of everyday life (Butler 1991). Bearing this in mind, it can be summarised that a holiday may provide a field of learning conducive to general improvements in awareness of, and behaviour towards, the environment, but that—realistically—the possible benefits are likely to be limited.

12.2 INTEREST IN AND DEMAND FOR ENVIRONMENTALLY FRIENDLY TOURISM

If it is considered difficult to define 'soft' tourism, then it is even more problematic—and perhaps virtually impossible—to provide even a generalised estimate of the extent of the demand for 'environmentally harmless' travel. Therefore, all that it is possible to do here is outline the potential for 'soft' tourism, and to attempt to assess awareness of the environmental damage in the holiday region.

Table 12.2. Survey of 'soft' partial tourism potential in Germany: percentages supporting particular statements

One should modify one's usual life style and comfort while on holiday	49
I would use public transport in the holiday resort when it was cheaper, more comfortable and quicker	61
One should leave oneself ample time on holiday, even if a particular place on the itinerary has to be omitted	84
One should respect the conventions and customs of the native population	95
One should treat the environment as carefully as possible, even if the native population do not show it respect	94
In most holiday regions, tourism places too great a strain on the native population and on nature	80

Source: Prepared by the author on the basis of Studienkreis für Tourismus e.V. (1989).

A useful starting point is the assessment made by the Studienkreis für Tourismus—as part of a larger study of travel behaviour in Germany—of the total 'soft' potential among the German population as a whole (Table 12.2). The results suggested that there was a total 'soft' potential among 20% of the German population. This was based on the fact that one-fifth of those interviewed displayed environmentally conscious attitudes when questioned about their views of environmentally friendly behaviour on holiday. However, these results have to be treated cautiously, for there is an important difference between 'soft tourism potential' defined in this way, and the proportion of holidaymakers who would actually behave in an environmentally friendly manner in a variety of situations. There is bound to be an important difference in this respect if only because environmentally friendly behaviour usually demands more money, time or a trade-off with certain comforts. In addition, it must also be remembered that interviewees may respond in ways that they perceive to be socially acceptable, even if they do not always act in line with such intentions.

Some social groups were disproportionately represented among those who responded positively to questions about 'soft tourism', especially the younger age groups, people with a higher class social background, those with travel experience, and those who seek out activity holidays. Yet, interviews conducted among members of BUND, the leading German environmental protection organisation, and interviews among sympathisers of the 'Green' political party, revealed that these groups do not travel in a particularly environmentally friendly manner. They travel often, to long-distance destinations, they make above-average use of aeroplanes, and are disproportionately likely to visit regions which can be considered exotic—whether in terms of different races or of untouched nature—and they are also likely to be well informed about the places that they are visiting (Hallerbach 1993). These tourists therefore have a potentially strong impact on local cultures and environments. This apparent contradiction only serves to underline the difficulties encountered in transforming rational attitudes into appropriate action against the backdrop of prevailing social conditions.

The problem of the gap between social concern and effective social action is evident in mass tourism as in 'soft' tourism. An analysis of survey data reveals that, in 1985, only 30% of German holidaymakers compared to 58% in 1988 and 1989 were aware of damage caused to the environment by tourism in their holiday resort. This shows a clear increase in awareness, although that has since stagnated. But once again there is a discrepancy between the formation of attitudes sympathetic to the tourism–environment relationship, and actually putting these into practice. Environmental damage is also not necessarily off-putting to these tourists since the regions and countries in which German tourists most commented (more than 68%) on such degradation—such as Spain, France and Schleswig-Holstein—have also experienced major increases in the number of arrivals from Germany. It therefore seems that, in the holiday regions, environmental pollution is apparently seen, to an extent, as being an acceptable or necessary part of the costs of developing tourism.

12.3 NEW AND 'GREENER' FUTURES? DEVELOPMENTS IN ENVIRONMENTALLY FRIENDLY TOURISM

If there is to be a more environmentally friendly structuring of the travel business then three differing approaches are possible—and probably necessary—at various levels: on a business basis, at a highly localised level as well as for larger regions where conservation is an issue, and at the state or the EU level.

12.3.1 The holiday accommodation sector

The approach of businesses to environmental issues tends to be structured by their scale and forms of capital organisation. In general, smaller hotels and guest-houses tend to be more environmentally friendly: they have more sympathetic building styles, they are mostly well integrated into the townscape, they make extensive use of local services, and they tend not only to be owned by local people but also primarily employ local people. In these respects, therefore, the smaller hoteliers are more socially compatible with their host communities. On the other hand, their contribution to the communal income via various forms of local or trade taxes is mostly well below the average for local businesses, or may even be zero if firms' profits do not exceed their tax-exempt allowances. Within the framework of policies to support small and medium-sized businesses, the construction of new buildings and the modernisation of smaller-sized guest-houses receive particular support, but more general programmes for stimulating regional economic growth are supported almost independently of their size. It is important, however, to be careful not to associate smallness positively with environmental friendliness, leastways not in any simplistic manner. For example, camping sites are often considered to be socially compatible and to be near to nature, and yet they significantly influence the landscape. They can also damage the surrounding vegetation—especially at the water's edge; for example, a great strain is placed on the soil and on ground water by oil leaks and insufficient purification of sewage.

There is certainly increasing awareness of environmental issues among business owners and managers in this sector, if only because of the dictates of changes in demand. In order to encourage reorganisation of the day-to-day running of hotels in a more environmentally friendly manner, catering associations in most countries have organised awareness campaigns and also award seals of quality. This often involves relatively small initiatives such as the abandonment of individual jampots and a daily change of hand towels, or the use of environmentally friendly washing powder and cleaning agents, or the use of recycled paper for correspondence and advertising. This is not just the prerogative of small businesses. International hotel and restaurant groups, such as Interconti or McDonald's, are also engaged in such initiatives. Since many of these measures do not involve any additional direct costs, they have been adopted by a large proportion of the guest-houses. Hotels and guest-houses do have considerable potential for presenting an environmentally friendly image, not least because they offer scope for guests to participate actively in environmental initiatives. For example, guests are requested to show understanding of environmental issues and have the opportunity to feel involved with—and to contribute in some way to—conservation of the environment. The overall effects of these measures, however, must not be overestimated, for they remain only a first step in the right direction.

Although there has been a shift to greater environmental awareness, there are very few examples of businesses which even approach a state which can be termed 'total environmental friendliness'. An outstanding example is Hotel Ucliva in Switzerland: it is architecturally well-integrated into the village of Waltensburg, has good public transport links, the construction is harmonious with the typical style of the region, the building materials are ecologically sensitive, it is heated by wood fuel and solar panels, the kitchen and dining room rely as far as possible on local produce, and environmentally friendly washing and cleaning agents are used. Refuse is avoided as far as possible, or composted, and a programme of environmental conservation events is offered to guests. A discount is also offered to those who help with the enterprise's activities, such as working in the woodland. The hotel is organised as a cooperative and, as many of the members do not originate from the region, they receive interest on their shares in the form of rights to overnight accommodation in the hotel. This example is important because it shows that a successful eco-marketing strategy can be pursued by an ecologically committed hotel: although its prices are relatively high, it secures above-average bookings and makes a substantial economic profit.

There are other, if less spectacular, examples of businesses which are more or less environmentally friendly, especially in Middle and Western Europe, but also occasionally in the Mediterranean from Spain to Turkey (Hamele and von Lassberg 1991). In general they demonstrated that it is possible to operate successfully within a more environmentally aware framework, but—especially in the Mediterranean—they only secure a marginal share of the market.

There is considerable debate as to what constitutes genuinely environmentally friendly enterprise behaviour. One of the most controversial debates has surrounded the claims of the Center Parcs to be ecologically sensitive. These large-scale holiday centres, with between 3000 and 6000 beds, and their trademark 'subtropical bathing resorts', together with a shopping mall, are built in one of two styles: either an open or an enclosed version. The covered-in model has such extensive facilities that only a small number of the guests ever leave the holiday centre in order to undertake any type of excursion. Critics argue that the construction volume of the Center Parcs, the streams of traffic they generate, their very high energy and water consumption, as well as their high volumes of refuse, place considerable strain on the environment of the surrounding area. In addition, their capital originates in the congested metropolitan areas, and the parks are externally controlled; only minor additional income opportunities are created for local businesses. However, there is a counter-argument that, due to the 'ghettoisation' of the holidaymakers in the Center Parcs, it is possible to protect other, more sensitive recreation areas, from these tourist pressures. It is precisely this effect which has led to a re-assessment of Center Parcs in many circles in Germany, so that such developments are no longer automatically rejected as a matter of course, as they once were. Furthermore, there is also sympathy for the arguments that to develop Center Parcs in Germany would contribute to reducing the net outflow of tourists to foreign destinations, including the large number of Center Parcs located near by in the Netherlands. As such, this is an important illustration of the implications of there being a single market for many forms of tourism activities, at least on a regional scale.

12.3.2 Community-level involvement with environmentally friendly tourism

There is considerable scope for communities to play an important role in the introduction and implementation of ecologically based tourism: on the one hand, they can support the attempts of hotels and guest-houses to provide more environmentally friendly tourism services, and on the other hand they may have the powers to carry through comprehensive ecologically based conceptions of how their areas should be developed. The key point is that with respect to achieving improvements in or implementing environmentally friendly tourism, each community has the jurisdiction—at least in central Europe—to take decisions as to which type and scale of facility is to be provided at which sites in the community, and how these are to be designed and embedded in their surroundings. For example, dreary swimming-pools and indoor tennis courts in unimaginative factory-style architecture can be prohibited. It must be emphasised, however, that except where the community is itself the developer, then its powers are largely negative and persuasive. It can refuse permission for non-conforming developments, and can indicate to developers the types of developments which will be permitted, but it ultimately relies on private investors to undertake these.

Once a community has formed a clear concept of the environmentally friendly local tourism it seeks to develop, then this serves to highlight the need to at least partly redesign existing facilities, while at the same time dispensing with more highly technical facilities (e.g. ski-lifts, airfields for sports planes, marinas). There can be a cost to pay for this: dispensing with such amenities—which are usually very profitable—can mean that, at least in the short term, the average economic rate of return will decline. However, there is a counter-argument that, in the long run, environmental protection can actually cut costs. A community which is able successfully—and on a permanent basis—to reshape its tourism around more conservationist lines, has the medium-term opportunity to demand higher prices for its environmentally friendly product.

A convincing conceptualisation of ecologically friendly tourism development in a community involves more than environment-friendly hotels, guesthouses and tourist facilities. Other sectors of the community also need to be orientated along similar lines:

- In traffic areas, there is a need to introduce pedestrian precincts and restricted traffic areas, while pedestrian and cycle traffic—as well as local public transport services—should be supported.
- A more ecologically oriented agriculture should be introduced, in conjunction with diversification of rural economic structures; farmers should adjust their products to the changing demands and needs of the (more environmentally conscious) catering trade and should concentrate on direct sales to guests.
- Housing developments should be in keeping with the typical architectural style of the region.

When planning these and other sectors, the communities can use their supreme power of planning to good advantage—within the framework of foreseeable regional planning—by influencing freedom of design, which they can implement by means of development plans, statutes and persuasion work in the sense of an environmentally friendly development of tourism in conjunction with coordinated town planning. The aspect relating to persuasion is extremely important, since large numbers of the population must be able to identify themselves with the conservationist style of tourism. In order to gain total acceptance by the general public, it is necessary to involve the local population in decision-making.

At least in northern and central Europe, where communities have real planning powers, the community is the decisive administrative level at which environmentally friendly tourism objectives can be forumulated and, systematically and concretely, developed and implemented. At higher administrative levels (see below), it is only really possible to formulate general principles. In contrast, it is at the community level that endogenous potential can be employed intensively and optimum solutions can be sought for ecologically minded tourism.

Tourists do not spend all their time in the holiday resort but make excursions to surrounding destinations. Bearing this simple fact in mind, it is essential that not only must the holiday resort itself be designed for ecological tourism, but where possible this should also apply to the surrounding countryside. This wider regional approach requires intercommunal cooperation. Even if communities are at loggerheads in other respects, it is absolutely essential that there is cooperation so that each community puts its endogenous potential to maximum use and also develops, in conjunction with neighbouring communities, its own specific strong points. In this way a network-like system may be formed with several functional focal points, which is also geared around the needs of the environment. One of the advantages of such a tourist region, with key functional focal points, is that traffic volumes can be better managed and controlled; for if there are attractive towns and villages in the vicinity, then long excursions to distant attractions will be reduced.

Larger nature-oriented sites present different types of developmental and managerial challenges; these sites are to be found in the form of various large-scale conservation areas, such as national parks, biosphere reserves or nature parks. In the case of these large-scale conservation sites, the main aim is the protection of 'unoccupied' or 'unspoilt' areas, although an environmentally friendly structure of built-up areas within and at the edge of the large-scale conservation areas is possible and necessary. Because of their natural beauty, these open spaces are subject to large numbers of visitors and are often major focal points of attraction for tourism. In order to resolve the central conflict between the demands of holidaymakers and of nature conservation, a number of managerial strategies are required: the areas are often divided into zones which control the flow of visitors, admission fees are charged, and the development and furnishing of sites are pursued in a sensitive and conservatonist manner with an emphasis on making visitor information available. The aim is to encourage greater understanding among visitors for the preservation of nature and for the restrictions which are essential to achieving this aim (Heukemes 1993).

There have been several attempts to conceptualise the development of environmentally friendly tourism in individual communities or in tourist areas. As always, however, one of the major problems has been implementation. In northern and central Europe, at least, there has not yet been an example where a tourist area or even an individual community has been converted to an ecologically self-sustaining tourist resort in all aspects. Until the present, only partial projects have been realised, as for example with regard to road traffic, agriculture or individual tourist facilities. Good examples of partial success with regard to traffic are the islands of Langeoog, Spiekeroog and Wangerooge in the German North Sea, as also are Saas Fee, Braunwald and Zermatt in the Swiss and Kleinwalsertal in the German Alps. Convincing attempts to develop balanced associations between tourism and agriculture are to be found in Hindelang in the German and Innervillgraten in the Austrian Alps.

In contrast to hotels and guest-houses, for which very clear ecological standards can be laid down, it is difficult to establish a set of convincing criteria for conservationist-minded tourist communities. As a result, it is very difficult to be able to award a seal of quality for the environment, which would serve to both encourage communities in this field as well as providing examples of good practice. In particular, the aspects of a balanced ecological structure for road traffic, housing development or even for individual tourist communities can hardly be measured in quantitative criteria. In Germany this process is made more complicated by a court ruling stating that seals of quality for the environment must be 'court-proof', that is, they must be based on verifiable and applicable criteria. But even if an approved seal of quality for communities offering ecological tourism could be developed, it will be very problematic to put this into practice. This is underlined by the fact that in Germany there are as yet no tourism communities which fulfil all potential criteria satisfactorily. On the other hand, communities and travel companies have a strong interest in developing a seal of quality for the environment—as in the case of the EU's 'Blue Flag' for beaches—as these are valuable for marketing their tourism products. In practice, in the absence of comprehensive ecological criteria, conformity with standards for a single ecological component within the supply side is considered to be sufficient to declare the whole package to be environmentally friendly.

12.3.3 Ecological approaches at national and regional level

Environmentally friendly tourism is not the sole preserve of local communities. Both national and regional governments can be involved in this sphere, as can be seen in the case of Germany. Within the Ministry of Economics an 'Advisory committee for matters of tourism' was formed, which issued an interim report in 1993 (Der Beirat für Fragen des Tourismus 1993). This presents a view of current problems and makes a series of recommendations which are directed at the travel agency business, and a list of measures which need to be instigated at state level. In contrast, the tourism programme formulated by the Social Democratic Party in 1993 is much more detailed and is dependent, to a considerable extent, on public funds. Only to a limited degree does either programme contain concrete recommendations which meet with public consent and there is no guarantee that these will be put into practice. No special promotion programmes have been introduced nor have contractual guidelines been rewritten with regard to ecological demands. Indeed, in practice, the UVP (programme for conservation of environment) guidelines of the EU have only been adjusted as far as has been absolutely necessary.

At county level, the Ministries of Economic Affairs are responsible for setting out recommendations for conservationist tourism. They organise competitions, present pilot projects relating to conservation of the environment in tourist regions, and support programmes involving 'soft tourism'. However, the incomplete and fragmentary policy guideline for tourism is illustrated by the fact that the guidelines for regional development, which seek to promote investments by the tourist trade and in tourist facilities, were not supplemented by criteria to protect the environment. And yet, in other ways, the county and regional planning authorities have intensified their efforts to adapt their planning principles so as to influence ecological planning at the community level. These planning principles seek to prevent any obvious actions or developments which are hazardous to the environment, but they are negative in character and do not necessarily lead to what really constitutes environment-friendly development.

Despite these reservations, there does seem to be a genuine shift in values in at least parts of the tourism industry in northern and central Europe. For example, the German Hotel and Catering Association has recently issued a *Catalogue of Criteria for the Environmentally Friendly Hotel and Catering Industry* containing 40 individual criteria covering such topics as water/sewage treatment, avoiding and managing refuse, and energy (Der Beirat für Fragen des Tourismus 1993), and this is becoming more and more widely used. Similarly, the regional tourist associations are switching over, to a greater or lesser degree, to conservation of the environment in their marketing activities, strongly emphasising such holidays in their advertising and public relations work. They also organise corresponding competitions in the hotel and catering industry and publish lists of environmentally friendly hotels and guest-houses as well as encouraging their guests to display more environment-friendly behaviour patterns. However, while such initiatives are important—not least in fostering a cultural change in the tourism sphere—they remain largely limited to the roles of persuasion, demonstration and, as a last resort, denial of planning permission. The ultimate success of developing environmentally friendly tourism continues to rely, as always, on the actions of operators and investors, to which we turn in the next section.

12.3.4 Travel organisers and agencies: ecologically informed initiatives in a changing policy environment

Despite the changes in the policy environment, genuinely 'soft' holidays are still rarely to be found on offer in the catalogues of the large tour operators in Germany. However, there is some progress even in this section. The well-known travel organisers have usually appointed a member of their staff to be responsible for environmental matters, even if this is rarely their function within the company. The task of these 'environmental representatives' is to try and reduce or eliminate from the company's brochure those holiday destinations which present significant environmental hazards, to try to encourage ecological thinking within the travel organisation, to use environmentally friendly advertising materials, and to convince clients to adopt more ecologically sensitive behaviour patterns.

In contrast, there is a large number of small tour operators who try to create a market niche for themselves, by presenting an image of being an ecologically oriented travel specialist. Without exception, these are small travel companies with one or only a few employees, who sell between 150 and 5000 holidays per year. Some are non-profit-making organisations, but most are commercially organised. The holidays offered are, on the whole, environmentally friendly although they often have minor weak points in their make-up: their outward journey is often made without the use of public transport, the participants are insufficiently prepared for the holiday experience, there is a lack of information concerning the ecological context of the holiday, etc. Although in absolute terms, the soft tourism products of these companies only account for a marginal proportion of the total market, they do contribute to 'softening' the overall range of travel organisation.

12.4   THE UNEVEN SPATIAL DISTRIBUTION OF ECOLOGICAL TOURISM IN EUROPE

The spatial distribution of environmentally friendly tourism is highly polarised. It is particularly concentrated in central, western and northern Europe, especially in those regions which have a relatively poorly developed tourist trade. In part, this is because the severe ecological damage which has been caused to the environments of these areas by non-tourist activities (industrialisation, urbanisation, etc.) has led to greater sensibility. In the area around the Mediterranean, in contrast, there are relatively few examples of environmentally friendly tourism. And, in part, these were initiated by committed environmentalists from the northern European home areas of the tourists. This is because, arguably, there is only a shallow level of ecological consciousness among the indigenous communities of the Mediterranean region. Examples of this are provided by Prodec in Andalusia, tourism cooperatives in Greece, the Club Natura Complex and the Half Moon Hotel in Bodrum in Turkey (Hamell and von Lassberg 1991).

In the present discussions about new forms of 'soft' tourism, it should not be forgotten that large-scale conservation areas, some of which were established before the Second World War and many more in the following decades, make an important contribution to environmentally friendly tourism. In Germany and France alone, there exist—besides several national parks—64 and 27 nature parks, respectively, which constitute 22 and 8% of the national territory (Job 1993a, b). Even if, as a rule, nature parks tend to be frequented more by local residents than by tourists, nature conservation and information concerning these have a high priority in these areas. In France these nature parks are seen as model landscapes and receive four times more subsidies from public funds than do such parks in Germany. On the one hand, there is carefully controlled expansion of infrastructure in these areas in France while, on the other hand, financial aid is available for structural changes in agriculture and for village renewal schemes.

The most favourable conditions for a conversion to 'soft' tourism exist in rural areas and in those regions where the tourist trade is not overdeveloped. In these areas, it is still possible to realise conservationist goals by building environmentally friendly hotels, guest-houses and facilities, and by modernising existing buildings. In tourist resorts which have already been fully developed, only limited restructuring is possible because of the difficulties of reversing intensive over-building of the countryside. However, an improvement in quality can be achieved even in such resorts while at the same time preserving nature if upper capacity limits are established, measures to save energy and water are taken, purification plants are built, the traffic volume is reduced, inter-company measures are taken to protect the environment, more green belts are planted, more 'soft' holidays and leisure activities are provided, and more information is made available. In this way, overdeveloped tourist areas can experience the rejuvenation phase of the resort life-cycle model.

In urban tourism, in which hotel chains claim increasing shares of overnight reservations, efforts are being concentrated on inter-company measures and on preventing 'overloading' of established tourist 'highlights', by opening up and promoting alternative tourist attractions.

12.5   CONCLUSIONS

In the course of the profound changes which have taken place in value systems in Western Europe, the volume and variety of leisure activities have increased so that the damage inflicted on the environment by excursionism and tourism is increasing. At the same time, however, there is greater awareness of the environment. Nevertheless, there continues to be a substantial gap between social concern and effective social action, and there is no prospect that this will be reduced until at least such time as the present younger generation become adults. Therefore, it has already become necessary to turn towards sustainable tourism, so as to initiate qualitative economic development which is compatible with ecological and social goals. There is a need to manage a shift from finite to renewable resources and to minimise the consumption of non-renewable resources.

Until the present time, the term 'sustainable development' has primarily been discussed on a global basis and among economists. It is not surprising, therefore, that there has been a failure to determine criteria which can be applied at the regional or local level. This applies equally to sustainable tourism. There are, however, some advances with respect to tourism. For example, in the German-speaking area of Europe, the Arbeitskreis Freizeit- und Fremdenverkehrsgeographie (Working Group on the Geography of Leisure and Tourism) is active in studying sustainable tourism. This does at least offer the hope that such research may lead to the incorporation of sustainable tourism in tourism policies.

The potential role of the EU in promoting sustainable tourism development in Europe is rather limited. There is, however, potential room for the EU to be active in the following areas:

- The EU can promote model projects, can award prizes for excellence, and can improve the circulation of information about sustainable tourism development.
- The EU should insist that the principles of sustainable tourism development are incorporated within the framework of its regional economic development programmes and other policy areas.
- The EU should support the transfer of experiences of soft or sustainable tourism from northern and central Europe to the Mediterranean region.

13 Tourism Change in Central and Eastern Europe

DEREK R. HALL
University of Sunderland, UK

13.1 INTRODUCTION

This chapter discusses some of the major elements of change in international tourism development in Central and Eastern Europe (CEE) and their significance for Western Europe. It reflects on the trends developing during the last years of state socialism as a means of providing a context for addressing the structural changes taking place during the transitional, post-communist period. The focus is placed specifically on the international dimension: tourism data for the region present the usual range of analytical problems (Hall 1991), and domestic tourism statistics tend to be limited and inconsistent. Internationally, the data are not always able to distinguish different forms of cross-border movement: (overnight) tourism, excursionism, transiting, petty trading, migrant labour or refugee flight.

The region boasts a wide range of mass and specialist niche attractions, some of which far surpass anything Western Europe can offer (Hall 1990a, 1991). Its diversity of physical and cultural environments and attractions provides the potential for substantial market segmentation. The image of poor service and inadequate infrastructure, often, perversely, reinforced by cheapness arising from favourable exchange rates, is gradually being overcome (Hall 1992a, b, c). Current discussion about targeting high-spending groups, with minimal adverse social and environmental impacts, and season-extending activities, emphasises the importance of attracting conference/business tourism and exploiting West European and North American incentive travel. The region's substantial heritage potential, and varied health resorts, can be employed to supplement such activities. With a heightened awareness of nationality in the region, ethnic tourism is also important (Ostrowski 1991).

The impact of tourism activities on the region's environmental diversity and fragility requires careful planning and monitoring. While official recognition is now being given to the need for 'sustainable', 'green' and 'eco' tourism, as, for example, in the Romanian national tourism programme (RMTT 1990, p. 3)

European Tourism: Regions, Spaces and Restructuring. Edited by A. Montanari and A.M. Williams.
© 1995 European Science Foundation. Published in 1995 by John Wiley & Sons Ltd.

and the UK Environmental Know-How Fund for ecotourism development in
Bulgaria's Pirin and Rila Mountains, there is often too little conceptual discussion and analysis of the appropriateness or otherwise of the adoption of what
are often little more than fashionable buzz words. This can result in contradictory and conflicting statements of policy, particularly between individual
ministries and other government agencies. Further, a newly unleashed entrepreneurial sector may have neither the resources nor the inclination to take a
broad view of tourism's potentially detrimental consequences.

Within contemporary CEE, tourism development cannot be isolated as an
independent variable, but it is an element of, and is heavily influenced by,
processes of economic, political and social restructuring. Significant among
these have been the loosening of constraints on personal mobility, enhanced
and reoriented foreign trade and investment, price liberalisation, encouragement of entrepreneurial activity, programmes of large- and small-scale privatisation, deregulation, divestment and internal currency convertibility. An
upgrading of existing, and the pursuit of new, transport and communications
infrastructure would appear pivotal in both the spatial and structural development of tourism and tourism relations in linking the new Europe's component
parts, upgrading the region's domestic infrastructure, and influencing the
mobility of the region's residents.

As post-1989 processes begin to blur the east–west division of Europe, they
also emphasise the diversity within the former socialist bloc. The individual
distinctiveness of nations and countries east of the Elbe has been reinforced by
the resurgent role of nationalism, a force which has both been harnessed by
and has, in its turn, employed as a vehicle of expression, international tourism
development.

13.2   EVOLUTION OF CEE TOURISM

Although tourism became increasingly popular in CEE in the first half of the
century, particularly in upland areas and spa towns (e.g. Rogalewski 1980;
Hall 1991, pp. 81–82; Jordan 1992), the post-war imposition of the Soviet
model of political, economic and social development cut short previous
development paths and introduced new roles and patterns for recreational
activity (Buckley and Witt 1990).

Priority was given to domestic recreation. This was subsidised to provide
cheap accommodation and transport for (usually urban/industrial) workers
and their families to take a holiday at least once every 2 years. But this trade
union and enterprise-supported activity did exclude a substantial element of
the rural population, rendering them unsubsidised and relatively immobile.
Despite the human rights clauses of the 1975 Helsinki agreement, the region's
nationals, other than Yugoslavs, were rarely permitted to travel westwards:
currency inconvertibility, restricted access to hard currency, relatively low
living standards, and stringent vetting and exit visa policies proscribed most

forms of extra-bloc tourism. Thus cross-border movement often entailed exchanges of 'friendship groups' between like-minded countries.

However, the trusted élite—the *nomenklatura*—were able to travel to the capitalist world using hard currency often either drained from the state coffers and/or illegally acquired. Thus there existed a multi-tiered tourism underclass:

1. rural peasantry unable to afford or gain access to domestic recreation because of their structural and/or spatial positions within the economy;
2. those workers denied access to overseas vacations within the socialist bloc because of their structural position, lack of access to hard currency or record of non-compliance;
3. most of the population denied access to non-bloc overseas visits because of their lack of ideological–bureaucratic status and connections.

Political change in the region has profoundly affected this social and economic order. The consequences of this process, converging through economic restructuring and the 'peace dividend', can be illustrated from the experience of the Bumar Labedy engineering enterprise. This was one of Poland's largest military equipment manufacturers, specialising in tanks and artillery tractors. In common with most large state enterprises in the region, it also embraced a significant welfare provision for its employees. With the introduction of a market economy nationally, and the collapse of the Warsaw Pact internationally, 3600 of the plant's workforce were made redundant and the company's 3500 homes, workers' hotels, clubs and holiday centres had to be sold to the private sector in order to pay off the plant's creditors (BBC 8.4.93). In one of the most popular areas for Polish domestic tourism, the Tatra Mountains, recorded visits were reduced by one-half between 1989 and 1992, from 3 to 1.5 million (Karpowicz 1993, p. 31). The imposition of 22% value added tax on goods and services in June 1993, in Poland, further exacerbated this situation. Put crudely, with the privatisation of previously subsidised infrastructure and a reordering of political and social élites, restructuring has brought a more simplified determining factor to domestic access to tourism and recreation in CEE: ability to pay.

13.3 INCOMING TOURISTS AND VISITORS

Economic barriers, constraints on mobility, ideological hostility and the low priority given to service industries, coupled with general cold war perceptions, rendered Europe behind the 'Iron Curtain' inhospitable to many Western vacationers before 1989. Anticipation of Western ideological contagion and social corruption constrained the pursuit of international tourism by the region's governments as a means of generating employment opportunities and of promoting positive national images abroad (Hall 1984, 1990a, b, 1991). This was further inhibited by centralised and inflexible social and economic planning systems.

Table 13.1.   CEE: international visitor arrivals 1980–92 (millions)

	1980	1985	1987	1989	1991	1992	% change 1985–89	1989–91	1980–91
Albania	n.d.	n.d.	n.d.	n.d.	n.d.	n.d.	n.d.	n.d.	n.d.
Bulgaria	5.5	7.3	7.6	8.2	6.8	n.d.	12.3	–17.1	23.6
Czecho-slovakia	5.1	16.5	21.8	29.7	64.8	83.5[a]	80.0	118.2	1 170.6
GDR	1.5	1.6	2.1	3.1	—	—	93.8	—	—
Hungary	14.0	15.1	19.0	24.9	33.3	33.5	64.9	33.7	139.3
Poland	5.7	3.4	4.7	8.2	36.8	46.0	141.2	348.8	545.6
Romania	6.7	4.8	5.1	4.9	5.4	6.4	2.1	10.2	–19.4
USSR	n.d.	4.3	5.2	7.8	6.9	—	81.4	–11.5	60.5[b]
Yugoslavia	6.4[c]	23.4	26.2	34.1	—	—	45.7	16.1[d]	—
Greece	4.8	6.6	8.0	8.5	8.3	n.d.	28.8	–2.4	72.9
Turkey	0.9	2.2	2.9	4.5	5.5	n.d.	104.5	22.2	511.1

[a] 85% went to the Czech Republic; for 1993 the Czech Republic reported 71.7 million visitor arrivals.
[b] 1985–91.
[c] Notified arrivals at all registered accommodation.
[d] 1989–90.
n.d. = no data.

Sources: Business Eastern Europe 14.3.94; Czech Tourist Authority (1993); Economist Intelligence Unit (1994d, pp. 25–26); Flint (1993b); Hungarian Tourist Board (1993, p. 4); WTO (1993, p. 26, 42, 62, 72, 123, 128, 158, 162, 171); Hall (1991, p. 26); author's additional calculations.

Therefore CEE was ill-equipped to respond to the rapid expansion of the West European package-holiday industry in the 1960s, and was largely bypassed by Western tour operators. Adopting a pragmatic attitude to labour and tourism mobility, however, Yugoslavia was the exception in experiencing a substantial growth in tourist arrivals from the West. This was one legacy of Yugoslavia's breaking away from the Soviet bloc in 1948. It accompanied, in the mid 1960s, a series of labour mobility agreements with Western governments and an admission, heinous in the eyes of other socialist governments, that Yugoslavia had unemployment.

Absolute numbers of international tourists to Yugoslavia were not significantly greater than those to several other countries in the region (with 'visitor' statistics swelled by transit travellers: Table 13.1). However, the dominance of the Western market did secure a significantly higher level of tourist income, which, by the end of the 1980s, was greater than the total for the rest of the region (Table 13.2).

During the last half-decade of state socialism (1985–89), CEE experienced an increase in international tourist arrivals of 20–35%, with growth of 13–17% over the 1989–91 watershed period (Table 13.3). During the second half of the 1980s CEE experienced a slight increase in its share of European arrivals. Excluding Yugoslavia (classified by the World Tourism Organization

Table 13.2. CEE: international tourist receipts 1987–91 (US$ millions)

	1980	1985	1987	1989	1991	% change 1985–9	% change 1989–91	% change 1980–91
Albania	n.d.	n.d.	n.d.	n.d.	n.d.	—	—	—
Bulgaria	260	343	494	495	n.d.	44.3	–18.6[a]	51.5[b]
Czecho-slovakia	338	307	493	581	825	89.3	42.0	144.1
GDR	n.d.	n.d.	n.d.	n.d.	n.d.	—	—	—
Hungary	504	512	784	798	1 037	55.9	29.9	105.8
Poland	282	118	184	202	149	71.2	–26.2	–47.2
Romania	324	182	176	167	103	–8.2	–38.3	–214.6
USSR	n.d.	163	163	250	n.d.	—	8.0[a]	65.6[c]
Yugoslavia	1 115	1 061	1 668	2 230	468	110.2	–79.0	–58.0
Greece	1 734	1 428	2 268	1 976	2 566	38.4	29.8	48.0
Turkey	327	1 482	1 721	2 557	2 654	72.5	54.2	711.6

[a] 1989–90.
[b] 1980–90.
[c] 1985–90.
n.d. = no data.
Sources: WTO (1992b, vol. 1, p. 114; 1993, pp. 26, 44, 72, 123, 128, 162, 171); author's additional calculations.

(WTO) as part of their southern Europe region), the region's share of total world arrivals in the late 1980s was only half that for the Western and southern Europe regions. This was set within a context of an overall declining European share of the world market (down from 65.07% in 1985 to 62.88% in 1989 and 61.97% for 1990 (WTO 1992b, vol. 1, pp. 2, 24).

Growth in international arrivals during the second half of the 1980s was particularly notable for the non-beach holiday states of central Europe; Czechoslovakia (63.3%), the German Democratic Republic (93.8%) and Hungary (49.5%), together with the Soviet Union (81.4%) (Hall 1992b, 1993a). Interesting niche roles emerged as a consequence of the artificial division of Europe: Hungary, for example, became a common meeting ground for East and West Germans who could not otherwise easily interact. The sun, sand and surf destinations showed modest growth between 1985 and 1988—Yugoslavia (6.9%), Bulgaria (15.8%) and Romania (15.5%)—but both Yugoslavia and Romania saw downturns in 1989. This trend continued, subsequently, in Yugoslavia, even though visitor arrivals continued to increase until 1990, reflecting that former country's important transit role. Numbers of international arrivals in Romania fluctuated—decreasing in 1989, rising in 1990 (to 6.5 million), only to decrease again in 1991 (figures for visitor arrivals and tourist arrivals are not differentiated in Romanian statistics: Table 13.1). At the same time, Romanian tourist accommodation capacity was reduced by a quarter between 1985 and 1991, with no compensatory increase in smaller-scale accommodation (Economist Intelligence Unit 1994d, p. 26).

Table 13.3.   CEE: comparative international tourism statistics, 1985–91

		1985	1988	1989	1990	1991	% increase 1985–89	% increase 1989–91
1. International	(a)	31.44	35.43	42.74	50.25	50.12	35.94	17.27
tourist arrivals	(b)	39.88	44.45	51.38	58.13	—	28.84	13.14[a]
(millions)	(c)	35.54	38.44	43.63	50.92	—	22.76	16.71[a]
2. % Share of	(a)	14.96	15.09	16.38	18.27	18.03	9.49	10.07
European	(b)	18.99	18.93	19.69	21.13	—	3.69	7.31[a]
arrivals	(c)	16.92	16.37	16.72	18.51	—	−1.18	10.71[a]
3. % Share of	(a)	9.74	9.27	10.28	11.32	11.01	5.54	7.10
world arrivals	(b)	12.36	11.63	12.36	13.10	—	0.00	5.99[a]
	(c)	11.01	10.06	10.49	11.47	—	−4.72	9.34[a]
4. International	(a)	1 625	2 318	2 360	2 506	2 893	45.23	22.58
tourist receipts	(b)	2 686	4 342	4 590	5 280	3 361	70.89	−36.97
($US millions)	(c)	n.d.	4 126	4 340	5 010	—	—	15.44[a]
5. % Share of	(a)	2.79	2.26	2.25	1.87	2.09	−19.35	−7.11
European	(b)	4.61	4.23	4.37	3.94	2.43	−5.21	−44.39
receipts	(c)	n.d.	4.02	4.13	3.74	—	—	−9.44[a]

[a] 1989–90.

Notes:
(a) The region of 'Eastern Europe' as defined by the WTO (which includes the former Soviet Union but excludes Yugoslavia, which is placed in 'Southern Europe').
(b) This comprises the countries of (a) with the addition of Yugoslavia.
(c) This comprises the countries of (b) but with the exclusion of the Soviet Union.

Sources: WTO (1992b, vol. 1, pp. 2, 24, 137–138, 157–158; 1993, pp. 171, 176, 193); author's additional calculations.

In the early transition period, the most spectacular growth in tourist arrival numbers came about in Hungary, with increases of 37.2% for 1989 and 41.5% for 1990 (Hall 1993a). In terms of visitor arrivals, however, Hungary showed a 33.7% gain for the 1989–91 period and a 75.5% overall increase for 1987–91. This was significant in that Hungary began to liberalise its attitudes to visitor promotion well ahead of the 1989 political changes. These figures are, however, eclipsed by increases in visitor numbers for Czechoslovakia— 118.2% for 1989–91 and 197.9% for 1987–91—and Poland—348.8 and 676.0%, respectively. By contrast, visitor decline set in for Bulgaria (influenced by the loss of transit traffic with increasing disruption in Yugoslavia), and the Soviet Union, and from 1991 for Yugoslavia.

13.4   TOURIST MARKETS

During the communist period, the vast majority of international tourists to the countries of the region were from other Eastern European states. Even by the end of the 1980s, with the exception of Yugoslavia (10.7%) and

Bulgaria (48.8%), the majority of those arrivals were from within the Soviet bloc (Hall 1991, pp. 91–93).

The subsequent picture, albeit blurred by German unification and refugee flight from parts of the former Yugoslavia, is different in both quantity and quality; there has been an increase in the proportion of Western arrivals and a changing complexion of intraregional patterns. At one extreme, Czechoslovakia, a forbidding destination for many Westerners before 1989, saw the number of Austrian visitor arrivals rise from 230 200 (1.2% of total visitors) in 1986 to 9.07 million (10.9%) in 1992, while visitors from Hungary declined from 16.3 to 4.3%, but increased in number from 3.1 to 3.6 million. At the other extreme, Slovenia, a favourite package holiday destination for Germans (28.5% of all bed-nights in 1985) and Britons (14.7%), has recently begun to emphasise high-income niche tourism. As a result, the shares of traditional tourist package markets have fallen compared to the market shares of immediate neighbours Italy (the proportion of bed-nights trebled to 32.5% between 1985 and 1992) and Austria (more than doubling to 24.7%) (Economist Intelligence Unit 1994a, p. 50).

13.5 ECONOMIC SIGNIFICANCE OF TOURISM

The second half of the 1980s witnessed increases in tourism receipts for all countries in the region except Romania and Poland (Table 13.2). Considerable increases over the 1985–89 period in particular countries—110.2% for Yugoslavia and 89.3% for Czechoslovakia—reflected the role of high-spending tourists from the West: substantial for the former and rapidly increasing for the latter. Romania, by contrast, experienced a massive 214.6% decrease for the 1980–91 period, reflecting the country's unattractive social and economic environment, while Poland saw a fall over the same period of 47.2%, despite a substantial increase in 1990.

The economic impact of international tourism in the region has remained relatively small by global standards, generating only about 4% of total European tourism receipts, despite attracting around a fifth of all Europe's international tourist arrivals (Table 13.3). In 1988, the last full year of state socialism in the region, Bulgaria's tourist income was just 2.2% of that of Spain, while Czechoslovakia earned just 10.3% of that of Switzerland (Hall 1991). That Turkey could raise its level of tourism receipts by over 700%, between 1980 and 1989, did not go unnoticed in the region.

Subsequently, the quantitative and qualitative differences between the spending power of Western and Eastern visitors have begun to blur. Polish estimates concerning visitors to Warsaw in 1993, for example, suggested that those from the former Soviet Union, comprising more than one-half of all overseas visitors to the capital, came mostly for shopping purposes and spent an average of $450 [sic] per head, while North American visitors, predominantly leisure tourists, spent an average of $782 (PAP 23.2.94).

The collapse of the Yugoslav tourist industry in the early 1990s has had a sharply deflating effect on receipts when that former country is included in the regional picture. In terms of purely tourist arrivals, with domestic troubles looming, Yugoslavia had begun to experience decline in 1989 (–4.1%), followed by an 8.8% reduction for 1990, the greatest in the region (Hall 1993a). During the first 7 months of 1991, tourism earnings dropped by 69% with 62% fewer foreign visitors. A $2 million tourism publicity campaign launched in Austria and Germany was soon overtaken by domestic events, and the Yugoslav tourism industry was subsequently dismantled. After gaining independence, however, both the Slovenian and Croatian authorities reinstated the organisational infrastructure for a tourism industry in their respective countries. This has included maintaining a significant presence at international tourism fairs.

In Croatia, tourist earnings collapsed from $2200 million in 1990 (about 78% of the registered Yugoslav total), when they were the republic's most important source of foreign currency, to $300 million in 1991. They have subsequently begun to recover, with $550 million generated in 1992 and an estimated $800 million in 1993 (Economist Intelligence Unit 1994a, p. 32), and by May 1994 a 60% increase in tourist arrivals was being claimed compared to the same month the previous year. For Slovenia, only briefly involved in a war of succession, the 1.1 million (non-Yugoslav) tourist arrivals of 1990 slumped to less than 300 000 in 1991, recovering in 1992 to 423 000 and for the first half of 1993 to 267 000 (Economist Intelligence Unit 1994a, p. 50). For the whole of 1993 some $278 million income was derived from the industry—three times the amount spent by Slovenes travelling outside of their country (STA 28.2.94), and tourism receipts for the first 2 months of 1994 were up 15%.

That the region's receipt increases have generally not kept pace with those elsewhere is reflected in its decreasing share of total European receipts. These, in themselves, increased in relative importance from 50.1% of the world total in 1985 to 51.9% in 1988 and 52.6% in 1990, despite a declining world share of international tourist numbers. The average annual rate of increase for receipts within the region, at 4.1% for the watershed years of 1988–90, was less than a third of that for Europe as a whole (15.3%) (WTO 1992b, vol. 1, pp. 2, 24).

13.6 PATTERNS OF OUTBOUND TOURISM FROM CEE

In attempting to assess patterns of outbound tourism from CEE, even within Europe, substantial problems of data incompleteness and inconsistency arise, as Tables 13.4 and particularly 13.5 suggest. None the less, the data in Table 13.4 provide an interesting indicator of the relative level of liberality of each of the region's state socialist societies in their waning years, and of the impact of subsequent transition.

Table 13.4.   CEE: travel abroad 1987–91

	Number of trips (thousands)					% change		
	1987	1988	1989	1990	1991	1987–89	1989–91	1987–91
Bulgaria	540	505	922	2 395	2 045	70.7	121.8	278.7
Czecho-slovakia	7 506	7 258	8 569	20 654	39 613	14.2	362.3	427.8
Hungary	7 197	10 797	14 476	13 596	14 317[a]	101.1	–1.1	98.9
Poland	5 230	6 923	19 323	22 131	20 754	269.5	7.4	296.8
Romania	1 020	948	874	11 247	9 096	–14.3	940.7	791.8
Soviet Union	3 447	4 243	8 009	9 086	10 820	132.3	35.1	213.9
Yugoslavia	20 013	21 284	24 923	36 290	n.d.	24.5	45.6[b]	81.3[c]

[a] 12 803 for 1992.
[b] 1989–90.
[c] 1987–90.

Sources: Hungarian Tourist Board (1993, p. 4); WTO (1993, pp. 26, 44, 72, 123, 128, 162, 171); author's additional calculations.

In the second half of the 1980s, Hungary and Poland were less austere and dogmatic in their social and economic policies than some of their neighbours, despite the period of martial law in Poland following the rise of Solidarity in the early 1980s. The Soviet Union, in the later 1980s, following Gorbachev's rise to power, was, through *glasnost* and *perestroika*, emerging from half a century of authoritarian centralism which had severely restricted outward travel. In the last years before 1989, these three countries' policies towards outbound tourism for their citizens had become more pragmatic than those of their fellow bloc members.

Comparing patterns of outward travel in the two short periods 1987–89 and 1989–91, therefore, Table 13.4 reveals that most growth during the 1987–91 period in Hungary, Poland and the Soviet Union actually took place up to 1989. In Hungary there was a 101% increase for 1987–89, compared to a decline of 1% during 1989–91; in Poland an almost 270% increase for 1987–89, with only 7% growth between 1989 and 1991; and in the Soviet Union 132 and 35% increases respectively were recorded. In the latter two countries, at least, the role of petty cross-border trading, taking advantage of differentials in prices, currency conversion rates and consumer goods availability, and the increasing tolerance of private markets, provided a significant element in the growth of outbound travel (e.g. Gołembski 1990).

In the hitherto relatively austere Bulgaria, most significant growth in outbound travel took place from 1989; 122% for 1989–91 compared to 71% during 1987–89. Overwhelmingly greater proportional increases in trips out of the country took place from 1989 to 1991 in the two former hard-line states of Czechoslovakia and Romania—362% compared to 14% in 1987–89 for Czechoslovakia, and 940% compared to a decrease of 14% in Romania (Table 13.4), where an enormous pent-up demand was released

Table 13.5.   CEE outbound tourists: % of all foreign tourists in European countries 1989–90

Host country	1989 No.	1989 % of all inbound tourists	1990 No.	1990 % of all inbound tourists	1989–90 % increase
Austria[a]	574 930	3.15	692 508	3.63	20.5
Cyprus[b]	28 671	1.96	n.d.		—
Denmark[c,d]	359 618	4.19	391 508	4.19	8.9
Finland[e]	336 362	13.36	355 818	14.41	5.8
France[f]	207 000	0.41	n.d.		—
Germany[a]	495 215	3.37	610 196	3.90	23.2
Greece[f]	571 573	7.06	847 556	9.54	48.3
Iceland[f]	1 485	1.13	1 764	1.24	18.8
Ireland[d,f]	35 000	1.00	49 000	1.33	40.0
Italy[b]	6 716 545	12.16	10 709 195	17.75	59.4
Liechtenstein[g]	2 153	2.79	3 805	4.90	76.7
Luxembourg[a]	n.d.		8 071	0.98	—
Malta[a,b]	2 266	0.27	6 015	0.68	165.5
Netherlands[a,d]	155 600	2.98	210 700	3.63	35.4
Norway[d,e]	265 117	7.72	320 390	9.05	20.8
Portugal[b]	52 559	0.31	63 542	0.33	20.9
Spain[b]	381 027	0.70	363 593	0.69	–4.6
Sweden[c,d]	424 704	5.59	431 156	6.55	1.5
Switzerland[a,i]	157 057	1.55	210 650	2.00	34.1
Turkey[b]	692 193	15.52	1 444 193	26.79	108.6
United Kingdom[b,i]	307 000	1.76	501 000	2.77	63.2
Bulgaria[b]	4 247 874	51.66	5 446 985	52.72	28.2
Czechoslovakia[b]	27 523 766	92.72	n.d.		—
Hungary[f]	9 214 000	63.58	15 100 000	73.61	63.9
Hungary[b]	15 590 902	62.56	27 664 241	73.49	77.4
Poland[b]	6 672 500	81.04	15 582 928	85.56	133.5
Romania[b]	4 298 500	88.57	5 697 008	87.18	32.5
Soviet Union[b,j]	5 357 500	69.10	4 292 652	59.58	–19.9
Yugoslavia[a]	1 000 042	11.56	927.872	11.77	–7.1

[a] International tourist arrivals at all accommodation.
[b] International visitor frontier arrivals.
[c] International tourist nights at all accommodation.
[d] data only for 'Other Europe'.
[e] International tourist nights at hotel accommodation.
[f] International tourist frontier arrivals.
[g] International tourist arrivals at hotel accommodation.
[h] Data only for Yugoslavia.
[i] Data only for Yugoslavia and 'Other Europe'.
[j] Data only for 'Other Southern Europe' and 'Region not specified'.

Source: WTO (1992b, vol. 2, pp. 38, 43, 50, 52, 59, 151, 158, 160, 172, 181, 203–204, 206, 214, 222, 261, 296–297, 304, 306–307, 313).

in 1990. In Czechoslovakia, despite the obvious response to the lifting of travel restrictions in December 1989, outward travel continued to be constrained by very unfavourable currency exchange rates.

Movement out of their country had been far less restrained for Yugoslavs since the mid 1960s, and the significant 1989–90 increase in outbound trips perhaps reflected both growing internal tensions, with Serbs turning away from Croatian Adriatic resorts for their holidays, and the greater ease and attractiveness of visiting CEE neighbours. Yugoslavs also dominated the flow of Central and East Europeans (CEEs) into Italy—88% of total arrivals in 1989 and 83% in 1990. For those 2 years just under a quarter of all outbound trips from Yugoslavia were to Italy.

13.7 DISTRIBUTION OF OUTBOUND TRAVELLERS

As Table 13.5 suggests, by 1990, for those 'Western' European countries not contiguous to the region, CEEs made up less than 5% of inbound tourists. For contiguous Austria and Germany, the figure was still less than 4%, but this excludes very considerable numbers of excursionists. Data for Germany are also complicated by unification in 1990. In these two countries very unfavourable exchange rages have been a major deterrent to high levels of CEE overnight tourism, although the data for both countries exclude excursionists. In other countries contiguous to the region, CEEs made up 7–10% of arrivals in Greece, 12–18% in Italy and Finland, and up to 27% in Turkey. In the region itself, the proportion of inbound tourists from other CEE countries ranged from 53% in Bulgaria (influenced by transit traffic to and from Turkey) to 87% in Romania; this, perhaps, reflects not so much the ability to attract neighbours' citizens (although again the local role of cross-border petty trading is significant), as the differential ability to attract Westerners.

The combination of relatively small numbers, coupled to substantial volatility in the overseas movement of CEEs in the early years of transition, renders any coherent analysis of patterns of change rather tenuous. Aside from Malta, the country revealing the largest proportional increase of CEE arrivals for 1989–90 was Turkey, with a rise of 165% (Table 13.5). This reflected strong increases from most countries of the region, with spectacular growth in arrivals from Bulgaria (366%), the Soviet Union (415%), Czechoslovakia (455%) and Romania (753%). Indeed, the latter country provided the source of 7% of Turkey's total arrivals for that year and 26% of CEE arrivals. The rapid increase in the role of small-scale Turkish investment in Romania, not least in the travel industry, may be significant here.

Otherwise, most major countries of Western Europe experienced increases of CEE arrivals, in the watershed 1989–90 years, of between 20 and 60% (Austria, Portugal, Germany, the Netherlands, Ireland, Greece, Italy), although Spain actually recorded a 4.6% reduction. Along with Austria and Portugal, Spain experienced a decrease in the arrival of Bulgarians and Poles.

Soviet arrivals also decreased, as they did in Italy and Austria, but they increased in Portugal and Germany, in the latter case as the group with the highest increase (54%).

Spain (82%), Greece (57%) and Italy (51%) experienced substantially increased numbers of arrivals for 1989–90 from Yugoslavia, although the fastest-growing incomers for Spain were the few hundred Albanians visiting the country (639% increase). For Greece, however, Bulgarians were the fastest-growing group (82%), contrasting with their reduction elsewhere.

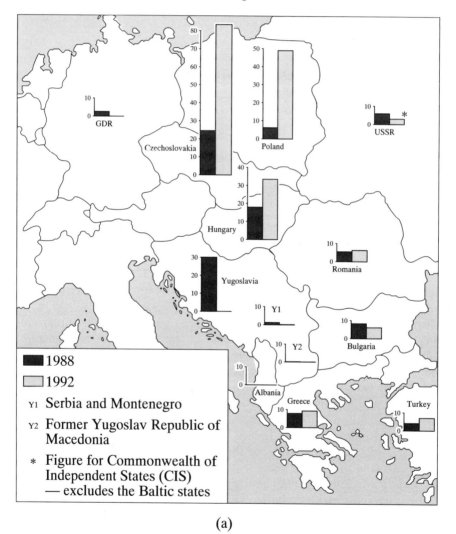

(a)

Figure 13.1. (a) International arrivals in CEE, 1988 and 1992; (b) Principal countries of origin of international arrivals in CEE 1988 and 1992. Source: WTO (1994, Vol. 2)

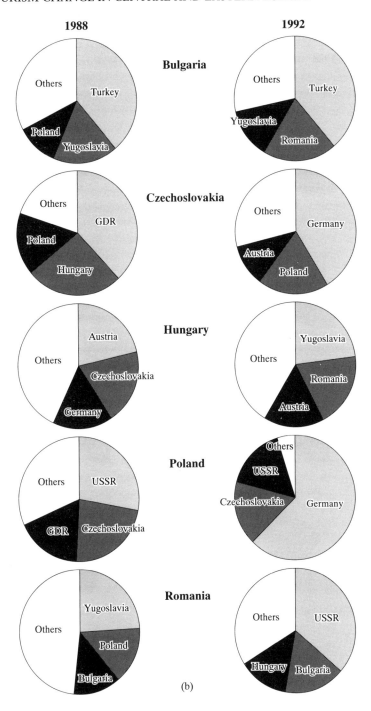

(b)

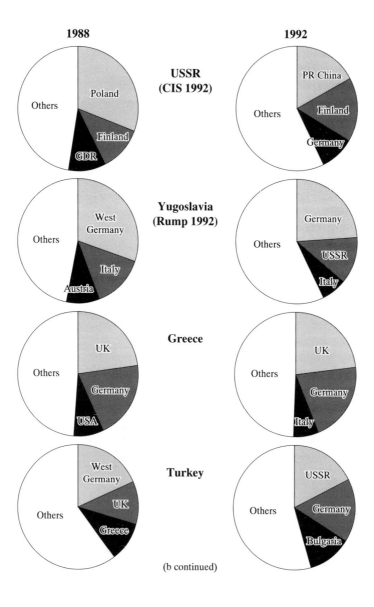

1988   **1992**

USSR
(CIS 1992)

Yugoslavia
(Rump 1992)

Greece

Turkey

(b continued)

Figure 13.1.   (b) Cont.

13.8 LONGER-TERM IMPACTS FOR WESTERN EUROPE OF OUTBOUND CEE TRAVELLERS

Four structural dimensions of the impact of CEE travellers may be considered significant.

1. Large numbers of low spenders will continue to travel to the West. The early 1990s witnessed several, often sensationalist, media reports of busloads of CEEs, armed with their own food supplies, in-bus sleeping arrangements and little hard currency, converging on such cities as Venice and Paris to pose congestion and other problems while spending very little. While such images may have been overstated, there will none the less remain for some time a vast tourist underclass in CEE, for whom collective, minimal cost, excursionist and other 'non-accommodation' visits will be their only realistic means of travelling to Western European tourist centres.

2. However, just when many analysts have been predicting the death of Western mass tourism, with the development of niche, special interest and 'quality' products, there is now a growing CEE market for just the types of package holidays which were popular with Western Europeans in the 1960s–1980s. One characteristic of the restructuring and privatisation processes within CEE's tourist industry has been the rapid growth of travel agents and holiday companies providing Mediterranean coast packages. For the summer of 1994, the Czech airline CŠA, for example, was planning a large number of charter flights out of Prague, including 95 to Split and Dubrovnik to convey some 10 000 Czech tourists to currently inexpensive Dalmation coast resorts.

With the long-term movement in the region's economic stability and in standards of living, increasing numbers of relatively low-income households will improve their mobility and access to international travel, although this process will be both uneven and dependent on a number of variables. In Hungary in 1991, for example, the dollar quota that individual Hungarians were permitted to take out of the country was raised from $50 to $350. In April 1994 the quota was again raised, to $800 per person (*Business Eastern Europe* 28.3.94). By contrast, in the spring of 1993 the Slovak National Bank set a limit of 7500 Slovak koruna (about $230) for individual purchases of foreign currencies (Economist Intelligence Unit 1994c, p. 52).

Reflecting the political, economic and administrative restraints of pre-1989 days, this 'delayed deflection' raises an interesting hypothesis: the diffusion of market reforms, and likely longer-term economic stability and improved living standards throughout CEE and the lands of the former Soviet Union, will result in a series of demand waves for mass tourism. This diffusing revival of the product cycle will telescope Western 1960s–1980s experiences into a relatively brief time period for each transitional society.

3. A small élite of high spenders will grow and will employ their disposable (convertible) income for tourism and other 'luxury' purposes in the West and in more exotic destinations. For example, while in part representing the

airline's transit role for non-Czech (or Slovak) travellers, in early 1994 CŠA's most popular destination outside Europe was Thailand, with over 6200 passengers having been carried there in the first 2 months of the year. In 1993, official assets from the former Soviet Union held by Western banks doubled to around $18 billion, almost a quarter of which was held in London. Anecdotal evidence suggested significant increases in high-spending Russian visitors to luxury goods shops there such as Cartier and Garrards (*East European Markets* 18.2.94).

4.   Overall, numbers from CEE countries will continue to fluctuate, reflecting varying national circumstances. As a leading source of outbound tourists from the region, Hungary, for example, witnessed the growth of outbound trips from 3.5 million in 1975 and 5.5 million in 1985 (Próbáld and Hosszú 1991) to 14.5 million in 1989. However, the country experienced fluctuations subsequently—13.6 million in 1990, 14.3 million in 1991 and 12.8 million in 1992 (Table 13.4).

13.9   KEY TRENDS

13.9.1   Competition for tourism investment

This has three basic components: (a) competition between CEE countries for inward investment; (b) competition between Western companies for CEE business; and (c) competition between East and West Europe for multinational tourism investment from North America and Japan. With its (for now) cheaper labour and newly opening markets, CEE does certainly present attractions to the movement of capital.

A major source of finance for supporting infrastructure projects and encouraging inward investment is multilateral aid from the major Western institutions. During the 4 years 1990–93, international assistance to the countries of the larger region totalled nearly $16 billion: $12.5 billion to CEE, $2.8 billion to the CIS states and $0.3 billion to the Baltic states (*East European Markets* 13.5.94). But with a number of different agencies involved—World Bank, International Monetary Fund (IMF), European Bank for Reconstruction and Development (EBRD) and European Investment Bank (EIB), among others— the distribution has been very uneven and the criteria for the disbursements are decidedly obscure and seldom published. Disparities in the distribution of such financial commitments for 1990–93 are reflected in per capita figures which range from $0.7 in Ukraine to $280 in Hungary, with Russia ($12.7), Albania ($44), Bulgaria ($92), Poland ($132) and Romania ($185) representing different positions within those extremes.

Further disparities are reflected in the sources and distribution of private investment, reckoned at $18 billion over the same period. For the Czech Republic, in the first half of 1993, the largest source of foreign investment by a considerable margin was the United States (58.6% of total capital), followed by Germany (9.2%) and France (6.6%). Here, consumer goods, transport and construction were the most favoured sectors (*Business Eastern Europe* 30.8.93). In the most favoured country for private foreign investment, Hungary, $7 billion was invested between 1990 and 1993, representing a level of approximately $700 per capita; by contrast, only $800 million had been deployed in Romania, a level of just $35 per head.

Such attractions for Western investors as access to trained labour, relatively low wages, minimum regulatory powers and encouragement from official agencies are very variable; while the best trained labour and most sophisticated market tastes can be found in Central Europe, regulatory controls may be least effective in the Balkans and former Soviet republics. In the Czech Republic, for example, there is now intense competition for qualified labour, while a shortage of personnel with foreign language skills has become a pressing problem.

Foreign investment in the tourism industry has been particularly notable in the hotel sector, with international chains supporting new construction and buying into existing capacity. In June 1994, for example, over 20 companies were said to be interested when 51% of the equity of the Hungar Hotels chain was put up for sale by the Hungarian State Property Agency. Marriott has invested $78 million in the Budapest Duna Intercontinental, bought earlier from the state, much to the chagrin of Intercontinental, who had been operating the lucrative hotel—particularly popular with Middle Eastern visitors—on a franchise for 20 years (*East European Markets* 10.6.94; Whitford 1993).

Next to accommodation, transport and communications have attracted most tourism-related foreign investment in the region. That most tourist and transit traffic employs road transport has been a major stimulus to foreign investment in upgrading and extending the region's highway system. Most notably, both Hungary and Poland have opted for the tendering of contracts to foreign interests for the construction and operation of motorways, on which tolls will be collected to reimburse the contractors. Czechoslovakia also began to pursue this line of development, but in November 1993 the Czech Republic abandoned the building of motorways by means of concessions. Foreign investors had demanded high tolls which, the Czech government estimated, would exclude 45% of the country's motorists from using the motorways because of their prohibitive level. Motorway construction will therefore be financed fully from the state budget and Czech companies will be expected to share 95% of the work. Part-funding will be derived from levying a single all-inclusive yearly fee on the country's road users.

Hungary is employing French-led international concessionaires HUMIC and Transroute, the first of which includes Austrian and South African as well as Hungarian interests. The Polish government's ambitious plan is to develop 2571 km of motorway in 15 years at a cost of some $6.4 billion. With Łodz rather than Warsaw acting as its hub, tolls charged on the system will aim to cover investors' costs within 7 years. The Polish government has emphasised that bidders for the contracts should have an established company in Poland—

representing a growing trend in the region to involve local partners—and a high local content (Lavell 1994).

Buying into privatised Eastern airlines (Hall 1993c; Symons 1993) has seen a number of variations in partnerships and approaches to structural questions, including the purchase or lease of Western aircraft, route rationalisation, internal restructuring and image overhaul. When Alitalia took a 30% stake in the Hungarian flag carrier MALÉV, when it was privatised, the latter company continued to keep its fleet of fuel-inefficient Russian-built Tupolevs specifically for niche charter flights and other secondary activities. Poland's LOT, however, deliberately aimed to eliminate all Russian-built aircraft before it was put on to the market in 1994, although a number of subsidiary services, such as in-flight catering, duty-free shops and ticketing, have been franchised out, and a strategic alliance with American Airlines has been established. Air France, controversially in tandem with the EBRD, took a 19.1% share of the equity in CSA, the Czech carrier, but the relationship did not prove successful, and has subsequently ended.

With an apparently deteriorating air safety record among Aeroflot's successors, certain Western airlines are identifying niche roles to be filled in operating to smaller locations otherwise poorly served: Lufthansa offers routes to Alma Ata, Tashkent, Riga and Tallinn, THY (Turkey) to Baku and Ashkhabad; and Austrian Airlines provides services to some 10 cities which do not have direct links from London, Paris, New York or Tokyo.

The developmental chasm within post-Trabant Europe has appeared to be growing ever wider as East-Central Europe's (Hungary, Poland, the Czech and Slovak republics, Slovenia, Croatia(?)) initial advantage and relative stability have attracted the bulk of inward investment (Gibb and Michalak 1993; Michalak and Gibb 1993; Murphy 1992). By contrast, the countries of south-eastern Europe (most of the former Yugoslavia, Bulgaria, Romania and Albania), have been later, less enthusiastic or ambivalent in their approaches to systemic political and economic change, or have been otherwise occupied—in at least one case literally so. Lower levels of economic and infrastructural development and living standards, general political uncertainty and continuing conflict, have inspired very limited confidence in potential Western and Japanese investors and visitors. In Romania, for example, by May 1994 there were just 27 joint ventures in the tourism sector, with an estimated investment value of $250 million (Rompres 19.5.94).

The Balkan countries, despite possessing the most favourable climatic and coastal conditions for mass tourism, have experienced stagnation or even decline in tourist numbers, reflecting an initial lack of clarity of political change, continuing instability, and a generally lower degree of road transport accessibility from major Western European markets. Furthermore, tourists from the northern part of the region, no longer restricted to Soviet bloc vacation destinations, started to abandon their post-war Black Sea coast holiday playgrounds for more enticing Western venues. This picture may now be changing, however.

In Bulgaria, benefiting from coastal tourism deflected away from the troubled Adriatic, investors' interests have focused on particular sectors—Spanish companies have been interested in gambling sites, Scandinavians in tour operation, Japanese in ski centres and US and UK companies in the hotel industry. Sheraton and Club Méditerranée have committed investment funds, and Ideal Standard (Belgium), part of the American Standard hotel fixtures and fittings group, has a plant in the country (Flint 1993a). The Black Sea countries have also started to become attractive for the North American fast food and soft drinks industries. As a Pepsico subsidiary, Pizza Hut opened the first of what was planned to be 15 restaurants in Bulgaria in 1994. Both Pepsico and Coca-Cola have been accompanied by the Swiss investment company Talladium, which has put $12 million into the Bulgarian drinks container producer Razvitie. Coca-Cola have invested heavily in Romania, the second largest market in the region outside of the former Soviet Union. The company has built bottling plants in several cities, including Bucharest and Braşov, while McDonald's was planning to open its first restaurant in the country by mid 1995.

Elsewhere, investment in catering has seen McDonald's establishing a high profile, initially in Budapest in 1990 and, subsequently, most notably in Moscow. In Poland, for example, the company has been developing a drive-through establishment in Czestochowa, the pilgrimage centre for the shrine of the Black Madonna, together with restaurants in Lublin and the southern mountain resort of Zakopane. In Kraków, however, a group of prominent residents have protested to the government against the opening of a Big Mac emporium in the city's historic Florianska Street and against the proposed opening of a second outlet in a former palace on Kraków's market square. The daily *Gazeta Wyborcza* quoted the protesters as arguing that 'The activity of this company, which is a symbol of industrialised mass civilisation and superficial moral cosmopolitanism, is in clear contradiction with the unique character of Kraków's town square' (*Business Eastern Europe* 9.5.94).

13.9.2 Competition for tourism markets

The market leaders, Hungary and the Czech Republic, are now undertaking a reappraisal of their tourism roles and marketing as conditions begin to move away from the immediate post-communist phase of economic and social transition. With a levelling off in tourist arrivals and revenues, Hungary has shown an explicit awareness of growing competition. For the 1994 season it adopted a more aggressive and coordinated marketing campaign to regain its leading role in the sector (*East European Markets* 10.6.94). With recent influxes of low-spending visitors from the former Yugoslavia and former Soviet Union, occupancy rates in Hungary's up-market hotels have decreased dramatically: in 1990 the rate for five-star hotels was 83%, but this had dipped below 60% by 1993. That Budapest has 4000 high-class hotel rooms to Prague's 1500 (Whitford 1993) emphasises Hungary's need to sustain the top end of the market through the sponsorship of conference and business tourism.

In the Czech Republic there is an acknowledgement that the rate of increase in tourist arrivals has been falling since 1990. This is attributed in part to rising crime rates, rising prices (including the imposition of 23% VAT) and the poor treatment of visitors by local tourist businesses (*Business Eastern Europe* 30.8.93). None the less, in 1993 $1.4 billion in tourism receipts were received, a 24% increase over the previous year (*Business Eastern Europe* 14.3.94). In Slovakia, the tourist industry has been identified as one of five priority sectors for the encouragement of foreign investment (Slovak National Agency for Foreign Investment and Development 1993), and new hotels have opened in Bratislava and other cities. In the longer term, as stability gradually returns to the Balkans and the beach holiday resorts there, the land-locked Central European states may actually benefit by being able to emphasise high-value niche activities embracing cultural, 'green' and business tourism.

13.9.3   Local cooperation and competition

Opportunities for cross-border cooperation have been opened up both in terms of tourism development (such as integrated day tours from Corfu to southern Albania), and for protecting environments hitherto located in inaccessible borderlands (Karpowicz 1993; Hall and Kinnaird 1994). Attempts to involve local communities, particularly in 'sustainable' tourism development processes, have been constrained in some cases by the lack of experience of bottom-up development upon which citizens could draw (Hall 1993b).

Cross-border economic differentials have seen the generation of substantial petty trading within the region since the early 1980s. With the opening of borders between East and West, often much more marked disparities and economic anomalies have been exploited by 'tourists' from both sides: for some time, Austrians have been crossing the border into Hungary to take advantage of lower prices on a whole range of goods and services, including dentistry and marriage services.

13.9.4   Restructuring of the tourism industry

At the end of the 1980s, the quality of the region's tourist services was low and very variable by accepted Western standards: accommodation, catering, utilities, transport and telecommunications had suffered from decades of neglect in which the economic and ideological cost of upgrading infrastructure to meet the needs of foreigners was often considered too high. In accommodation, for example, the newly developing private sector has needed to generate substantial growth in the availability of modest to medium-grade accommodation. In Bulgaria, 1988 legislation permitted private citizens to operate hotels and inns, and after December 1989 there occurred a major expansion of hotel building in Czechoslovakia, together with a growth in the opening of private guest-houses, notably in Prague's suburbs. Joint ventures for investment in top-quality accommodation and transport have been required to develop and consolidate high-spending conference and business tourism.

While by no means confined to tourism requirements, the encouragement to upgrade transport infrastructure, and particularly road systems, has been reinforced by the high use of the region's road systems by tourists and transit travellers: in 1992, for example, 90% of Hungary's 33.5 million international visitors entered the country by road (Hall 1993c, d).

The question of human resources within the tourism industry is now being addressed. With a history of mediocre quality of service, especially in the state sector, a poor image was often projected which did not encourage return tourist visits. The requirement for staff training in hotel management, catering, travel agenting, and in such areas as computing, telecommunications and foreign languages, has been recognised in a number of multilateral aid projects emphasising training and skills enhancement; one such example is the EU's 4.5 million ECU PHARE programme project for developing Polish tourism skills through the training of 5000 industry employees. The private sector has seen a number of multinational companies training nationals of the region, either *in situ* or in Western training institutions. One of the more high profile private ventures saw American Express launching a $500 000 fund to develop tourism personnel skills in Czechoslovakia, Hungary and Poland (Hamilton 1991).

For some time, however, there will continue to exist a great deal of uncertainty over the future organisation of the tourism industry, as decentralisation of state-controlled systems gives way to privatisation. Legislative and regulatory frameworks appropriate for a restructured industry may be slow in coming about, particularly for potential foreign investors. In Bulgaria, for example, a Tourism Reconstruction Board, supported by the EU's PHARE programme and the UK Know-How Fund, was established in 1993 to attract foreign investment for privatisation. This began in earnest in 1994 in the accommodation sector alongside plans to sell off Balkan Air, the national flag carrier. Overall, the Bulgarian Privatisation Agency envisaged the privatisation of 315 enterprises during 1994, representing about 10% of all state-owned companies. Equally over-optimistic, the Romanian government planned to privatise most tourist companies by 1996, with 52 scheduled for 1994 along with 20 hotels (Flint 1993b).

In the travel agency sector, the privatisation of state sector companies has taken place in tandem with the growth of new competing private enterprises: in Poland, for example, there are now some 4500 travel agencies. In Hungary, Ibusz, the former monopoly travel agent, has experienced some difficulty in maintaining its market share, which has been reduced to

25–30% of total tourism revenues. Lack of market experience saw the company diversifying too rapidly after privatisation, resulting in the costly liquidation of two key investments and an abandonment of its banking operations. By mid 1993 there were some 650 registered competing travel agencies in Hungary, although the real number could be as high as 1200 (Whitford 1993). Following privatisation, Cedok, the former Czechoslovak state tourist agency, had to compete with numerous domestic travel companies, as well as with well-known foreign tour operators such as Fischer Reisen, American Express Travel Service and Thomas Cook; the latter two have been able to locate offices at prime sites in Wenceslas Square, Prague (Gomez 1993). The Slovak part of Cedok emerged in 1993 as the Slovak Travel Agency (SATUR), with 52 branches in the country, together with overseas representation in Berlin, Vienna, Zurich and Budapest.

13.9.5   The continuing impact of Yugoslav disintegration

There are three main impacts of Yugoslav disintegration which can be considered here.

Deflection

After an initial post-communist decline in international arrivals, with a halving of CEE arrivals between 1990 and 1992 and a reduction by a third of arrivals from other sources, Bulgaria appears to have been benefiting subsequently from the deflection of coastal tourism away from Dalmatia. By 1993 its tourism receipts totalled $900 million—three times the previous year's figure—and were expected to be maintained at that level for 1994 (*Business Eastern Europe* 7.3.94). As long as conflict continued in the former Yugoslavia, and while alternative destinations such as Greece and Turkey remained relatively more expensive, Bulgaria appeared to be in a competitive position at the lower end of the market (Flint 1993a).

Restitution: Dalmatia

As noted earlier, both Slovenia and Croatia are again pursuing the international tourism market. In March 1993, the deeply symbolic reopening of Pula airport to international traffic was marked by an outbound flight of Croatia Airlines resuming its service to London. For the 1994 summer season, the Croatian authorities began upgrading transport links to tourist destinations, with daily ferry sailings scheduled for the Rijeka–Dubrovnik route and improved services on the links between Ancona (Italy) and Split and Zadar. Croatia Airlines had plans for 210 charter flights to such centres as Split, Dubrovnik and the island of Brac (*Business Eastern Europe* 9.5.94). International investors were also beginning to look at coastal resorts, encouraged by both Slovenian and Croatian governments. In April 1994, for example, Israeli interests were examining the investment possibilities of hotels on the Istrian and Kvarner north Adriatic coasts and on the island of Krk.

Distortion: UN sanctions busting

Informal means of circumventing UN sanctions against rump Yugoslavia (Serbia—including Kosovo and Vojvodina—and Montenegro), have entailed substantial cross-border traffic, further distorting, along with refugee flight, international visitor statistics. For example, when the Bulgarian authorities proposed limiting the number of car journeys across the border into Serbia, permitting drivers to make only one journey every 15 days, it was estimated by the customs office at the Vidin crossing point alone that more than 3000 Bulgarian motorists had travelled into Serbia to sell petrol during the month of April 1994 (*Business Eastern Europe* 6.6.94).

13.10   CONCLUSIONS

Several major conclusions can be drawn from this analysis:

1. The volatility which has been experienced since the end of the 1980s in terms of patterns and numbers of international tourists and visitors into and out of the region is likely to continue for some time.
2. Inward investment in the tourism industry appears to be gaining momentum, especially from sources outside of Europe. This will diffuse to the Balkans as stability gradually takes hold there. For the short to medium term, however, the bulk of Western investment is likely to be focused on those countries whose economic and political circumstances are most favourable for entry into the EU.
3. With privatisation, infrastructural elaboration and restructuring processes likely to continue for several years to come, those investment opportunities in tourism will continue to be spread across the construction, accommodation, catering, transport, agenting and training sectors.
4. The tourism market for the region, and particularly in land-locked Central Europe, will become increasingly specialised and niche-oriented. Cultural, environmental and conference considerations will be particularly important in this respect.
5. For outbound tourists, however, the mass tourism package will hold substantial attractions for some time to come, diffusing spatially eastwards and socially through each nation as access to disposable income and increased leisure time broadens. This sector of the international market is far from reaching its peak. Additionally, increasing numbers of

high-spending CEEs may be expected to visit Western Europe in an individual capacity, while low-spending groups will provide substantial numbers of excursionists.

6. The lands of the former Soviet Union represent potential major yet unpredictable actors in the international tourism industry.

Part V

CONCLUSIONS

14 The Impact of Tourism on the Restructuring of European Space

PAUL CLAVAL

Université de Paris-Sorbonne, France

14.1 TOURISM AND THE TRANSFORMATION OF EUROPE

Europe today is experiencing a major phase of urban and regional restructuring. It results from the creation of the European Community (now Union), the globalisation of trade and the ensuing crisis in many traditional sectors of the economy. New distributions of population and new hierarchies of urban centres are developing.

The forces at work behind this emerging geography are well known: labour productivity in primary and secondary activities is rising, computers and telecommunications are impacting strongly on service activities and the organisation of enterprises. People are also travelling at a lower cost and more quickly. While communication costs were high, footloose activities tended to concentrate in the more densely settled—and generally central—economic spaces. In contrast, today counter-urbanisation and metropolitanisation compete with centralisation in the process of restructuring economic space.

Leisure and recreation are playing an increasingly important role in modern societies: there is an increasing tendency for people to work for only 4 or 5 days, 32–40 hours a week. They enjoy more and longer holidays. They retire earlier, with higher pensions, especially if these are privately funded. These trends are reflected in the simple statistics that in the EU countries, in 1983, it has been estimated that 43.4% of the time of individuals was needed for biological uses (sleeping, feeding, etc.), 34% was work related, 7% was obligated (mainly travel) and 15.7% was free (Shaw and Williams 1994, p. 5). Not surprisingly, then, tourism is one of the few activities which has grown almost permanently since the end of the Second World War. Its share in the European GNP now exceeds even that of agriculture.

Tourist flows are becoming increasingly internationalised. The European population is becoming increasingly mobile in moving from one European

European Tourism: Regions, Spaces and Restructuring. Edited by A. Montanari and A.M. Williams.
© 1995 European Science Foundation. Published in 1995 by John Wiley & Sons Ltd.

country to another. In addition, the share of those who choose to spend a few weeks every year on tropical sunny seashores, travel through America, or visit the birthplaces of the great cultures of the Middle East, South Asia and the Far East is also rising and assuming increasing significance. At the same time, travelling in Europe has become popular among American and Japanese tourists. There is also a growing number of tourists arriving in Europe from the new economic 'dragons' of East and South Asia.

These geographical shifts are reflected in the facts that, in 1989, Europe attracted 62% of the world's international tourists, the Americas 20%, Africa 4% and Asia/Pacific and the Middle East 15% (WTO, quoted by Shaw and Williams 1994, p. 25). This is a quite significant change in comparison with 1971, when Africa accounted for 1% and Asia/Pacific and the Middle East for only 5%. The share of America was more or less static in this period (rising from 19 to 20%). Europe, in contrast, experienced a relative decline in world market share, but although this represented a significant shift, Europe remains by far the main focus of tourist activities globally. Europe, therefore, also receives the largest share of the receipts generated by international tourism; in 1989 it received 50.5% of world tourism receipts, compared to 27% for the Americas and 17% for Asia/Pacific and the Middle East (Shaw and Williams 1994, p. 29).

The financial flows resulting from tourism have an increasing impact on the current accounts of individual European countries, and indeed of the whole European community *vis-à-vis* the rest of the world: the UK, Scandinavia, the Benelux and especially Germany have a huge deficit, while the Mediterranean countries, Switzerland, Austria and France benefit from net international tourism receipts.

Tourism is a solid economic reality—as measured in income flows, jobs and business creation—but it results, more than any other sector of the economy, from images and representations. Today, people are visiting the places which were made famous in the eighteenth and nineteenth centuries by poets, novelists, kings and courtiers. The impact of films and of television programmes is becoming increasingly significant. In this book, the authors analyse the way in which the main European tourist regions express, at the same time, both myths and realities. For example, they measure the impact of the literary models of the north on travelling to the British Isles or Scandinavia, of the romantic image of the Alps on visiting Switzerland or Austria, and of the classical representations of the Mediterranean on touring in Italy, Spain or Greece. Hence, the scene-setting chapters in the first part of the book devoted to the British Isles (Williams and Gillmor, Chapter 4), Scandinavia (Nyberg, Chapter 5), the Alps (Zimmermann, Chapter 2) and the Mediterranean (Montanari, Chapter 3).

Another theme in the volume has been the exploration of new forms of tourism—rural (Cavaco, Chapter 7), or metropolitan (Shachar, Chapter 8)—and the impact of mega-events, such as the Olympic Games (Carreras, Chapter

11). Some restructuring is happening: there is a crisis in the dominant model of coastal tourism, which has been explored by Marchena Gomez and Vera Rebollo (Chapter 6). At a time when people are increasingly conscious of the problems of pollution, it has also been important to analyse environmental issues linked with tourism (Becker, Chapter 12). Similarly, since Central and Eastern Europe is experiencing such extensive and rapid change, it has been important to consider how these changes relate to tourism in Europe as a whole (see Hall, Chapter 13).

The changes identified in these and other chapters in this volume raise a number of important issues for those concerned with regional and urban restructuring. It is evident that tourism has to be explained in a theoretical perspective. In this respect, the essential contribution of Walter Christaller (1954, 1964) to the explanation of touristic locations is already well known. Industrial and service activities were traditionally attracted by central places or areas. However, tourists were seeking out nature, low densities, pleasant environments and possibilities for outdoor recreation, which meant that peripheries were attractive to them. They also had a taste for historical landscapes, either rural or urban, which induced a different driving force: thanks to these preferences, central areas also received visitors. However, for Walter Christaller, this aspect was not the most significant, because he considered that the forces behind tourism were overwhelmingly centrifugal. Since sports and outdoor activities were the dominating motivations of the majority of tourists, the peripheral regions which enjoy sun, sea and mountains were the most popular.

Traditional location theory relied on a simple assumption: in all sectors of the economy, transport costs weighed heavily in economic returns and, as a consequence, distance was the overwhelming factor in choosing the place where to develop an activity. This was also true for tourism. The heterogeneity of space was surely influential, but less constraining than distance. Southern sunny areas were more valued than rainy cold ones, but only in so far as they were within reach of the departure areas. Walter Christaller's general hypotheses were well adapted to the situation which prevailed before 1960. Jean-Marie Miossec's (1976, 1977) reflections on the location of touristic activities covered the situation in the early 1970s. Conditions, however, have changed considerably from the 1960s to the 1990s, and it is important to analyse prevailing contemporary trends.

14.2   TOURIST ACTIVITIES IN THE 1990S: A MORE DIVERSIFIED DEMAND, A MORE SOPHISTICATED SUPPLY

In modern industrialised societies everyone is a potential tourist but, statistically, the proportion of people leaving their homes during weekends or for annual holidays is higher in urban areas. This proportion depends on income, occupation and location. It grows with wealth. It is higher for the upper classes or upper-middle classes, and lower for farmers. People living in small cities or rural areas with pleasant sunny environments are also less prone to travel than the dwellers of large industrial metropolises in cold, rainy and cloudy regions.

The demand for tourism is increasingly differentiated. Accommodation is provided by camping sites, hotels or rented rooms or apartments. The range of services which is sought is also becoming wider: the majority of travellers today expect the same quality of health services as are to be found in the large cities, and a wide range of entertainment and recreation facilities. They come to practise tennis or golf, skiing, climbing, swimming or boating. At night, they are pleased to find ethnic restaurants, bars and night clubs. Some, however, prefer trekking in a difficult environment or rafting down mountain streams. There is also an important demand for culture: museums, art galleries, opera or concert halls, or fine historical environments. Tourism is increasingly diverse: this trend runs counter to the tendency towards standardised consumption, which was characteristic of industrial societies and the mass tourism they generated until the beginning of the 1960s.

The supply of tourism comes from areas equipped with hotels and other forms of accommodation, entertainment and recreation facilities, and a wide range of commercial, leisure and health services. Traditionally, the enterprises which ran them were predominantly small or medium size, especially those serving middle-class customers. The heavy investments involved in big hotels were mainly reserved for the highest income brackets.

Massification transformed these conditions from the 1930s. The amount of money to be extracted from each tourist decreased as the majority of visitors were now middle or lower class, but it was still possible to earn profits on them because of the sheer numbers involved. Accommodation was the first sector to be transformed. Hence there was the development of large, comfortable but non-luxury hotels, and camping or mobile home sites.

Since the range of entertainment facilities required by tourists was becoming wider and wider, it became increasingly difficult to rely on natural conditions and the dispersed initiatives of small firms to provide these. Investors discovered that it was possible to make profits from what may be termed 'distraction' or 'amusement' parks. Disneyworld provided one model for such tourist realisations. As a result, tourist destinations ceased to rely only on history, the beauty of natural landscapes and the quality of past monuments to attract visitors. Their environment is increasingly an artificial device planned and realised by large companies.

Visitors expect a wider range of facilities and attractions than in the past: it is not possible to provide them everywhere. At the time when Christaller was studying tourist activities, they were still characterised by a highly dispersed supply. In contrast, today a growing share of tourists frequent densely equipped areas since they are the only ones where the expected wide range of facilities and the sought-after high level of interaction can be met.

The concentration of tourist flows towards fewer but better equipped destinations coexists—almost paradoxically—with a demand for lower densities, wilder or quieter environments, and the ensuing development of an adapted supply: the attraction of virgin lands, rural areas or natural parks is growing.

14.3 THE INFLUENCE OF TRANSPORT MODES

14.3.1 Trains and ships

Transport and communications play a strategic role in the geography of leisure and recreation. Time constraints are always essential for tourists. They move for a weekend, one or two weeks, one month or more. Depending on the available free time and tastes of individuals, and on the characteristics of itineraries, travel is experienced as a pleasure or as a burden. In the first case, tourism is often a nomadic activity: people spend one day here, two or three days in the next place. In the second case, the trip is just a transition between two sedentary periods.

Tourism was first associated with ships and railways. Destinations had to be situated on, or close to, rail itineraries or seashores. It limited the spatial diffusion of tourism equipment to relatively small areas, and explained the urban atmosphere of the majority of destinations. Rivieras are good examples of touristic regions of that period. There were, however, other forms of tourist mobility: many people chose to move to rural areas either to visit their relatives or to live in second homes, often linked with landed property.

14.3.2 Automobiles

Automobiles have had a tremendous impact on tourism: they gave tourists the scope to be autonomous in their movements, allowed them to change their itineraries at any time, and potentially to visit all the places connected by the road network. This also provided the possibility for travelling with more luggage: one side-effect of this was that the expansion of camping was stimulated. With mobile homes, this evolution went a step further: people ceased to depend on fixed accommodation. In low-density areas, they could stay almost anywhere. In urbanised environments, they needed only parking lots of a special kind.

In many ways it is more pleasant to travel by car than by train, but it is tiring and time-consuming. It means that tourism by car is mostly practised only within a radius of 200 km around the emission zones for weekend breaks, and generally of 1200–1800 km for longer vacations. It opens the northern part of the Mediterranean to people coming from the colder or wetter environments of north-western or Central Europe. The southern parts of the Mediterranean peninsulas and Mediterranean islands are too distant for most car drivers, especially if they live in northern UK or Scandinavia.

14.3.3   Aeroplanes

Air travel has transformed tourism: faraway destinations can be reached in a short time. Until the 1950s in North America and the Caribbean, and the 1960s in Europe and the Mediterranean, prices were so high that air transport was reserved for an élite and did not significantly modify the spatial distribution of tourist activities. The situation changed when air companies began to offer cheap fares to travel agencies in order to fill their planes in periods when demand was low. In order to sell the seats which were offered to them at a low price, tour operators chose to offer their customers a new kind of tourist product in which travel and accommodation were integrated. Since tourists were often ignorant of the languages and customs of many of the destinations of these long-distance trips, they were generally pleased to rely on an organisation which provided them with all they needed.

Jumbo jets gave air tourism even more specific features: low fares could be offered thanks to the chartered flights as soon as planes were full. The size of tours changed: operators had to attract 300 to 400 people at a time for each destination, and to provide accommodation on this scale. Since it was only possible to have 20 kg luggage when travelling by plane, camping was only marginally important. Instead, hotels or new forms of accommodation (of the 'Club Méditerranée' style) were needed. In tourist zones, the life style of the majority of tourists was largely sedentary, since mobility was only possible through (generally expensive) rented cars or the services offered by local bus operators.

A new type of tourist area developed under these conditions: within a radius of 40 or 50 km from airports with runways long enough for large jets, accommodation was provided for visitors by standardised large hotels of the 300–400 rooms range (equivalent to the passenger load of a Boeing 737 or an A 300-310 Airbus). Major historical centres also benefited from these new possibilities. A new kind of nomadic tourism developed: 'Europe in a week', with London, Paris, Amsterdam, Munich or Vienna, the Swiss Alps, Rome and Venice included in the tour!

Since there were considerable investment costs involved in these new developments, they had to be operated through most of the year: hence the attractiveness of mountains and the southern shores of Mediterranean countries within Europe, and the growing success of non-European destinations. From Cyprus to Marbella, a new southern European belt of tourist regions resulted from this type of development.

14.4   THE IMPACT OF IMPROVED COMMUNICATIONS SYSTEMS

One of the major problems of all tourist activities stems from their characteristic spatial dissociation between demand and supply. With traditional communication techniques, there was no simple or effective solution to the problem. The difficulty in obtaining information on destinations was less for weekend activities: they were often repetitive and car owners could easily explore different places before electing to patronise one of these. The cost of becoming acquainted with the choice of accommodation or recreation in distant places was higher. People had to rely on the information diffused by the owners of hotels, apartments or camping sites in the tourist areas. Since there was no means of controlling the quality of advertisements, the risks were considerable. Individual tourists could never, for example, be sure that the house they had rented by mail would match the enthusiastic description they had read in the 'ad'. There was also a problem of delay: would the order that has been sent arrive in time for the reservation they aspired to make? As a result, planning for the tourist season acquired a relatively long lag time and they had to start early—characteristically during the winter for the next summer.

14.4.1 Cars, communications and the dispersion of touristic activities

When moving by car, it is possible to travel without preset itineraries and reservations if the area or country to be visited is well equipped with hotels and other forms of accommodation. At its simplest, this means that the driver just stops when a place looks pleasant. If there is no accommodation, he (she) just moves to the next settlement. This style of travel involves a high density of tourist equipment, and many small or medium-size facilities in villages or small towns. These conditions are generally met in the regions in which tourism developed early. Switzerland, Austria, France, the UK and southern Germany are all suitably equipped for this style of travel. They are within easy reach for many car drivers since they are close enough to the major urban concentrations in Europe. Some Mediterranean regions also have a high level of equipment, but this form of tourism is still marginal there since the majority of visitors come on chartered flights.

14.4.2 Tour operators, prospecting dispersed demand and concentrating flows

Modern conditions for tourism are different. Tour operators are active agents in the solution of the tourism information problem: instead of selling only accommodation, or travel, or recreation, they sell a package. Tourists are offered a description of the itinerary, the facilities they will enjoy, and the overall price. In order to maintain or enlarge their share of the market, the image of these companies has to be positive, which forces them to give precise information—leastways to a certain degree. They also offer different forms of insurance within their package. In total, they significantly reduce the risk inherent in any travel.

Because the main tour operators are large companies, they can pay for expansive publicity campaigns. The information which they provide is broadcast over wide areas. All the segments of the market are targeted. Travel agencies throughout a country are provided with leaflets which specify the trips and sojourns offered by each operating company. Just-in-time reservations can be made via telephone calls, faxes or other modern telecommunication devices. Customers know at the moment of decision whether there are still vacancies.

The modernisation of communications technologies favours the development of the larger operators in the tourism market: because there are 300 or 400 seats in chartered planes, and hotels have been built in order to accommodate such groups, large segments of the market have to be prospected. Virtually all places and classes in a country are tapped, which allows for the mobilisation of a structurally dispersed demand. However, flights depart from the airports of major cities, and there are few destinations: therefore, the net effect is that tour operators are mainly directing low- or high-density demand towards high-density concentrations of modern tourist facilities.

14.4.3   Modern communications and the development of low-density tourist areas

Modern communication technologies do not always favour concentration. Potential tourists live in different places. They look for various types of environments, activities and prices. Through electronic reservation systems, it is easier to match demand and supply. Many travel agents all over Europe are able to provide information on bed and breakfast accommodation in Austria, the Netherlands, Switzerland or France. For example, French departmental associations of *gîtes ruraux* publish catalogues in which all the capacities of accommodation offered by their members are listed, with indications as to how to make electronic reservations. It is mainly through the effectiveness of this system, that this kind of tourism became popular in France and abroad.

14.5   THE DIFFERENTIATION OF THE MAIN TOURIST BELTS IN EUROPE

It is more difficult, costly and time-consuming to make individual reservations in different places than it is to buy a package offered by a tour operator. As a result, dispersed forms of tourism have more appeal to the upper or middle classes than to the working classes. Hence a curious social geography of tourism has emerged in Europe: in its mid-latitude belt, within 1200 or 1800 km from the main urban concentrations in the UK, Benelux, Germany and France, visitors often tend to be middle class and travel by car. One part of this group congregates in the high-density coastal developments of ex-Yugoslavia, northern Italy, southern France and northern Spain, but others—and they are numerous—have a taste for low-density areas, rural settings or historical small cities. Further south, the proportion of both élite and lower-class tourists is higher. Tour operators have a more important share of the market, especially for winter sojourns. Tourist regions are of the concentrated type: they are composed of important cities or coastal belts with large hotels which accommodate the cohorts which have disembarked from chartered jets.

The development of the central tourist belt of Europe, from southern UK and the North Sea coast to the northern Mediterranean, started early, during the late eighteenth or early nineteenth century. It expanded to Yugoslavia and northern Spain in the 1950s and 1960s. Many of the features of this belt are inherited from the time when people travelled mainly by train. However, the car and modern communication facilities played a decisive role in the rise of tourism in rural low- or medium-density areas and the development of new forms of accommodation (mainly camping sites), for lower-middle-class travellers. Air travel is significant, especially during the winter season. It benefits the major cities, which attract visitors from Europe, Japan and North America. The major Mediterranean urban centres, Athens, Rome, Madrid, Barcelona and Lisbon, are often incorporated in the same tours.

The restructuring of tourism during the last 30 years had its maximum impact on the southern tourist belt of Europe, extending from Cyprus to the Algarve through Crete, Sicily, Malta, the Balearics and the Costa del Sol, or further afield including the Canary Islands and Madeira. In this area, the winter season is always significant. Tourism equipment is mainly concentrated within a short range—about one hour—from the major charter airports.

14.6 TOURISM AND REGIONAL AND URBAN RESTRUCTURING IN EUROPE: THE DIRECT IMPACT

The impact of tourism on regional and urban restructuring in Europe is manifold. It is direct, through the facilities which are developed for transport, accommodation and entertainment, and also through the money spent by visitors, and the salaries and income they generate in the tourist regions. It is also indirect, since the facilities developed for tourists often attract permanent residents and may induce the growth of new sectors of production.

Tourism was never overwhelmingly a peripheral activity. There was always a significant proportion of people who did not wish to spend all their free time in areas where they could relax and indulge in outdoor activities. Many tourists preferred to visit the places where important historical events had occurred, where there were prestigious monuments, or where their ancestors first settled. In the seventeenth or eighteenth centuries, the Grand Tour of wealthy young English people ran through Amsterdam and the Netherlands, the Rhine Valley, Milan, Venice, Florence, Rome, Naples, the Swiss Alps and Paris (Figure 14.1). In this form of travel, nature was something which occurred in between areas of cultural interest: the preferred

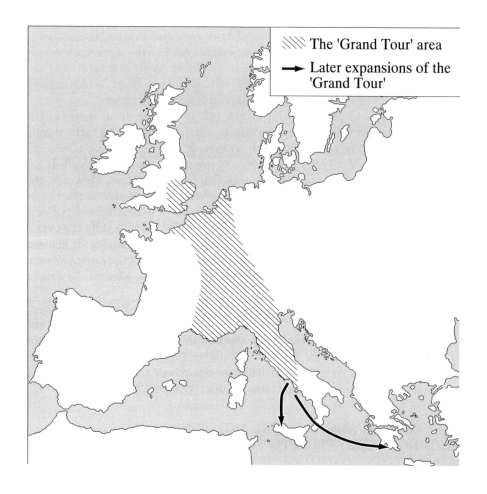

Figure 14.1. The Grand Tour

forms of landscape were provided by the wild tracts along the itinerary, either coastal or mountainous.

14.6.1 The ninteteenth-century geography of tourism in Europe

The new forms of sensibility developed during the eighteenth century had a major impact during the following century: they explained the growing popularity of sport and outdoor recreation among the middle classes. Tourism became increasingly oriented towards nature, mountains, lakes, seashores and rural areas. Spas and sunny regions were also visited for health reasons. By the end of the nineteenth century, tourism had become mainly a peripheral region activity, but since it relied on railways, its impact favoured narrow strips along

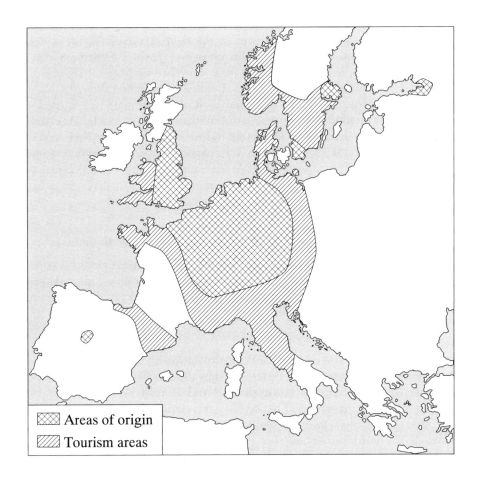

Figure 14.2.   Tourism in the nineteenth century

the routes from the urban concentrations of industrialised Europe (Figure 14.2). These processes led to the urbanisation of some relatively peripheral areas: coastal resorts along the North Sea, the Channel and the Atlantic shores of the UK and France, the rivieras of the Alpine lakes or the northern Mediterranean coasts, and spas. These 'peripheries' attracted a large part of the new tourist flows in Europe. They were located within a radius of 1200 km from the major urban concentrations. Tourist Europe was larger than the area visited at the time of the Grand Tour, but it was centred on the same core, since an increasing flow of tourists became enthusiastic about the Alps or visited the major historical cities from Naples and Rome to the cathedral cities of the Rhine Valley, northern France and southern UK.

As soon as a region or a city had acquired tourist functions, it ceased in many ways to be a part—sociologically—of the periphery of modern society. Many of the most original experiences in the field of urbanism, life styles, fashions and attitudes first appeared in cities like Bath, Cheltenham, Spa, Vichy, Luchon, Aix-les-Bains, Baden-Baden, Carlsbad or Marienbad, and in another style, in places such as Brighton, Deauville, Arcachon, Biarritz, Nice, Montreaux, Lucerne, the Lido, Viareggio or Rapallo. In many ways, tourist areas were integrated into the core areas of modern civilisation whatever their native population: detached fractions of industrialised societies were superimposed upon peasant societies. This was particularly conspicuous in some parts of the Alps or Pyrenees, and the Mediterranean coastal areas. It can even be argued that the whole urban setting of major European cities was a by-product of the laboratory constituted by spas and seaside resorts.

14.6.2   Tourism in Europe during the first part of the twentieth century

During the first part of the twentieth century, tourism development was increasingly peripheral. Because of the automobile revolution, accommodation and other forms of tourism supply and facilities expanded rapidly in remote areas. The impact of tourism ceased to be restricted to narrow zones. It affected much wider areas, but within the same distance range as in the late nineteenth century (Figure 14.2).

A growing proportion of travellers came from the middle or lower classes. Their attitudes to tourism were different. They did not like the formal setting of nineteenth-century tourism towns or cities and, instead, preferred less sophisticated tourism atmospheres. The sociological relations between tourist areas and the regions from which the visitors came remained, however, practically unchanged. The optimal places for social innovation in life styles and built environments continued to be the new tourist centres. Since informality, outdoor activities, sports and youth were much emphasised at that time, there was a break in the approach to planning tourist landscapes. Many of the architects and town-planners of the time adhered to anti-urban ideologies, and tried 'to dissolve the city into nature'. Tourist landscapes were designed in order to look more natural, which meant more peripheral, but they were still sociologically a part of the centre.

The share of large cities in tourist activity remained high, even if this aspect was generally not much stressed. However, there was widespread consciousness of the impact of tourism on capital cities such as Paris, Rome and Vienna, or on major historical centres like Venice or Florence.

14.6.3   A new geography of tourism in Europe

During the last 40 years, the geography of tourism has profoundly changed (Figure 14.3). This transformation is less conspicuous in the central tourist belt

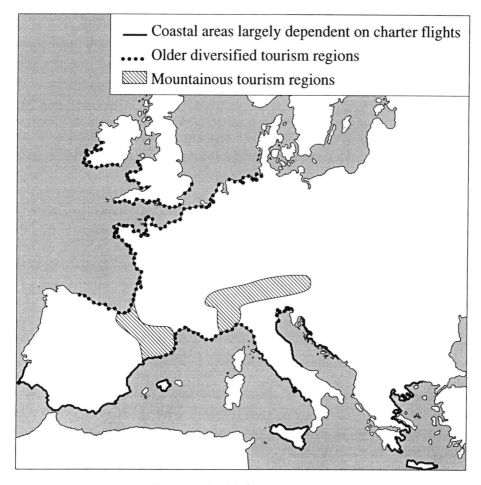

Figure 14.3. Modern mass tourism

of Europe, where people predominantly use cars for their holiday trips. It means that there dispersion is one of the major features of tourist distribution. Nineteenth-century tourist areas or cities generally retain a reasonable share of their former customers, but the increase in tourism activities has favoured the colonisation of less accessible tracts of coasts, mountains and rural areas (Figure 14.3).

Dispersion is, however, limited. Contemporary tourists are seeking more and more diversified activities and facilities. It is impossible to provide these when visitor densities are too low: hence the spectacular growth of new forms of tourist resorts in many parts of the mountains or coastal areas of Europe. Rural resorts develop only in so far as they attract sufficient tourists to pay for expanding their modern facilities.

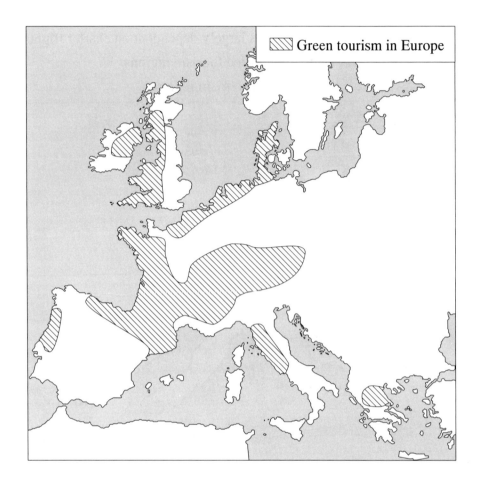

Figure 14.4.   Green tourism in Europe

New life styles and urban settings are frequently launched in tourist centres. For example, marinas as new forms of urban landscape, first appeared in Florida and the Caribbean, were then adopted on the Mediterranean shores (Port Grimeau close to Saint-Tropez, for instance), and then imported to major harbours all over the industrialised world: Baltimore, Boston, Sydney, London, Manchester, or Genoa and Barcelona are all capitalising on their new water-fronts as they seek to improve the quality of their built environments.

In the new tourism belt further south, and in part of the older tourist areas, tourism is more evidently a concentrated activity. It is the result of the growing significance of charter flights which feed the new hotel tracts along the sunny coasts of this part of the world. The airports of Palma de Majorca, Las Palmas, Malaga, Malta or Larnaca have more volumes of passengers than the airports of many European metropolises. It means that tourism begins, in this way, to be a factor of metropolitanisation.

14.6.4   Tourism and the urban and regional restructuring in Europe: the indirect impact

The impact of tourism on regional and urban restructuring is increasingly indirect. Good quality tourist facilities and services are important for local communities; they provide important advantages for the permanent residents. Some of these are former tourists who have chosen to retire to the second homes or apartments they had bought several years earlier. Others are economic immigrants, attracted by the idea that it is more pleasant to work in an enjoyable environment.

Tourist areas do, however, suffer important handicaps. First, many of them are highly seasonal, which means that the majority of their commercial and service activities are operational for only a few months of the year. As a consequence, those high mountains and southern regions which enjoy two seasons, are better placed to attract non-tourism activities. Second, land prices are often so high that housing is more expensive than in non-tourist cities of the same size elsewhere.

Some mid-density tourist areas are sufficiently well equipped as to be able to attract new forms of teleworking: they benefit from a large share of the ongoing process of counter-urbanisation. This can be observed in the rings of weekend tourism settlements around the major cities, as well as in the rural zones set back from the most attractive seashores (in the Mediterranean hills of Provence for instance) or mountains (in the Bavarian Alps or Black Forest of southern Germany).

The success of many enterprises now relies on the availability of rapid transport to major centres of contacts and communications. The growing share of air transport in tourist travel thus has a significant impact. Some tourist airports have higher volumes of traffic than large metropolitan areas. As a result, they have been able to attract metropolitan activities. This is particularly the case when regular flights represent a significant proportion of their traffic; Nice, for example, is increasingly becoming an industrial and high tech service city. It has attracted laboratories and the European headquarters of some international corporations. The tourist function is also significant in the service development of Geneva, and relies partly on the quality of its airport.

In most of the tourist areas which were popular before the Second World War, the share of upper-class customers remains high. Many of their visitors travel individually and use regular rather than scheduled flights. As a result, the share of charters is relatively low in their airport traffic. This is particularly favourable for the development of non-tourist enterprises.

In the resorts in the south of Europe, charter flights are predominant. Even if Palma de Majorca is one of the major airports in Europe, it does not provide the same accessibility to major central or control points as do Nice or Geneva. As a result, many foreign immigrants who have chosen to settle permanently in the island rely on the possibilities of teleworking, since the place is still not attractive enough for international enterprises. Many of the permanent British residents earn their living in this way.

Until now, the effect of tourism on the metropolitanisation of the southern European tourist belt has been limited by the nature of the region's air connections. During the next 10 or 20 years, air links will almost certainly improve to this region. Tourism will then become a more significant force in the process of metropolitanisation than it is today.

Finally, it should be emphasised that for other types of tourist activities, metropolitan attractiveness is already a decisive location factor: for example, it is not because of their climatic advantages that Paris and London rank first and second in the world as congress centres.

14.7   CONCLUSIONS

Tourism has been a major force in the shaping of European geography from the seventeenth century. From the beginning, it favoured more peripheral regions than was the case with many other activities, even if the limited mobility of the time meant that the Grand Tour developed in a rather restricted belt stretching from the UK to Italy (Figure 14.1).

Changing public tastes, and later the impact of new transport technologies, have extended the area open to European tourists (Figure 14.2). Today tourism is in many respects a global phenomenon, but distance from the source or emitting areas is still a significant factor both for weekend and longer vacation trips. The majority of tourists originating from the main urban concentrations of north-western and Central Europe still predominantly frequent a central tourist belt (Figure 14.3) which covers the UK, southern Scandinavia and continental Europe from the North Sea to the northern Mediterranean shores. However, during the last 40 years, it is further south—in a zone in which charter flights are more significant—that the most spectacular developments took place. However, tourism in this southern region remains restricted to narrow coastal strips which have had to experience massive changes in order to meet the expectations of modern travellers (Figure 14.3).

Tourist areas have benefited from the processes of counter-urbanisation and metropolitanisation which are an essential part of the ongoing process of urban and regional restructuring in Europe, but in some respects their experiences have been significantly different. The relatively recent sunbelt developments of the southern Mediterranean are less attractive destinations for counter-urbanisation than are the regions of green tourism in the older central tourism belt of Europe (Figure 14.4), or its major cities. In this way, traditional central areas maintain a relative advantage in an evolutionary process in which peripheries are, only at first glance, favoured.

References

Agarwal, S. (1994) 'The resort cycle revisited: implications for resorts', in C.P Cooper and A. Lockwood (eds), *Progress in Tourism, Recreation and Hospitality Management*, Vol. 5, Chichester: Wiley.

Albrechts, L., Moulaert, F., Roberts, P. and Swyngedouw, E. (eds) (1989) *Regional Policy at the Crossroads*, London: Jessica Kingsley.

Alvarez, J.R.D. (1988) *Geografia del Turismo*, Madrid: Editorial Sintesis.

Amin, A. and Thrift, N. (1992) 'Neo-Marshallian nodes in global networks', *International Journal of Urban and Regional Research*, 16, 571–587.

Anastasopoulos, P.G. (1989) 'Italy's importance in the development of tourism in the Mediterranean', *Annals of Tourism Research*, 16(4), 568–572.

Andolf, G. (1989) *Turismen i Historien, i Längtan till landet Annorlunda*, Stockholm: Gidlunds.

Arcangeli, F., Borzaga, C. and Goglio, S. (1980) 'Patterns of peripheral regions in Italian regions, 1964–77', *Papers of the Regional Science Association*, 44, 19–34.

Ardittis, S. (1988) *Migration de Retour en Europe du Sud*, Geneva: International Labour Office, Migration Working Paper 39.

Argullol, R. and Trias, E. (1992) *El Cansancio de Occidente*, Barcelona: Ed. Destino.

Aronsson, L. (1989) *Turism och Lokal Utveckling*, Göteborgs Universitets Geografiska Institutioner, Series B No. 79.

Ashworth, G. and Tunbridge, J. (1990) *The Tourist-Historic City*, London: Belhaven Press.

Ashworth, G.K. and Voogd, HJ. (1990) *Selling the City*, London: Belhaven Press.

Atkinson, J. (1984) *Flexibility, Uncertainty and Manpower Management 1*, Falmer: University of Sussex, Institute of Manpower Studies, Report 89.

Bäck, I. and Primeus, E. (1988) 'Fritidshusägare i Norrtälje kommun—en vistelsevaneundersökning' (unpublished), Examensarbete No 105, Turismlinjen, Högskolan i Ostersund.

Bagguley, P. (1990) 'Gender and labour flexibility in hotel and catering', *Services Industries Journal*, 10, 105–118.

Bagguley, P., Mark-Lawson, J., Shapiro, D., Urry, J., Walby, S. and Warde, A. (1989) 'Restructuring Lancaster', in P. Cooke (ed.), *Localities*. London: Unwin Hyman.

Barbaza, Y. (1970) 'Trois types d'intervention du tourisme dans l'organisation de l'espace littoral', *Annales de Géographie*, 443, 446–469.

Barbier, B. (1978) 'Ski et stations de sports d'hiver dans le monde', *Wiener Geographische Schriften*, 51–52, 130–148.

Bätzing, W. (1993) 'Der sozio—ökonomische Strukturwandel des Alpenraumes im 20 Jahrhundert', *Geographica Bernesia*, 26, Bern.

Barucci, P. and Becheri, E. (1990). 'Tourism as a resource for developing Southern Italy', *Tourism Management*, 11, 227–239.

Baučić, I. (1972) *The Effects of Emigration from Yugoslavia and the Problems of Returning Migrant Workers*, The Hague: Nijhoff, European Demographic Monographs 2.

Bayerisches Staatsministerium für Landesentwicklung und Umweltfragen (ed.) (1980) *Landesplanung in Bayern, Erholungslandschaft Alpen*, Munich.

BBC *Summary of World Broadcasts: Eastern Europe*, London: BBC, weekly.
Becheri, E. (1993) 'Economia internazionale e turismo. Il caso italiano', in *Ministero del Turismo e dello Spettacolo, Quinto Rapporto sul Turismo Italiano*, Milan: Il Sole 24 Ore SEME, pp. 1–23.
Becker, C., Job, H. and Koch, M. (1991) *Umweltschonende Konzepte der Raumordnung für Naherholungsgebiete. Belastungen, Lösungs- und Planungsansätze, Verwaltungsstrukturen*, Trier: Materialien zur Fremdenverkehrsgeographie, 22.
Bel Adell, C. (1989) 'Extranjeros en Espana', *Papeles de Geografia*, 15, 21–32.
Bennett, B.C. (1979) 'Migration and rural community viability in central Dalmatia (Croatia), Yugoslavia', *Papers in Anthropology*, 20(1), 75–83.
Beratende Kommission für Fremdenverkehr des Bundesrates (1979) *Das schweizerische Tourismuskonzept—Grundlagen für die Tourismuspolitik*, Berne.
Bernt, D. and Pauer, W. (1988) *Internationale und nationale Trends im Tourismus. Rahmenbedingungen für die Fremdenverkehrsentwicklung in Österreich*, Vienna.
Berriane, M. (1983) 'Tourisme et employ: le cas d'Agadir,' *Revue de Geógraphie du Maroc*, 7, 21–33.
Bishop, J. and Hoggett, P. (1989) 'Leisure and the informal economy' in C. Rojek (ed.), *Leisure for Leisure: Critical Essays*. London: Macmillan.
Blacksell, M. (1994) 'Environmental policies and resource management', in M. Blacksell and A.M. Williams (eds), *The European Challenge: Geography and Development in the European Community*, Oxford: Oxford University Press.
Bohlin, M. (1982) *Fritidsboendet i den regtionala ekonomin*, Uppsala: Geografiska regionstudier No. 14, Kulturgeografiska institutionen, Uppsala universitet.
Bonertz, J. (1981) *Die Planungstauglichkeit von Landschaftsbewertungsverfahren in der Landes- und Regionalplanung*, Trier: Materialen zur Fremdenverkehrsgeographie, 7.
Boniface, B. and Cooper, C. (1994): *The Geography of Travel and Tourism*, Oxford: Butterworth-Heinemann.
Bonifazi, C. (1994) 'Size and characteristics of foreign immigration in Italy', *Labour*, 81(1), 173–190.
Bonneville, M. et al. (1992) *Villes Européennes et Internationalisation*. Lyons: Programme Rhône-Alpes.
Bord Fáilte (1992) *Tourism Marketing Plan 1993–97*, Dublin: Bord Fáilte.
Bote, V. (1993) 'La necesaria revalorización de la actividad turistica española en una economia terciarizada e integrada en la CEE', *Estudios Turisticos*, 118, 5–26.
Bote, V. and Sinclair, T. (1991) 'Integration in the tourism industry: a case study approach', in T. Sinclair and M. Stabler (eds), *The Tourism Industry: An International Analysis*, Wallingford: CAB International.
Brinchmann, K.S. and Huse, M. (1991) 'Scandinavia: challenging nature in Norway', in A.M. Williams and G. Shaw (eds), *Tourism and Economic Development: Western European Experiences*, London: Belhaven Press.
Britton, S. (1991) 'Tourism, capital and place: towards a critical geography', *Environment and Planning D: Society and Space*, 9, 451–478.
BTA/ETB (1993) *Tourism Intelligence Quarterly*, 15(2).
Buckley, P.J. and Witt, S.F. (1990) 'Tourism in the centrally-planned economies of Europe', *Annals of Tourism Research*, 17(1), 7–18.
Bundesamt für Statistik (1991) *Länderbericht Schweiz*, Berne.
Business Eastern Europe, London: Economist Intelligence Unit, weekly.
Butler, R.W. (1980) 'The concept of a tourist area cycle of evolution: implications for management of resources', *Canadian Geographer*, 14, 5–12.
Butler, R.W. (1991) 'Tourism, environment, and sustainable development', *Environmental Conservation* 18, 201–209.
Bywater, M. (1992) *The European Tour Operator Industry*, London: Economist Intelligence Unit, Special Report No. 2141.

Cabanne, C. (1993) 'Problèmes du développement touristique sur la côte sud-est de la Crimée', *L'information Géographique*, 57(1): 9–14.

Canogar, D. (1992) *Ciudades Efimeras. Exposiciones Universales: Espectáculo y Tecnologia*, Madrid: Julio Ollero Editor.

Carreras, C. (1988) 'Barcelona de 1929 a 1992, del pasado al futuro', in R. Grau (ed.), *La Exposición Internacional de 1888. El Libro del Centenario*, Barcelona: Ed. L'Avenc.

Carreras, C. (1992) 'La politica urbanistica en Barcelona durante el periodo 1975–1985', in AAVV (ed.), *Cambios Urbanos y Politicas Territoriales*, Pamplona: Eunsa, pp. 255–269.

Carreras, C. (1993) *Geografia Urbana de Barcelona. Espai Mediterrani, Temps Europeu*, Vilassar de Mar: Ed. Oikos-tau.

Carreras, C. (1994) 'Els serveis al consum', in C. Carreras (ed.), *Geografia General desl Països Catalans*. Barcelona: Enciclopédia Catalana, Vol. 5, 107–167.

Castells, M. (1989) *The Informational City*, Oxford: Blackwell.

Castles, S. and Kosack, G. (1973) *Immigrant Workers and Class Structure in Western Europe*, London: Oxford University Press.

Castles, S. and Miller, M.J. (1993) *The Age of Migration*, London: Macmillan.

Cavaco, C. (1980) *Turismo e demografia no Algarve*, Lisbon: Editorial Progresso Social e Democracia.

Cavaco, C. (1993) 'A place in the sun: return migration and rural change in Portugal', in R. King (ed.) *Mass Migrations in Europe: the Legacy and the Future*, London: Belhaven.

Cazes, G. (1992) *Fondements pour la Géographie du Tourisme et des Loisirs*, Paris: Ed. Breal.

CBS (Central Bureau of Statistics) (various years), *Statistical Abstracts of Israel*, Jerusalem: CBS.

CEC General Directorate of Transport (1986) *Les Européens et les Vacances*, European Omnibus Survey.

CEC (Commission of the European Communities) (1987), *Europeans and their Holidays*. Brussels.

CEC (1991) *Leader. Programme d'actions de développement rural à l'initiative de la Commission*, Brussels.

CEC (1992) *Europa 2000. Pespectivas de Desarrollo del Territorio del la Communidad*, Luxembourg.

CEC (1994) *5th Periodic Report on the Social and Economic Situation and Development of the Regions in the Community*, Luxembourg.

Central Marketing Department (1988), *We've Been to Ireland*, Dublin: Central Marketing Department, Bord Fáilte Eireann.

Central Statistical Office (1991) *Regional Trends*, London: Central Statistical Office.

Charmes, J., Daboussi, R. and Lebon, A. (1993) *Population, Employment and Migration in the Countries of the Mediterranean Basin*, Geneva: International Labour Office, Mediterranean Information Exchange System on International Migration and Employment, Paper 93/1E.

Christaller, W. (1954) 'Beitrage zu einer Geographie des Fremdenverkehrs', *Erd kunde*, 9(1), 1–19.

Christaller, W. (1964) 'Some considerations of tourism location in Europe', *Papers, Regional Science Association*, 95–105.

Clary, D. (1993) 'Les motivations récentes des touristes et l'émergence de nouveaux produits touristiques', in M. Marchena, F. Fourneau and V. Granados (eds), *Crisis del Turismo? Las Perspectivas en el Nuevo Escenario Internacional*, Seville: IDR.

Clout, H.D. (1984) *A Rural Policy for the EEC?* London: Methuen.

Cohen, R.B. (1981) 'The new international division of labor, multinational corporations and the urban hierarchy', in: M. Dear and A. Scott (eds), *Urbanization and Urban Planning in Capitalist Society*. London: Methuen, 287–315.

Cohen, R. (1987) *The New Helots: Migrants in the International Division of Labour*, Aldershot: Avebury.

Cohen, E. (1992) 'Pilgrimage centers: concentric and excentric', *Annals of Tourism Research*, 19(1): 33–50.

Cohen, E. (1993) 'Contemporary tourism—trends and challenges', in E. Nocifora (ed.) *Il Turismo Mediterranea come Risorsa e come Rischio—Strategie di Communicazione*, Rome: Edizioni SEAM.

Cooke, P. (ed.) (1989) *Localities*, London: Unwin Hyman.

Cooper, C.P. (1990a) 'The life cycle concept and tourism', Conference paper presented at 'Tourism Research into the 1990s', University of Durham.

Cooper, C.P. (1990b) 'Resorts in decline. The management response', *Tourism Management*, 11(1), 63–67.

Cooper, C. (1992) 'The life cycle concept and strategic planning for coastal resorts', *Built Environment*, 18(1), 57–66.

Coopers Lybrand Deloitte Tourism Leisure Consultancy Services (1990) *U.K. Conference Market Survey 1990*, London: Coopers Lybrand.

Corbin, A. (1993) *El Territorio del Vacio. Occidente y la Invención de la Playa (1750–1840)*, Barcelona: Ed. Mondadori.

COS (Central Office of Statistics) (various years), *Annual Abstracts of Statistics*, Valletta: COS.

Czech Tourist Authority (1993) 'Tourism statistics' (unpublished), Prague.

Daniels, P.W. (1991) *Services and Metropolitan Development*, London: Routledge.

Danish Tourist Board (1994) *Dandata*, Danish Tourist Board.

Dann, G. (1981) 'Tourism motivation. An appraisal', *Annals of Tourism Research*, 9(2), 187–219.

Davidson, F. (1992) *Tourism in Europe*, London: Pitman Publishing.

Dawes, B. and D'Elia, C. (1995) 'Towards a history of tourism: Naples and Sorrento (XIX Century), *Tijdschrift voor Economische en Sociale Geografie* (forthcoming).

Debbage, K.G. (1990), 'Oligopoly and the resort cycle in the Bahamas', *Annals of Tourism Research*, 17(5), 513–527.

Der Beirat für Fragen des Tourismus beim Bundesministerium für Wirtschaft (1993), *Förderung eines umweltschonenden touristischen Angebots*, Bonn: BMWi Dokumentation No. 330.

DIA (Plan) (1993) *Plan de Desarrollo Integral del Turismo de Andalucia*, Seville: Junta de Andalucia.

Dicken, P. (1992) *Global Shift: The Internationalization of Economic Activity*. London: Paul Chapman.

Doganis, R. (1985) *Flying Off Course*, London: Allen and Unwin.

Doxey, G.V. (1976) 'When enough's enough: the natives are restless in Old Niagara', *Heritage Canada*, 26–27.

Dunford, M. (1990) 'Theories of regulation', *Environment and Planning D: Society and Space*, 8, 297–322.

Dunning, J.H. (1977) 'Trade, location of economic activity and the MNE: a search for an eclectic approach', in B. Ohlin, P.O. Hesselborn and P.M. Wijkman (eds), *The International Allocation of Economic Activity*, London: Macmillan.

Dunning, J.H. and McQueen, M. (1982) 'The eclectic theory of the multinational enterprise and the international hotel industry', in A.M. Rugman (ed.), *New Theories of the Multinational Enterprise*, London: Croom Helm.

Durbiano, C. and Radvanyi, J. (1987) 'Aspects des systèmes touristiques et récréatifs du littoral soviétique de la mer Noire et de la mer Caspienne. Etude comparative avec le littoral méditerranéen français', *Revue Méditerranée*, 2

East European Markets, London: *Financial Times*, fortnightly.

Economist Intelligence Unit (1986) *International Tourism Reports*, No. 1, London: EIU.

Economist Intelligence Unit (1991) *Travel and Tourism Analyst*, No. 2, London: EIU.
Economist Intelligence Unit (1992) *International Tourism Reports*, No. 1, London: EIU.
Economist Intelligence Unit (1993) *International Tourism Reports*, No. 3, London: EIU.
Economist Intelligence Unit (1994a) *Bosnia-Herzegovina, Croatia, Slovenia: Country Profile 1993–94*, London: EIU.
Economist Intelligence Unit (1994b) *Bulgaria, Albania: Country Profile 1993–94*, London: EIU.
Economist Intelligence Unit (1994c) *Czech Republic, Slovakia: Country Profile 1993–94*, London: EIU.
Economist Intelligence Unit (1994d) *Romania: Country Profile 1993–94*, London: EIU.
Elling, B. (1993) *Nordens Infrastructurelle Farce*, Nordrevy No. 3/4 1993, Oslo: Scandinavian University Press.
English Tourist Board (1991a) *The Future for England's Smaller Seaside Resorts: Summary Report*, London: English Tourist Board.
English Tourist Board (1991b) *Tourism and the Environment. Maintaining the Balance*, London: English Tourist Board.
Ericsson, B. (1992) *Reiseliv som Sysselsettningsfaktor i Distriktene?* Lillehammer: Ostlandsforskning.
Estudios Turisticos (1988) 'Concentracion y asociacionismo empreserial en el sector turistico', *Estudios Turisticos*, **103**, 3–33.
Eurostat (1991) *Tourism 1990*, Luxembourg: European Communities.
Fielding, A.J. (1993) 'Mass migration and economic restructuring', in R. King (ed.), *Mass Migrations in Europe: the Legacy and the Future*, London: Belhaven.
Findlay, J.M. (1992) *Magic Lands. Western Citiscapes and American Culture After 1940*, Berkeley: University of California Press.
Finnish Tourist Board (1994) *Finland Handbook*, Helsinki: Finnish Tourist Board.
Flakstad, A.J. (1989) 'Befolkningsutviklingen fra et tokjonnet perspektiv—en annerledes historie?' *NoredRefo*, **1**, Helsinki.
Flint, A. (1993a) 'Tourism: Bulgaria's first success story', *Business Eastern Europe*, **22**(34), 5.
Flint, A. (1993b) 'Romanian tourist market growing', *Business Eastern Europe*, **22**(38), 8.
Flognfeldt, T. Jr, (1993) 'Fritidshusets plass i stedsutvikling av reiselivstilbud, in V. Jean-Hansen and J.V. Haukeland (eds), *Riselivsforskning i Norge*, Oslo: Transportokonomisk Institutt 194.
Formez (1982) 'The advanced service sector in Southern Italy', *Formez Researches and Studies*, **34**, Rome.
Forte, C. (1986) *Forte: the Autobiography of Charles Forte*, London: Sidgwick and Jackson.
Friedmann, J. (1986) 'The world city hypothesis', *Development and Change*, **17**, 69–84.
Friedmann, J. (1993) 'Where we stand: a decade of world city research', Paper prepared for the Conference, 'World Cities in a World System' held in Stirling, Virginia, April.
Fuá, G. (1983) 'Rural industrialization in later developed countries: the case of northeast and central Italy', *Banco Nazionale del Lavoro*, **147**, 351–377.
Genty, M. (1992) 'Tourisme en Perigord Noir. Une chance de développement,' *Des Régions Paysannes aux Espaces Fragiles*, Clermont-Ferrand: Université Blaise Pascal.
Gershuny, J.I. and Miles, I. (1983) *The New Service Economy*. London: Frances Pinter.
Gibb, R. and Michalak, W. (1993) 'The European Community and Central Europe: prospects for integration', *Geography*, **78**(1), 16–30.
Gilg, A.W. (1991) 'Switzerland: structural change within stability', in A.M. Williams and G. Shaw (eds), *Tourism and Economic Development. Western European Experiences*, 2nd edn, London: Belhaven Press, pp. 130–152.

Gillmor, D.A. (1993a) 'Tourism in the Republic of Ireland', in W. Pompl and P. Lavery (eds), *Tourism in Europe: Structures and Developments*, Wallingford: CAB International.

Gillmor, D.A. (1993b) 'Geographical patterns of tourism between Ireland and Europe', in R. King (ed.), *Ireland, Europe and the Single Market*, Dublin: Geographical Society of Ireland, Special Publication No. 8.

Godvin, S. (1988) 'Danske glesbygdsforskningsprofiler—oversigt av problem, metoder og milijoer', *NoredRefo*, 2, Helsinki.

Gołembski, G. (1990) 'Tourism in the economy of shortage', *Annals of Tourism Research*, 17(1), 55–68.

Golini, A., Bonifazi, C. and Righi, A. (1993) 'A general framework for the European migration system in the 1990s', in R. King (ed.), *The New Geography of European Migrations*, London: Belhaven, pp. 67–82.

Gomez, B. (1993) 'Tourism in Prague', *Business Eastern Europe*, 22(37), 8.

Gomez, B. and Sinclair, M.T. (1991) 'Integration in the tourism industry: a case study approach', in M.T. Sinclair and M.J. Stabler (eds), *The Tourism Industry: an International Analysis*. Wallingford: CAB International.

Goodall, B. (1992) 'Coastal resorts: development and redevelopment', *Built Environment*, 18(1), 5–11.

Goodall, B. and Ashworth, G. (1990) *Marketing in the Tourism Industry*, London: Routledge.

Gordon, I. and Goodall, B. (1992) 'Resort cycles development processes', *Built Environment*, 18(1), 41–55.

Gormsen, E. (1981) 'The spatio-temporal development of international tourism: attempt at a centre-periphery model', *La Consommation d'Espace par le Tourisme et Sa Preservation*, Aix-en-Provence: CHET, 150–170.

Graham, B.J. (1994) 'Regulation and liberalisation in the UK scheduled airline industry', *Environment and Planning C: Government and Policy*, 12, 87–107.

Gray, H.P. (1970) *International Travel—International Trade*, Lexington: D.C. Heath and Co.

Greenwood, J. (1992) 'Producer interest groups in tourism policy', *American Behavioural Scientist*, 36, 236–256.

Greffe, X. (1992) 'Tourisme rural, développement économique et emploi', *Entreprises et Emplois dans le Monde Rural, Initiatives Locales de Création d'Emploi*, OECD, Paris.

Grenon, M. and Batisse, M. (1989) *Futures for the Mediterranean: the Blue Plan*, Oxford: Oxford University Press.

Grolleau, H. (1987) *Le Tourisme Rural dans les 12 États Membres de la Communauté Économique Européene*, Brussels: EEC, D-G des Transports (Service du Tourisme).

Haggett, P. (1983) *Geography. A Modern Synthesis*. New York: Harper Collins.

Haimayer, P. (1984) 'Tourismus im Alpenraum', in *Geographische Rundschau*, 36(8), 417–423.

Hall, D.R. (1984) 'Foreign tourism under socialism: the Albanian 'Stalinist' model', *Annals of Tourism Research*, 11(4), 539–555.

Hall, D.R. (1990a) 'Eastern Europe opens its doors', *Geographical Magazine*, 62(4), 10–15.

Hall, D.R. (1990b) 'Stalinism and tourism: a study of Albania and North Korea', *Annals of Tourism Research*, 17(1), 36–54.

Hall, D.R. (ed.) (1991) *Tourism and Economic Development in Eastern Europe and the Soviet Union*, London: Belhaven and New York: Halstead.

Hall, D.R. (1992a) 'Skills transfer for appropriate development', *Town and Country Planning*, 61(3), 87–89.

Hall, D.R. (1992b) 'The challenge of international tourism in Eastern Europe', *Tourism Management*, 13(2), 41–44.

Hall, D.R. (1992c) 'The changing face of international tourism in Central and Eastern Europe', *Progress in Tourism, Recreation and Hospitality Management,* **4**, 252–264.

Hall, D.R. (1993a) 'Eastern Europe', in W. Pompl and P. Lavery (eds), *Tourism in Europe: Structures and Developments,* Wallingford: CAB International, pp. 341–358.

Hall, D.R. (1993b) 'Ecotourism in the Danube Delta', *Revue de Tourisme,* **3**, 11–13.

Hall, D.R. (ed.) (1993c) 'Impacts of economic and political transition on the transport geography of Central and Eastern Europe', *Journal of Transport Geography,* **1**(1), 20–35.

Hall, D.R. (ed.) (1993d) *Transport and Economic Development in the new Central and Eastern Europe,* Belhaven: London.

Hall, D.R. and Kinnaid, V.H. (1994) 'Eastern Europe', in E. Cater and G. Lowman (eds), *Ecotourism: the Sustainable Alternative?,* Wiley: London.

Hallerbach, B. (1993) *Das Reiseverhalten von umweltbewussten Personen. Eine empirische Untersuchung des Reisverhaltens von Mitgliedern in Umwelt-und Naturschutzvereinen,* Geogr. Diplomarbeit Trier.

Hamele, H. and von Lassberg, D. (1991) *Mehr Wissen—mehr Handeln. Bausteine für eine umweltverträgliche Tourismusentwicklung. Eine Planungs- und Orientierungshilfe für Anbieter im Tourismus,* Munich: ADAC.

Hamilton, G. (1991) 'Amex sets initiative for EE tourism development', *Business Eastern Europe,* **20**(46), 412.

Harvey, D. (1989) *The Urban Experience,* Oxford: Blackwell.

Haywood, M.K. (1986) 'Can the tourist area cycle of evolution be made operational?', *Tourism Management,* **7**(3), 154–167.

Healey, M.J. and Ilbery, B.W. (1990) *Location and Change. Perspectives on Economic Geography.* Oxford: Oxford University Press.

Henderson, D.M. (1975) *The Economic Impact of Tourism in Edinburgh and the Lothian Region,* Edinburgh: University of Edinburgh, Tourism and Recreation Research Unit.

Heukemes, N. (1993) *Loving Them to Death? Sustainable Tourism in Europe's Nature Parks,* Grafenau: Federation of Nature and National Parks of Europe.

HMSO (1985) *Pleasure, Leisure and Jobs: the Business of Tourism,* London: HMSO.

HMSO (1991) *London: World City Moving into the 21st Century,* London: HMSO.

Hudson, R. (1989) 'Labour-market changes and new forms of work in old industrial regions: may be flexible for some but not flexible accumulation', *Environment and Planning D: Society and Space,* **7**, 5–30.

Hudson, R. and Williams, A. (1989) *Divided Britain,* London: Belhaven.

Hughes, C. (1991) *Lime, Lemon and Sarsaparilla: the Italian Community in South Wales 1881–1945,* Bridgend: Seren Books.

Hungarian Tourist Board (1993) *Tourism in Hungary 1992,* Budapest: Hungarian Tourist Board.

Hymer, S.H. (1975) 'The multinational corporation and the law of uneven development', in H. Radice (ed.) *International Forms and Modern Imperialism,* London: Penguin.

INE (Instituto Nacional de Estatísticas) (1988) *Portugal. Estatísticas do Turismo,* Lisbon: INE.

Inskeep, E. (1991) *Tourism Planning. An Integrated and Sustainable Development Approach,* New York: Van Nostrand Reinhold.

Iso-Ahola, S.E. (1980) *The Social Psychology of Leisure and Recreation,* Dubuque: W.C. Brown.

ISTAT (Istituto Nazionale di Statistica) (1991) *Commercio, Alberghi e Servizi Vari per Commune al 31.12.1988,* Rome.

Jacobs, J. (1984) *Cities and the Wealth of Nations. Principles of Economic Life,* New York: Random House.

Jansen-Verbeke, M. (1988) *Leisure Recreation and Tourism in Inner Cities*, Amsterdam: Netherlands Geographical Studies, No. 58.

Jean-Hansen, V. and Haukeland, J.V. (1993) *Riselivsforskning i Norge*, Oslo: Transportokonomisk Institutt 194.

Jenner, P. and Smith, C. (1992) *The Tourism Industry and the Environment*, London: The Economist Intelligence Unit, Special Report No. 2453.

Jenner, P. and Smith, C. (1993) *Tourism in the Mediterranean*. London: The Economist Intelligence Unit.

Joannon, M. and Tirone, L. (1990) 'La Méditerranée dans ses états', *Méditerranée*, 70(1–2), special issue.

Job, H. (1993a) 'Braucht Deutschland die Naturparke noch? Eine Stellungnahme zur Diskussion um Grosschutzgebiete', *Naturschutz und Landschaftsplanung*, 25, 126–132.

Job, H. (1993b) 'Naturparks in Frankreich. Parcs naturels regionaux und Erfahrungen für deutsche Naturparke, *Naturschutz und Landschaftsplanung*, 25, 102–111.

Johansson, L. and Johansson, M. (1991) 'Säsongsanställda inom turismnäringen vintertid i Are kommun' (unpublished), Examensarbete No. 168, Turismlinjen, Högskolan i Ostersund.

Jordan, P. (1992) 'Slovakia in the scope of central European tourism—present state and outlook', *Geograficky Casopis*, 44(2), 105–119.

Jorgensen, H. and Lind, J. (1988) 'Decentrale politikker for jobskabelse og erhvervsudvikling i Norden', *NordRego*, 4, Helsinki.

Journal of Sustainable Tourism (1993) Clevedon, England.

Julius, DeAnne (1990) *Global Companies and Public Policy: the Growing Challenge of Foreign Direct Investment*, London: Frances Pinter.

Jungk, R. (1980) 'Wieviel Touristen pro Hektar Strand?', *Geo*, 10, 156.

Jurdao, F. and Sanchez, M. (1990) *España, Asilo de Europa*, Barcelona: Editorail Planeta.

Karpowicz, Z. (1993) 'The challenge of ecotourism—application and prospects for implementation in the countries of Central and Eastern Europe and Russia', *Revue du Tourisme*, 3, 28–40.

Kemper, F.J. (1978) *Probleme der Geographie der Freizeit*, Bonn: Ferd. Dümmlers Verlag.

King, R. (1993) 'European international migration 1945–90: a statistical and geographical overview', in R. King (ed.), *Mass Migration in Europe: the Legacy and the Future*, London: Belhaven Press.

King, R., Mortimer, J. and Strachan, A.J. (1984) 'Return migration and tertiary development: a Calabrian case-study', *Anthropological Quarterly*,57(3), 112–124.

King, R. and Rybaczuk, K. (1993) 'Southern Europe and the international division of labour: from emigration to immigration', in R. King (ed.), *The New Geography of European Migrations*, London: Belhaven.

Kolodny, E. (1992) 'Irruption du tourisme dans une île lointaine. Le cas d'Amargos (Cyclades)', *Des Régions Paysannes aux Espaces Fragiles*, Clermont-Ferrand: Université Blaise Pascal, pp. 659–670.

KPMG (1993) *Overview: Comparative Analysis of 34 European Cities*, Amsterdam: KPMG.

Krippendorf, J. (1975) *Die Landschaftsfresser, Tourismus und Erholungslandschaft—Verderben oder Segen?* Berne, Stuttgart.

Krippendorf, J. (1980) *Tourismus im Jahre 2010. Eine Delphi-Umfrage über die zukünftige Entwicklung des Tourismus in der Schweiz*, 3rd edn, Berne: Interpretationen und Schlußfolgerungen.

Krippendorf, J., Kramer, B. and Muller, H. (1986) *Freizeit und Tourismus. Eine Einführung in Theorie und Politik*, Berne: Berner Studien zum Fremdenverkehr, Vol. 22.

Krippendorf, J., Messerli, P. and Haenni, H.D. (1982) *Tourismus und Regionale Entwicklung*, Diessenhoven.

Lanfant, M.F. (1989) 'International tourism resists the crisis', in A. Olszewska and K. Roberts (eds), *Leisure and Life-Style: a Comparative Analysis of Free Time*, London: Sage Publications.

Lash, S. and Urry, J. (1987) *The End of Organized Capitalism*, Cambridge: Polity.

Lavell, T. (1994), 'Toll motorway project ready to go', *Business Eastern Europe*, **23**(20), 5.

Law, C. (1991) 'Tourism as a focus for urban regeneration', in S. Hardy, T. Hart and T. Shaw (eds), *The Role of Tourism in the Urban and Regional Economy*, London: Regional Studies Association, 11–18.

Law, C. (1992) 'Urban tourism and its contribution to economic regeneration', *Urban Studies*, **29**, 599–618.

Law, C. (1994) *Urban Tourism*, London: Mansell.

Lawson, F.R. (1982) 'Trends in business tourism management', *Tourism Management*, **3**, 298–302.

Leontidou, L. (1991) 'Greece: prospects and contradictions of tourism in the 1980s', in A.M. Williams and G. Shaw (eds), *Tourism and Economic Development: Western European Experiences*, London: Belhaven.

Lewis, J.R. and Williams, A.M. (1987) 'Productive decentralization or indigenous growth? Small manufacturing enterprises and regional development in Central Portugal', *Regional Studies*, **21**, 343–361.

Lewis, J. and Williams, A.M. (1988) 'Portugal: market segmentation and regional specialisation', in A.M. Williams and G. Shaw (eds), *Tourism and Economic Development: Western European Experiences*, London: Belhaven Press, pp. 101–122.

Lloyd, P.E. and Dicken, P. (1977) *Location in Space: a Theoretical Approach to Economic Geography*, London: Harper and Row.

Lowyck, E. and Wanhill, S. (1992) 'Regional development and tourism within the European Community', in C. Cooper and A. Lockwood (eds), *Progress in Tourism, Recreation and Hospitality Management*, Vol. 4, London: Belhaven Press.

Lozato-Giotart, J.P. (1991) *Mediterráneo y Turismo*, Barcelona: Ed. Masson.

Lozato-Giotart, J.P. (1993) 'Activites de Foyers touristiques in Méditerranée: scénarii pour un proche futur', in E. Nocifora (ed.), *Il Turismo Mediterranee come Risorsa e come Rischio: Strategie di Comunicazione*, Rome: Edizioni SEAM, 85–91.

McIntosh, R. W. (1977) *Tourism: Principles, Practices and Philosophies*, 2nd edn, Columbus, Ohio: Grid Inc.

McGowan, F. (1994) *The EEA Air Transport Industry and a Single European Air Transport Market*, Geneva: European Free Trade Association, Economic Affairs Department, Occasional Paper No. 47.

Mamday, J.F. (1992) 'Le tourisme de pays, vecteur du développpement local', *Des Régions Paysannes aux Espaces Fragiles*, Clermont-Ferrand: Université Blaise Pascal, pp. 605–616.

Marchena, M. (1987) *Territorio y Turismo en Andalucia*, Seville: Junta de Andalucia, 305.

Marchena, M. (1992) 'El turismo, una experiencia de "descurbrimientos"', *Estudios Turisticos*, **113**, 9–24.

Marchena, M. et al. (1992) *Ocio y Turismo en los Parques Naturales Andaluces*, Turismo l, Junta de Andalucia, Seville.

Massey, D. (1984) *Spatial Divisions of Labour: Social Structures and the Geography of Production*, London: Macmillan.

Meadows, D. and D. and Randers, J. (1992) *Die Neuen Grenzen des Wachstums*, Stuttgart.

Meadows, D. and D., Zahn, E. and Milling, P. (1972) *Grenzen des Wachstums*, Stuttgart.

Mendonsa, E. (1982) 'Benefits of migration as a personal strategy in Nazare, Portugal', *International Migration Review*, **16**(3), 635–645.

Mespelier-Pinet, J. (1993), 'Les nouveau contextes de la demande touristique Méditerranéenne' in E. Nocifora (ed.), *Il Turisme Mediterraneo come Risorsa e come Rischio: Strategie di Comunicazione*, Rome: Edizioni SEAM, 159–169.

Messerli, P. (1989) *Mensch und Natur im Alpien Lebenstraum—Risiken, Chancen und Perspektiven, Zentrale Erkenntnisse aus dem Schweizerischen MAB-Programm,* Bern/Stuttgart: Haupt.

Michalak, W. and Gibb, R. (1993) 'Development of the transport system: prospects for East/West integration', in D.R. Hall (ed.), *Transport and Economic Development in the New Central and Eastern Europe,* London: Belhaven.

MICYT (Ministerio de Industria, Comercio y Turismo) Secretaria General de Turismo (1992), *Plan Marco de Competitividad del Turismo Español,* Madrid: MICYT, Centro de Publicaciones.

Mill, R.C. and Morrison, A.M. (1992) *The Tourism System. An Introductory Text,* New York: Prentice-Hall.

Mingione, E. (1991) *Fragmented Societies,* Oxford: Blackwell.

Ministeriet for Kommunikation og Turisme (1994) *Turistipolitisk Redegorelse,* Copenhagen.

Miossec, J.M. (1976) 'Eléments pour une théorie de l'espace touristique', *Les Cahiers du Tourisme,* vol. C-36, Aix-en-Provence.

Miossec, J.M. (1977) 'Un modèle de l'espace touristique', *L'Espace Géographie,* 6(1), 41–48.

Montanari, A. (1992) *Il Turismo nelle Regioni Rurali della CEE: la Tutela del Patrimonio Naturale e Culturale,* Naples: Edizioni Scientifiche Italiane.

Montanari, A. (1993a), 'El impacto de la crisis en el mediterraneo turistico: nuevos equilibrios y nuevos competidores', in M.J. Marchena, F. Fourneau and V. Granados (eds), *¿Crisis del Turismo? Las Perspectivas en el Nuevo Escenario Internacional,* Malaga: Servicio de Publicaciones, Unviersidad de Malaga.

Montanari, A. (1993b) 'Food consumption, culture, quality of life and economic development in Mediterranean countries: mediation, integration and conflict', in A. Montanari (ed.), *Food Policy and Economic Development in Mediterranean Arab Countries,* Naples: ESI.

Montanari, A. (1993c) 'La geografia del brain drain. Il caso dell Italia nel contesto internazionale', *Rivista Geografica Italiana,* C3, 703–728.

Montanari, A. and Cortese, A. (1993a) 'Third World immigrants in Italy', in R. King (ed.), *Mass Migration in Europe: the Legacy and the Future,* London: Belhaven Press, pp. 275–292.

Montanari, A. and Cortese, A. (1993b) 'South to North migration in a Mediterranean perspective', in R. King (ed.), *Mass Migration in Europe: the Legacy and the Future,* London: Belhaven Press.

Montanari, A. and Williams, A.M. (1995) 'Tourism regions and spaces in a changing social framework', *Tijdschrift voor Economische en Sociale Geografie,* 86(1), 3–12.

Müller, H., Kaspar, C. and Schmidhauser, H. (1991) *Tourismus 2010. Delphi-Umfrage 1991 zur Zukunft des Schweizer Tourismus,* Bernel St Gallen.

Muñoz-Pérez, F. and Izquierdo-Escribano, A. (1989) 'Espagne, pays d'immigration', *Population,* 44(2), 257–284.

Murphy, A.B. (1992) 'Western investment in East-Central Europe—emerging patterns and implications for state stability', *Professional Geographer,* 44(3), 249–259.

Nacher, J. and Selma, S. (1993) 'Territorio Turistico: conceptos, fenómenos y perspectivas de gestión', *Papers de Turisme,* 12 (Valencia), 27–46.

National Atlas of Sweden (1993) *Cultural Life, Recreation and Tourism,* Stockholm: Almqvist & Wiksell International.

NordRefo (1991) *Statens ansvar 1991:3,* Copenhagen: Academic Press.

NUTEK (1993) *Skattereformen och Turismen.* Stockholm: Slutrapport juni 1993, Rapport No. 1993:20, Närings—och teknikutbecklingsverket.

Nyberg, L. (1989) 'Planning for public service in an expanding mountain resort', Paper presented to the Tourist Research Centre Meeting, March 1989, Birmingham, UK.

O'Cinneide, M. and Walsh, J.A. (1990–91) 'Tourism and regional development in Ireland', *Geographical Viewpoint*, 19, 47–68.

OECD (1974), *Government Policy in the Development of Tourism*, Paris: OECD.

Opaschowski, H.W. (1987) *Wie leben wir nach dem Jahr 2000? Szenarien über die Zukunft von Arbeit und Freizeit*, Hamburg: BAT Freizeit-Forschungsinstitut.

Opaschowski, H.W. (1988) *Urlaub 87/88. Traumziele und Urlaubsträume. Daten, Träume und Trends*, Hamburg.

Opaschowski, H.W. (1992) *'Freizeit 2001', Ein Blick in die Zukunft unserer Freizeitwelt*, Hamburg: BAT Freizeit-Forschungsinstitut.

Oscarsson, G. (ed.) (1989) 'A European resource based periphery in a knowledge economy, published by the Nordic Institute on Regional Research', *NordRefo*, 3, Helsinki.

Österreichisches Statistisches Zentralamt (1970-.) *Der Fremdenverkehr in Österreich im Jahre*, Vienna.

Ostrowski, S. (1991) 'Ethnic tourism—focus on Poland', *Tourism Management*, 12(2), 125–131.

PAP (Polish News Agency), Warsaw.

Parkinson, M., Bianchini, F., Dawson, J., Evans, R. and Harding, A. (1992) *Urbanization and the Functions of Cities in the European Community*, Liverpool: European Institute of Urban Affairs, Liverpool John Moores University.

Paulsson, B. (1985) *Turismarbetskraft i Are Kommun*, Hogskolan i Ostersund: Idéutveckling.

Pearce, D.G. (1987a) *Tourism Today: a Geographical Analysis*, New York: Longman.

Pearce, D.G. (1987b) 'Spatial patterns of package tourism in Europe', *Annals of Tourism Research*, 14, 183–201.

Pearce, D.G. (1987c) 'Mediterranean charters—a comparative geographic perspective', *Tourism Management*, 8, 291–305.

Pearce, D.G. (1989) *Tourist Development*, London: Longman.

Pearce, D.G. (1990) 'Tourism and the European Regional Development Fund: the first fourteen years', *Journal of Travel Research*, F30, 44–51.

Peck, J.G. and Lepie, A.S. (1977) 'Tourism and development in three North Carolina coastal towns', in V.L. Smith (ed.), *Hosts and Guests: the Anthropology of Tourism*, Philadelphia: University of Pennsylvania Press, pp. 159–172.

Peisley, T. (1992), *Ferries, Short Sea Cruises and the Channel Tunnel, Travel and Tourism Analyst*, London: The Economist Intelligence Unit.

Peters, M. (1969) *International Tourism: the Economics and Development of the International Tourist Trade*, London: Hutchinson.

Petersen, J. and Belchambers, K. (1990) 'Business travel—a boom market', in M. Quest (ed.), *Howarth Book of Tourism*, London: Macmillan.

Pigram, J. (1983) *Outdoor Recreation and Resource Management*, London: Croom Helm.

Piore, M.J. (1979) *Birds of Passage: Migrant Labour in Industrial Societies*, Cambridge University Press.

Pollard, J. (1989) 'Patterns in Irish tourism', in R.W.G. Carter and A.J. Parker (eds), *Ireland: a Contemporary Geographical Perspective*, London: Routledge.

Pompl, W. and Lavery, P. (eds) (1993) *Tourism in Europe. Structures and Developments*, Wallingford: CAB International.

Poon, A. (1993) *Tourism, Technology and Competitive Strategies*, Wallingford: CAB International.

Porter, M.E. (1985) *Competitive Advantage: Creating and Sustaining Superior Performance*, New York: Free Press.

Porter, M.E. (1986) *Competition in Global Industries*, Boston: Harvard Business School Press.

Próbáld, A. and Hosszú, K.P. (1991) *Tourism in Hungary 1990*, Budapest, Hungarian Tourist Board.
Racionero, L. (1983) *Del Paroa al Ocio*, Barcelona: Ed. Anagrama.
Reclus, DATAR (1989) *Les Villes Européennes*. Paris: La Documentation Française.
Renucci, J. (1985), 'Le tourisme et L'emploi en Corse', *I° Conférence Economique de la Méditerranée Nord-Occidentale*, Barcelona, June 1985.
Renucci, J. (1990) 'Tourisme international et tourisme national dans les États de l'Europe méridionale', *Annales de Géographie*, **551**, 21–50.
Requena, J.C. and Aviles, P.R. (1993) 'O agriturismo, uma forma de turismo rural a considerar', *LEADER Magazine*, **4**, 13–15.
Ritchie, B. and Hawkins, D. (eds) (1992) *World Travel and Tourist Review*, Vol. 2, Wallingford: CAB International.
Ritchie, J.R and Zins, M. (1978) 'Culture as a determinant of the attractiveness of a tourist region', *Annals of Tourism Research*, **5**, 252–267.
RMTT (Romania Ministry of Trade and Tourism) (1990) *The Programme of Modernization and Development of the Romanian Tourism in 1990–1992*, Bucharest: Ministry of Trade and Tourism.
Rogalewski, O. (1980) 'Intrenational tourism originating from Poland', *International Social Science Journal*, **32**(1), 114–127.
Rompres (Romanian News Agency), Bucharest.
Ryan, C. (1991) *Recreational Tourism. A Social Science Perspective*. London: Routledge.
Salt, J., Singleton, A. and Hogarth, J. (1994) *Europe's International Migrants: Data Sources, Patterns and Trends*, London: HMSO.
Salvá í Tomás, P.A. (1991), 'La population des îles Baléares pendant 40 ans de tourisme de masse (1950–1989)' *Méditerranée*, **1**, 7–14.
Santos, M. et al. (1993) *Fim de Século e Globalizaçao*, Sao Paulo: Hucitec-ANPUR.
SAR (Syrian Arab Republic), Central Bureau of Statistics (various years), *Statistical Abstract*, Damascus: SAR.
Sassen, S. (1991) *The Global City: New York, London, Tokyo*, Princeton: Princeton University Press.
Savitch, H.V. (1988) *Post-Industrial Cities*, Princeton: Princeton University Press.
Schweizer Tourismus-Verband (1993) *Schweizer Tourismus in Zahlen*, Berne.
Scott, A. (1988) *Metropolis: From the Division of Labor to Urban Form*, Berkeley: University of California Press.
Scoullos, M. (1992) 'Prefazione', *Il Turismo nelle Regioni Rurali della CEE: la Tutela del Patrimonion Natural e Culturale*, Rome: Edizioni Scientifiche Italiana.
Secretaria General de Turismo, Ministerio de Transportes, Turismo y Communicaciones (1990, 'Evaluación y Consequencias de la Oferta Extralegal en la Industria Turìstica Española, Madrid: Secretaria General de Turismo, unpublished paper.
Seers, D., Schaffer, B. and Kiljunen, M.L. (eds) (1979) *Underdeveloped Europe: Case Studies in Core Periphery Relations*, Hassocks: Harvester Press.
Selstad, T. (1993) *Nordic Tourism in Europe and European Tourism in Nordic Countries: Trends and Scenarios*, Copenhagen: NordRefo.
Sessa, A. (1983) *Manual of Tourism Economics*, Rome: CATAL.
Shachar, A. (1994) 'Randstad Holland: A world city?', *Urban Studies*, **31**, 381–399.
Shaw, G., Greenwood, J. and Williams, A.M. (1991) 'The United Kingdom: market responses and public policy', in A.M. Williams and G. Shaw (eds), *Tourism and Economic Development: Western European Experiences*, London: Belhaven.
Shaw, G. and Williams, A.M. (1990) 'Tourism, economic development and the role of entrepreneurial activity', *Progress in Tourism, Recreation and Hospitality Management*, London: Belhaven Press.
Shaw, G. and Williams, A.M. (1994) *Critical Issues in Tourism: A Geographical Perspective*, Oxford: Basil Blackwell.

Simms, J., Hales, C. and Riley, M. (1988) 'Examination of the concept of internal labour markets in UK hotels', *Tourism Management*, **9**, 3–12.

Simonazzi, M. (1993) 'Le abitazioni turistiche: un segmento storicamente sotto-valutato', in *Ministero del Turismo e dello Spettacolo, Quinto Rapporto sul Turismo Italiano*, Milan: Il Sole 24 Ore SEME, pp. 469–483.

Sirgado, J.R. (1993) 'Turismo nas regiôes portuguesas', *Inforgeo* (Asociación Portuguesa de Geógrafos), pp. 21–36.

Slattery, P. and Johnson, S.M. (1993) 'Hotel chains in Europe', *Travel and Tourism Analyst*, Economist Intelligence Unit, No. 1, pp. 65–80.

Slovak National Agency for Foreign Investment and Development (1993) *Slovakia Central Location*, Bratislava: Slovak National Agency for Foreign Investment and Development.

Smeral, E. (1985) *Längerfristige Entwicklung und Struktureller Wandel im Inter-Nationalen und im Österreichischen Tourismus*, Vienna: Österreichischer Strukturbericht 1984.

Smeral, E. (1986) 'Strukturwandel in der österreichischen Außenwirtschaft', in *Länderbank Report. Aktueller Wirtschaftsdiesnt*, **41**, 1–7, Vienna.

Smith, D.M. (1977) *Human Geography: a Welfare Approach*, London: Edward Arnold.

Smith, G.V. (1989) 'The European conference market', *Travel and Tourism Analyst*, **4**, 60–76. London: Economist Intelligence Unit.

Smith, G. V. (1990) 'The growth of conferences and incentives', in M. Quest (ed.), *Howarth Book of Tourism*, London: Macmillan.

Smith, V.L. (1992) 'Introduction: The quest in guest', *Annals of Tourism Research*, **19**(1), 1–17.

SOPEMI (1992) *Trends in International Migration*, Paris: OECD.

Sorkin, M. (ed.) (1992) *Variations on a Theme Park*, New York: Hill and Wang.

SPD Bundestagsfraktion Arbeitsgruppe Fremdenverkehr (1993) *SPD Fremdenverkehrsprogramm*, Bonn.

Spezia, G. (1992) *Eventi e Turismo*, Bologna: Ed. Calderini.

STA (Slovene Telegraph Agency): Ljubljana.

Statistical Office of the European Communities (1993) *Tourism 1991*, Brussels: Eurostat.

Statistics Sweden (1992) *Statistical Yearbook 1992*, Stockholm: Statistics Sweden.

Statistics Sweden (1993) *Accomodation Statistics 1993*, Stockholm: Statistics Sweden.

Steinecke, A. (1989) 'Wohin geht die Reise? Tourismus im Jahr 2000', in A. Steinecke (ed.) *Tourismus-Umwelt—Gesellschaft. Wege zu einem Sozial- und Umweltverträglichen Riesen*, Bielefeld: IFKA-Schriftenreihe, Vol. 8, pp. 7–28.

Storper, M. (1985) 'Oligopoly and the product cycle: essentials in economic geography', *Economic Geography*, **61**, 260–282.

Stringher, B. (1912) 'Su la bilancia dei pagamenti fra l'Italia e l'estero', *La Riforma Sociale*, **1–2**, 49–83.

Studienkreis für Tourismus e.V. (1989) *Reiseanalyse*, Starnberg.

Styrelsen füor Sverigebilden (1992) 'Image of Sweden in Europe' (unpublished), Stockholm.

Symons, L.J. (1993) 'Restructuring the region's air industry', in D.R. Hall (ed.), *Transport and Economic Development in the New Central and Eastern Europe*, London: Belhaven.

Tangi, M. (1977) 'Tourisme et environnement', *Ambio*, **6**(6), 339–345.

Tansey, Webster and Associates (1991) *Tourism and the Economy*, Dún Laoghaire: Irish Tourism Industry Confederation.

Tello, R. (1992) 'Les stratégies de Barcelone pour l'an 2000', in *Villes et Territoires*, pp. 43–56.

Thurot, J.M. (1982) *La Technique des Scénarios Appliquée au Tourisme: Aspects Méthodologiques*, Aix-en-Provence: CHET.

Tinardon, Ph. (1992) 'Une politique touristique pour le Crese', *Des Régions Paysannes aux Espaces Fragiles*, Clermond-Ferrand: Université Blaise Pascal.

Townsend, A. (1992) 'New directions in the growth of tourism employment: propositions of the 1980s', *Environment and Planning A*, **14**, 821–832.

Trinardon, Ph (1992) 'Une politique touristique pour la Creuse', *Des Régions Paysannes aux Espaces Fragiles*, Clermont-Ferrand: Université Blaise Pascal, pp. 593–604.

Tuppen, J. (1991) 'France: the changing character of a key industry', in A.M. Williams and G. Shaw (eds), *Tourism and Economic Development. Western European Experiences*, 2nd edn, London: Belhaven Press, pp. 191–206.

Turner, I. and Ash, J. (1991) *La Horda Dorada. El Turismo Internacional y la Periferia del Placer*, Madrid: Ed. Endymion.

Urry, J. (1987) 'Some social and spatial aspects of services', *Environment and Planning D: Society and Space*, **5**, 5–26.

Urry, J. (1990) *The Tourist Gaze: Leisure and Travel in Contemporary Societies*, London: Sage Publications.

Urry, J. (1992) 'The Tourist gaze "revisited"', *American Behavioural Scientist*, **36**, 172–186.

Valenzuela, M. (1988) 'Spain: the phenomenon of mass tourism', in A.M. Williams and G. Shaw (eds), *Tourism and Economic Development: Western European Perspectives*, London: Belhaven.

Van den Berg, L., Van der Borg, J. and Van der Meer, J. (1994) *Urban Tourism*, Rotterdam: EURICUR, Erasmus University.

Var, T., Cessario, E. and Mauser, G. (1985) 'Convention tourism modelling', *Tourism Management*, **6**, 194–200.

Veggeland, N. and Hedegaard, L. (1993) 'Nordens inflydelse pa EFs regional udvikling og spatiale organisation', excerpt from Final Report, *Impact of the Development of the Nordic Countries on Regional Development and Spatial Organisation in the Community*, NordRevy No. 3/4 1993, Oslo: Scandinavian University Press.

Velluti, Zati (1992) 'Edifici rurali: una risora culturale, ambientale et economica da salvaguardare e vallorizare', *Il Turismo nelle Regioni Rurali della CEE: la Tutella del Patrimonio naturale e culturale*, Rome: Edizione Scientifische Italiana, pp. 57–71.

Venturini, M. (1992) 'Immigration et marche du travail en Italie: données récentes', *Revue Européenne des Migrations Internationales*, **8**, supplement, 145–161.

Vera Rebollo, J.F. (1987) *Turismo y Urbanización en el Litoral Alicantino*, Alicante: Inst. Juan Gil Albert.

Vera Rebollo, J.F (1990) 'Turismo y territorio en el litoral mediterráneo español', *Estudios Territoriales*, **32**, 81–110.

Vera Rebollo, J.F. (1994) *Tourism and the Environment: Sustainable Development and New Culture for Tourist Consumption, Culture with a View of Nature*, Basle: Swiss Academy of Humanities and Social Sciences, UNESCO.

Viken, A. (1991) *Nordkalotturismen*, FDH Rapport 1991: 5, Alta.

Viken, A. and Slettvold, O. (1988) *Bilturisme i Finnmark*, FDH Rapport 1988:6, Alta.

Villes et Territoires (1992) *Barcelone–Toulouse Horizon 2000*. Toulouse: Presses Universitaires du Mirail, No. 4.

Warnes, A. (1992) 'Age related variation and temporal change in elderly migration', in A. Rogers (ed.) *Elderly Migration and Population Redistribution: a Comparative Study*, London: Belhaven.

Wheatcroft, S. (1990) 'Towards transnational airlines', *Tourism Management*, **11**, 353–358.

Wheatcroft, S. and Seekings, J. (1993) *Europe's Senior Travel Market*, Paris.

Whitford, R. (1993) 'Will tourism pick up in Hungary?' *Business Eastern Europe*, **22**(36), 1–2.

Wight, P. (1993) 'Ecotourism: ethics or eco-sell?', *Journal of Travel Research*, **31**(3), 3–9.

Williams, A.M. (1987) *The Western European Economy*, London: Hutchinson.

Williams, A.M. (1989) 'Management strategies for coastal conservation in South Wales, UK: Recreational uses of coastal areas', *The Geojournal Library*, 12, 19–38.

Williams, A.M. (1993a) 'Tourism', in J. Loughlin (ed.), *Southern European Studies Guide*, London: Bowker Saur, p. 173–192.

Williams, A.M. (1993b) 'Tourist and economic transformation in Greece and Portugal', *Inforgeo* (As. Portuguesa de Geógrafos, Lisbon), pp. 7–20.

Williams, A.M. (1994) 'L'internazionalizzazione del turismo e lo sviluppo ineguale nella CE: i casi di studio di Portogallo e Regno Unito', in C.S. Lezzi and A. Trono (eds), *Atti del Seminario Internazionale 1992 e Periferie d'Europa*, Lecce: Università Degli Studi di Lecce.

Williams, A.M. and Montanari, A. (1995) 'Tourism regions and spaces in a changing social framework', *Tijdschrift voor Economische en Sociale Geografie*, (forthcoming).

Williams, A.M. and Shaw, G. (1988) 'Tourism: candy floss industry or job generator?', *Town Planning Review*, 59, 81–104.

Williams, A.M. and Shaw, G. (eds) (1991a) *Tourism and Economic Development: Western European Experiences*, London: Belhaven.

Williams, A.M. and Shaw, G. (1991b) 'Tourism policies in a changing economic environment', in A.M. Williams and G. Shaw (eds), *Tourism and Economic Development: Western European Experiences*, London: Belhaven.

Williams, A.M. and Shaw, G. (1991c) 'Tourism in urban and regional development: Western European experiences', in S. Hardy, T. Hart and T. Shaw (eds), *The Role of Tourism in the Urban and Regional Economy*, London: Regional Studies Association, 5–10.

Williams, A.M. and Shaw, G. (1991d) 'Western European tourism in perspective', in A.M. Williams and G. Shaw (eds), *Tourism and Economic Development: Western European Experiences* Belhaven: London, pp. 31–39.

Williams, A.M. and Shaw, G. (1992) 'Tourism research: a perspective', *American Behavioural Scientist*, 36, 133–143.

Williams, A.M. and Shaw, G. (1994) 'Tourism: opportunities, challenges and contradictions in the EC', in M. Blackswell and A.M. Williams (eds), *The European Challenge: Geography and Development in the European Community*, Oxford: Oxford University Press.

Williams, A.M., Shaw, G. and Greenwood, J. (1989) 'From tourist to tourism entrepreneur, from consumption to production: evidence from Cornwall, England', *Environment and Planning A*, 21, 1639–1653.

Wolfe, R.I. (1983) 'Recreational travel, the new migration revisited', *Ontario Geography*, 19, 103–124.

World Commission on Environment and Development (1987) *Our Common Future*, Oxford.

WTO (World Tourism Organization) (1983) *Development of Leisure Time and the Right to Holidays*, Madrid.

WTO (1986) *Economic Review of World Tourism*, Madrid.

WTO (1990) *El Turismo hacia el Año 2000: Aspectos Cualitativos que Afectan al Crecimiento Global*, Madrid.

WTO (1991) *Tourism to the Year 2000: Qualitative Aspects Affecting Global Growth, A Discussion Paper*, Madrid.

WTO (1992a) *Sustainable Tourism Development: Guide for Local Planners*, Madrid.

WTO (1992b) *Yearbook of Tourism Statistics*, Madrid.

WTO (1993) *Compendium of Tourism Statistics 1987–1991*, Madrid.

WTO (1994) *Yearbook of Tourism Statistics*, Madrid.

World Travel and Tourism Review (1993) 'Indicators, trends and issues', Vol. 3, Wallingford: CAB International.

Yuill, D., Allen, K., Bachtler, J., Clement, C. and Wishlade, F. (1991) *European Regional Incentives 1991*, London: Bowker Saur.

Zelinsky, W. (1985) 'The roving palate: North America's ethnic restaurant cuisines', *Geoforum*, **16**(1), 51–72.

Zimmermann, F. (1989) 'Ende des Wachstums und Umbau des Fremdenverkehrs: Szenarien und Modellrechungen zum österreichischen Fremdenverkehr im Jahr 2000', in E. Lichtenberger (ed.) *Österreich zu Beginn des 3.Jahrtausend. Raum und Gesellschaft. Prognosen, Modellrechnungen und Szenarien*, Beiträge zur Stadt und Regionalforschung, 9, Vienna: Verlag der Österreichischen Akademie der Wissenschaften, pp. 177–202.

Zimmermann, F. (1991a) 'The organisation of tourism in Austria: marketing at the provincial level', in G.J. Ashworth and B. Goodall (eds), *Marketing Tourism Places*, London: Routledge.

Zimmermann, F. (1991b) 'Austria: contrasting tourist seasons and contrasting regions', in A.M. Williams and G. Shaw (eds), *Tourism and Economic Development: Western European Experiences*, 2nd edn, London: Belhaven Press.

Zimmermann, F. (1992a) 'Issues, problems, and future trends in the Austrian Alps: changes within traditional tourism', in *Proceedings of the Vail Conference on "Recreation Trends and Mountain Resort Development"*, Denver/Colorado, 160–170.

Zimmermann, F. (1992b) 'Prognosen in der Tourismusforschung: Trends, Szenarien, Delphi-Umfragen am Beispiel der Tourismusentwicklung in Österreich', in *Materialien zur Fremdenverkehrsgeographie*, Trier: vol. 25, pp. 9–69.

Index